# MUSTAPHA MATURA

# Six Plays

As Time Goes By
Nice
Play Mas
Independence
Welcome Home Jacko
Meetings

*Introduced by the author*

## METHUEN WORLD DRAMATISTS

This edition first published in Great Britain in 1992
by Methuen Drama, Michelin House, 81 Fulham Road, London SW3 6RB
and distributed in the United States of America
by HEB Inc., 361 Hanover Street, Portsmouth, New Hampshire NH 03801 3959.

*As Time Goes By* first published by Calder and Boyars Limited in 1972
Copyright © 1972 by Mustapha Matura

*Nice* first published by Eyre Methuen Limited in 1980
Copyright © 1980 by Mustapha Matura

*Play Mas* first published by Methuen London Limited in 1982
Copyright © 1982 by Mustapha Matura

*Independence* first published by Methuen London Limited in 1982
Copyright © 1982 by Mustapha Matura

*Welcome Home Jacko* first published by Eyre Methuen Limited in 1980
Copyright © 1980 by Mustapha Matura

*Meetings* first published by Methuen London Limited in 1982
Copyright © 1982 by Mustapha Matura

This collection copyright © 1992 by Mustapha Matura
Introduction copyright © 1992 by Mustapha Matura

The author has asserted his moral rights

A CIP catalogue record for this book
is available from the British Library

ISBN 0–413–66070–2

*The front cover shows* The Sleeping Gypsy *by Henri J F Rousseau (1844–1910),
The Museum of Modern Art, New York/The Bridgeman Art Library, London.
The photograph of Mustapha Matura on the back cover is by Michael Mayhew.*

Photoset by Wilmaset, Birkenhead, Wirral
Printed and bound in Great Britain
by Cox & Wyman Ltd, Reading, Berks.

# Contents

# A Chronology

# To Ann, Dominic, Cayal and Mia

# Introduction

As a child in Trinidad, my two influences were the cinema and the lives of the local people. Later on I read some literature, attended poetry readings sponsored by the British Council and a play by an expat British amateur company.

Arriving in England in 1961, my interests broadened to include continental films, painting, architecture, graphics: all the visual arts. Amongst other plays, I saw Edward Albee's **Death of Bessie Smith** and John Osborne's **Luther**. In Rome I pulled the curtains for a production of Langston Hughes' **Shakespeare in Harlem** but, having goofed that, no trumpets blared or angels rejoiced 'This is it, this is it'.

Then 1968 arrived. The social and economic changes amongst young people began to create other forms of expression: the fringe, the underground – the alternative culture was born. It was the time too of the Vietnam war; flower power; revolutionary politicians cohabiting with peace and love devotees; rallies at the Roundhouse in London, political as well as artistic in content. It was also a time of serious personal and psychological changes for me, my friends and other colonised people around the world; for as well as flower power in 1968 there was also Black Power.

Information and knowledge about my life and history was arriving at breakneck speed, the effects of which were so dramatic and inspiring I felt an urge, a need to speak, to tell it like it is, to pass it on, to confirm. The alternative culture had also given birth to alternative theatre, which attracted me by its accessibility and immediacy.

It was with all these conflicting changes and contradictory experiences, as well as an encouraging fee from the producer Michael White, that I sat down to write my first full length stage play: **As Time Goes By**. Drawing heavily on my memories of a Trinidadian sense of folk tale, of back yard, of personal lives being lived in the open for all to see, I wrote a story based on a friend I had stayed with on my arrival in London and, as well as his humorous attempts to come to terms with life in London at the time, I was able to show the pain and sense of dislocation felt by his wife and other members of the West Indian community.

Having left Trinidad before Independence and not returned for twelve years, I then went back and observed the different social and political changes that had taken place. On my return to England I wrote **Play Mas**, a story looking at the effects of the emergence of the Negro in Trinidadian society and politics, as seen through the eyes of an Indian tailor and his mother, with the theme of Carnival – a national celebration of make-up, make-believe – running through it.

In 1978 I returned to the theme of independence with a play of that name, this time a few years on, and looked at its effects on the lives of those who remembered colonialism: some with affection, some with regret and, in the case of Allen, a child of post-Independence having to live with the debris of it, rejecting it totally.

Moving back to England, I went on a speaking tour to Sheffield where I visited a youth community centre which was so desolate and hopeless and seemed to me to be just a terminus for young black men moving in and out of prison and struggling to discover some kind of Black identity. Out of this came **Welcome Home Jacko**. The play looks at the lives of four unemployed teenage West Indians in a youth club, forced to compete amongst themselves, experimenting with Rastafarianism and being confronted by the realities of the harsh outside world in the person of Jacko, newly released from prison.

Some days a writer sits down with a blank piece of paper before him and thinks, 'What shall I write?'. I did and then wrote a monologue: **Nice**. It's a simple story seen through the eyes of a simple man, a pure, unsophisticated newly-arrived immigrant in London and it looks at his attempts to preserve his innocence whilst having to deal with less kindly souls.

With **Meetings** I returned again to Trinidad, which was at that time suffering the pains of an economic boom due to the hike in oil prices which had in turn given birth to a new species, a heavily American influenced, young, prosperous, forward-looking middle class. And this time I looked at the effects of the loss of their cultural heritage amongst that group through the life of a couple, both searching for an identity. And the search continues.

Mustapha Matura, 1991

*As Time Goes By* was first performed at the Traverse Theatre Club, Edinburgh, on 13 July 1971, with the following cast:

| | |
|---|---|
| RAM | Stefan Kalipha |
| ARNOLD | Alfred Fagon |
| BATEE | Mona Hammond |
| UNA | Corinne Skinner |
| MARK | Robert Coleby |
| LUCILLE | Carole Hayman |
| BERTRAM | Oscar James |
| ALBERT | Frank Singuineau |
| SKIN HEAD | Robert Atiko |
| ALFRED | T-Bone Wilson |
| THELMA | Patricia Moseley |

*Directed by* Roland Rees

*Author's Notes On Characters:*

RAM – Indian origin between 30–40, dressed all in white
ARNOLD – Negro origin between 25–30, dressed in London Transport Underground Guards uniform
BATEE (Ram's wife) – Indian origin between 30–40, dressed plainly
MARK – White between 25–30, trendily dressed
LUCILLE – White between 20–25, trendily dressed
BERTRAM – Negro origin between 25–30, dressed in London Transport Bus Conductor's uniform
ALBERT – Negro origin between 40–45, dressed in Council Dustman's uniform
SKIN HEAD – Negro origin teenager, dressed in skin head gear
ALFRED – Negro origin between 30–40, dressed sharply
THELMA – Negro origin between 25–30, dressed trendily

## ACT ONE

### Scene One

*The action takes place in two rooms. Front room. Lavishly decorated with religious objects and pictures. Back room. Very shabby kitchen.*

RAM. Ram, Ram, salam, wale com, shalom, peace, hi, hello, good evening, welcome to the house of truth and reality, come in. Is this your first time, who told you about me?

ARNOLD. Am Alfred told me about you, he said you were very good, that you knew a lot, you see, am I told him a had a few problems, you see me wife left me and gone to live with me brother, you see, so a have a few problems.

RAM. Well that is no problem at all, as you will come to see in time.

ARNOLD. So how long you doing this kinda ting?

RAM. Well it's hard to say, the more I tink back, is the more I realise I've being doing all the time, but through different consciousnesses.

ARNOLD. Or a see, I uses to meditate too, you know, but nothing used to happen so I gave it up.

RAM. Well you know some of us attain higher planes of consciousness and it is our duty to pass on a higher vibration to others who haven't reached that level as yet but you will understand that as time goes along, you will see what I'm talking about, so why did yer wife leave yer?

ARNOLD. I don't know, dat's what I come ter see you for.

RAM. Or I see, you don't know, but you do know, it just hasn't reached your waking consciousness as yet, but it will in time, you know, deep down inside, why she left you, what you have to learn to do is to bring it forward, but you will learn to do that as time goes by, because it's only by realising the truth that you understand and overcome your problems.

ARNOLD. But she left me and living with me brother.

RAM. I know, I know.

ARNOLD. She say is because, a never used to take she out at all, but me brother don't take she out, an' she still living with he, so, how come she en lef' he, he says she en change.

RAM. Or I see so you are still friends with your brother?

ARNOLD. Of course, he is me brother, not because he take way me wife, a go fall out with him.

RAM. Well you see you are on the right path, by loving him, you relieve yourself of the burden of hate, and by doing so you bypass the normal reactions of the average human being, you have saved yourself years of suffering by doing so, as you will come to see, as time goes by.

ARNOLD. Yes, but he still living with she, an' he does beat she, I never used to beat she, a mean now an' then she used to get on me nerves, but I never beat she, a used to cuss she sometimes, but a never lay hands on de woman, except dat time when she forgot to post me pools coupon.

RAM. Was it a winning coupon?

ARNOLD. No, but supposing it had win.

RAM. Or I see.

ARNOLD. Yer see what a mean, supposing me coupon had win, what woulda happen, a woulda get no money because she didn't post it, she say she forget, a chance anyway, but a still didn't beat she.

RAM. Well that's good because if you were suppose to win she would have posted it you see but you will come to see what I am talking about as times goes by.

ARNOLD. But brother Ram, he don't buy she no clothes, he does carry she down de market an' till she pick one from de ten bob bundle. I used to buy she a new dress every month an' carry she to de pictures de same night, yer could ask fer more, a mean ter say, I en Henry Ford, I does work hard fer my money yer know, so after de bookies done with me, ter buy she a new dress an' den take she ter de pictures is a lot, so why she left me?

RAM. Well dat's what we have to find out, but that's not the end of it, we have to go further and learn to understand her and sympathise with her because she must have suffered just as much as you.

ARNOLD. She suffer, she en suffer, she had all she wanted, how she could suffer, she had notting to suffer for, she had food, a used to go down Shepherd's Bush an' buy she salt fish, and green fig an' sometimes I meself even used to come home an' cook it, so how she could suffer?

RAM. Well it's a hard case but as time goes by you and I will make it soft.

ARNOLD. Well brother Ram, that's good because if a could only know why she left me a would feel good but anyhow ita good talking to you a start to feel good already.

RAM. Yer see, that's what a was talking about all de time, it's through understanding an' talking about it you begin to feel better. So how long ago she left yer?

ARNOLD. Is three years now, an' I en see she since last independence dance an' when she see me she pass me straight straight, like a full trolley bus, a ask she fer a dance, she say she tired, but I was watching she, she only had one dance before, so a know she lie, but I en tell she nothin' I say dat alright maybe de next one but when de music start up a couldn't find she, is like de woman disappear. A feel like a tree fall down on me, da is how a feel, a tree ever fall on yer? Brother Ram.

RAM. No, never.

ARNOLD. Well one time when a used ter work Mr Gitten's land, dey cut a tree, but I didn't hear nobody call, tree falling so I en move, an' de tree hit me. A was in hospital fer a long time but nothing happen to me, dey say dey shout tree falling but I didn't hear dem, so I en move, how a go move if a en hear dem, dey must be joking, dey say dey shout but I have a feeling dey en shout at all because if dey had shout I wouldna hear dem because I was standing right next to de tree an' even when I come out a de hospital an' ask dem dey still say dey shout. Yer see how some people is, but is a good ting nothing happen to me or else a go mad an' chop up all a dem, hook, line an' sinker.

RAM. So nothing happened to you.

ARNOLD. No man dat's what a telling yer, after de tree fall on me an' when a say fall a mean fall yer know, not just de branches, is de whole tree, de trunk. A tell yer what kind a tree it was, yer know den tree does grow yellow flowers once a year, well is one adem. Yer know how dey big, well after de tree hit me, I get up and start ter cuss dem, de run round me, saying if alright, an' a should go an' see de hospital people, but I know it was a trick, because nothing was wrong with me, when I reached de hospital dey say me arm break in two places. I tell dem dey lie because I couldn't feel nothing, if it had break I was bound ter feel something at least a little pain or hurting somewhere but I didn't feel nottin' but a went along wit dem an' let dem put me hand in plaster an' stay in fer a few weeks till Carnival. A come out a hospital Carnival Monday morning an' jump in a band that was going up cascade so instead a taking a taxi de band carry me home. A change me clothes an' went an' play mas like a never play before. De few weeks in de hospital gave me a good rest, an' dat's when a met Una, she was in de same band.

RAM. Or I see you knew her in Trinidad.

ARNOLD. Well a knew her in Trinidad but since she come over here I en know her, she change, dat's what a come ter see yer about is dis change dat's boddering me, I en change so why she change, is de country dat change she, it en change me, de only ting is a does wear more clothes, more jumpers an' tings but yer have ter do dat or else yer go freeze, an' me en want ter freeze so a have ter wear all dem sweaters.

RAM. So you only saw her at that dance.

ARNOLD. No a saw after that at me other brother's child christening but she didn't say why when de music start a couldn't find she so I didn't mention it, but a wanted ter ask she, but me brother was der so a couldn't say nothing, I don't want him ter tink I still love she, because den he go feel he do a bad ting.

RAM. You see how much you know without even knowing it, well that's the way it works.

ARNOLD. But I en know nothing, brother Ram. Dat's what a come to find out.

RAM. I know, I know, but you don't know you know it, you see, as time goes by you will come to realise what you know and then you will know what you know if yer see what a mean.

ARNOLD. Well a tink a know what yer mean but a not sure.

RAM. Anyhow trust me, and you will see, I was just like you, I couldn't see anything but it was right in front a me all the time but I couldn't see it, is when I wasn't looking then it appeared but I wasn't worried, my time came and I saw it all, as you will see as time goes by.

ARNOLD. Yes, brother Ram, I see. I only hope she don't think I go take this lying down because if she tink so she badly mistaken. I go try and try until a find out why. She don't know me, she don't know me at all, she tink I soft but she go find out.

RAM. So is Alfred told you about me, eh?

ARNOLD. Yes I saw him in de bookie an' tell him me problems an' he say you know all about life.

RAM. What he tell yer, what he tell yer, how he say it, was he serious, or was he taking de mickey?

ARNOLD. Serious, man, if he wasn't serious I wouldn't be here, what's wrong with yer, man, yer don't believe me.

RAM. Yer yer, I believe yer but a know sometimes Alfred like ter take de mickey and a wasn't sure, but I believe yer.

ARNOLD. Or hor, because a carn't have you not believing me, you is de man who go have to know.

RAM. Yes, but is just Alfred, anyhow forget him, it's your problems we talking 'bout.

ARNOLD. A smell something burning.

RAM. Is de incense, man.

ARNOLD. No it smell like food, man, like rice run outa water.

RAM. A coming.

RAM *gets up and goes in the back. Voices from the back.*

A thought a tell yer ter watch de rice an' don't let it burn. Yer mean ter say yer carn't even do dat. Yer know when a have ter see somebody a carn't see them an' watch de rice at de same time. So yer stand up day an' let de rice burn, yer is me enemy or what, what yer trying to do?

BATEE. Why I must watch de rice an' you is de cook in dis house. If you put on rice you must know when de rice done so why I must watch it?

RAM. Alright, alright, I go see about it, you glong.

BATEE. When yer go put on the meat I hungry.

RAM. Well yer have ter wait. A have a very important client out ther so yer have ter wait and don't touch de potatoes I go see about them when a finish.

BATEE. When you go finish I want ter go and sit down, a tired staying in de kitchen every time somebody come in the house, de kitchen cold.

RAM. A won't be long, yer carn't wait fer a little bit.

BATEE. I cold.

RAM. Alright, alright but don't rush me, just don't rush me, okay. (RAM *returns*.) Yes it was de rice burning, me wife forget ter put water but that alright now.

ARNOLD. Yes I like burn rice too, dey say it have iodine in it, an' dat good fer de body.

RAM. Oh, yea, yea, it's good fer cuts too. So did she come to see you in hospital?

ARNOLD. No, man, yer wasn't listening or what, is after, after a came out a hospital a met she, in de band, a told yer.

RAM. Oh, yea, sorry. Boy a carn't leave dat woman to do notting, a leave she to cook some rice, she let me rice burn.

ARNOLD. Who dat, yer woman?

RAM. Yea.

ARNOLD. Or I see, yer lucky you have a woman, I have ter look after my own self, me en have nobody to wash and cook for me, I have ter go ter de laundrette myself, is a good ting it next ter de betting shop otherwise a don't know what a woulda do.

RAM. Or I see, and do you want her back, I mean if she wanted to come back would you have her?

ARNOLD. Of course I'd have her, I want her back, a just tell you man, I en have nobody ter do de washing and cooking, but she would have ter come back on my terms, me en buying she no more saltfish and green fig, she go have ter learn ter do without dat, she go have ter learn I is de boss. I was tinking you might go an' see she, an' you know have a talk with she.

RAM. I'm not sure that would be the right thing, I'd have to meditate on it and see what I come up with.

ARNOLD. But yer better be careful if yer go der because me brother is a ignorant kinda feller, he might go fer yer, so yer have ter go when he en dere.

RAM. I see, if I do go, I'm not saying I will go, I'll have ter go with his permission.

ARNOLD. Well forget it, he en go let you come in his house ter talk his woman into leaving he, ter come back ter live with me. What yer tink it is at all, you have ter go when he not dere, he mustn't know that I send anybody, he must think she leave on she own free will, yer see, otherwise he go come round here and beat all a we. A tell yer he's a ignorant feller my brother, yer carn't trust him at all.

RAM. Oh I see, well I don't think I can do that, we'll have to think of another way. What about her coming here?

ARNOLD. That's a better idea, brother Ram, yer really good yer know. It look like this meditation ting does really work. If we get somebody ter tell she that yer want ter see she, she go

come because all she want to know is some man want ter see
she an' she day, especially if is a swami like you.

RAM. Yes but we mustn't overdo the swami ting, she must
think I am just like anybody else and then she'll feel free to
talk to me. I don't want her preconcepting.

ARNOLD. What's, what?

RAM. What's what?

ARNOLD. This preconcepting.

RAM. Or it means making up yer mind before you know what
going happen.

ARNOLD. Brother Ram, yer really know what yer talking 'bout
yer know, she just like that, always preconcepting. A always
used ter tell her yer mustn't preconcept too much but she
never used ter listen to me. Now yer see where she
preconcepting get she, she living wit a man who beat she,
don't feed she and does only buy she ten bob dress.

RAM. Alright, alright, so can I leave the telling to you and you
just let me know when she's coming and I'll be ready, okay.

ARNOLD. Right, brother Ram, you leave the telling to me and
I go leave the rest ter you when de rice go finish. Alfred say
yer was a good cook too.

RAM. Well I'm afraid Alfred was joking that time.

ARNOLD. O I see. (*Sounds of a baby crying.*)

BATEE. And the next time I catch you doin' that a go kill yer,
yer hear. (*Smack, smack.*) An' yer could tell yer father is I hit
yer, I don't care. (*Smack. Cry, cry.*)

ARNOLD. Like she go kill de child in truth.

RAM *gets up and goes into the back.*

RAM. A coming. (*Inside.*) What yer beating der child for? How

many times a tell yer not ter beat der child, if she do
something wrong tell me and I'll talk to her, beating de child
don't help, yer only making things worse.

BATEE. Well look she day you talk ter her, I carn't talk to her.
She do something bad so I beat her, what's wrong with that
all you go do is talk one set a shit an' soon as yer turn yer
back she go and do the same ting yer tell she not to do, you
don't have ter look after she all the time yer know. Is I have
ter, I have to put up with all the bad things she do, you sitting
down in the front nice and warm whilst I in de kitchen
freezing with de child bawling. So you don't come and tell me
what ter do. I don't tell you how to fool people so you don't
tell me how to look after my child.

RAM. Who fooling people, I don't fool nobody. People come
ter me for help and I try ter help them dat's all and all I ask
fer is some peace and quiet but that's like is too much fer you
to give, if yer en killing the child with blows yer letting de rice
burn over so how am I expected to help people with all that
going on, eh, tell me. It looks very bad when people come
here to talk ter me and all that going on, yer hear, in case yer
didn't know.

BATEE. Ter hell with dem, dem nice and warm yer know, dem
could afford ter sit down and talk dey ass off, dem en freezing
so don't tell me about dem. All I know is I cold and hungry
and instead a you come and cook some food you sit in de
front room playing the ass.

RAM. Playing the ass yer call it, eh. So where yer think we get
de money ter buy de same food yer hungry fer, dat same food
yer waiting on, is those people does pay fer it, so, wait a go
get ten pounds off dis guy and yer could run down de road
and catch de butchers and buy a chicken, okay, so just give
me a little more time, alright. (RAM *returns*.) Boy a don't
know what happen ter women nowadays yer know, dey
carn't do nothing.

ARNOLD. A know is de same ting a was telling you about Una. She never do anything right even when she leave me. Instead a she go an' live with some man wit' some money so a could sue she fer divorce and get some, wha' yer call it, damages, she go an' live with me brother, a mean a man carn't sue me own brother fer damages, how dat go look.

RAM. Yea yea, a see what yer mean. Back home a found one a me cows lying dead an' a feel glad because de cow was sick and a know de only man in de village who had a big lorry was Mr Smithson. So a went ter see him. When a reach he house who a could see but me own brother driving Mr Smithson's lorry so a had ter make some excuse about losing me way, a mean a big man like me losing he way, boy a never feel so shame everybody laugh.

ARNOLD. Yes Mr Gittens had a lorry too but I never drive it, a never even get a drive in it, he used ter keep it fer he pigs, he prize pigs that's what he used ter call dem boy, a never see a man make such a fuss over a few pigs an' dat same lorry yer know, one day he leave de handbrake off an' it start ter roll down a hill, everybody run outa de way but I was de only one who try ter stop it. I chuck me foot under de wheels. De lorry didn't stop but a least a try yer know. De lorry pass over me foot an' nothing happen but at least a try an' he still wouldn't give me drive in it. Boy, some man hard yer know.

RAM. But you mustn't let other people reactions upset you. You must continue on you path.

ARNOLD. Brother Ram, yer keep trowing dem big words at me, yer go knock me down.

RAM. I mean the way other people behave towards you.

ARNOLD. Or a see, but people don't worry me, is just Una leaving me but people don't worry me as long as I don't wish nobody no harm dem nobody carn't harm me. (*Sounds of child crying.*) Dis time she go really murder de child.

RAM. A coming, a coming.

ARNOLD. Right, brother Ram, you deal wit' it.

RAM *goes into the back once more.*

RAM. What is it dis time?

BATEE. She want a ice cream dis freezing weather an' she say
she want a ice cream, so a beat she. I'd like ter beat the ice
cream man who ring de damn bell. I'd wring he damn neck
an' you, yer so good at talking ter people why yer don't go
an' tell him damn ice cream man not ter ring he damn bell,
eh.

RAM. Because dis is a free country dat's why an' if yer want ter
live here yer have ter allow other people their freedom dat's
why. Yer not back home in Trinidad yer know where yer
father was de big shot in de village so stop trowing yerself
about. A now know why he was happy when you get
married, he was laughing at me but he don't know I would
send yer back ter he, even after all these years.

BATEE. Send me na, send me na, I don't care. It only cold an'
dark over here. At least back home a could beat me child in
peace but over here as soon as a touch me own child is don't
do that, don't do this, is some reason or de other, send me
back home I'd don't care.

RAM. Like this time yer really looking fer a lash. All yer have
ter do is keep de child quiet fer a little while longer. Alright,
is that too much ter ask, eh. (RAM *returns.*) Ar, boy, is a
hard life but we have ter take it as it comes an' make it better
right. What kinda work yer do?

ARNOLD. I on de underground. Dat's something else Una used
ter say. She never like man in uniform but if yer work on de
underground yer bound ter wear uniform, it's in de
regulations, yer bound ter an' de hat but me brother working

on de buses an' she living with he so how come she don't like man in uniform, eh, woman funny, eh.

RAM. But a suppose dat's life.

ARNOLD. I, brother Ram, yer really know wat yer talking 'bout. A feel a could really trust yer.

RAM. So how much a week yer earn?

ARNOLD. Earn, or yer mean how much a week a does get? Only eighteen but sometimes with a little overtime it does reach twenty after dey take dey tax dat's something else. When she was living wit' me a never used ter pay tax on she now a have ter pay tax because me brother claiming fer she an' two an we carn't claim fer one woman. So you see a get hit all over every way a turn is licks.

RAM. But at least you don't spend as much as you used to.

ARNOLD. Dat's true but don't tell nobody. A never used ter buy she a new dress a used ter get dem with small damages dat nobody could see so it wasn't really a new dress.

RAM. Before yer go yer must tell me where yer buy dem dresses. Me wife could do with a new one, dat might keep she quiet.

ARNOLD. A could take yer, de Jew man is me friend, we is like brothers.

RAM. Ar yes, the Jews dey are nice people dey help us a lot. Dey are de only people ter trust us when we have no money ter pay fer clothes. Dey are de only people dat tells us is alright pay me when yer get it, dey are good people.

ARNOLD. Yea but dey smart too yer know, don't think dey foolish.

RAM. Nobody is foolish nobody is smart, we are all governed.

ARNOLD. Oh yer mean like how de Governor used ter be in Trinidad.

RAM. Well something like that but more powerful.

ARNOLD. Or a see, yer mean like God.

RAM. Shhh, shhh, we don't say his name. We can think about an' we can talk about him but never say his name.

ARNOLD. Alright sorry, brother Ram, a sorry.

RAM. He'll forgive yer because he knows yer didn't mean any disrespect.

ARNOLD. Oh no a didn't mean any a dat. It was just a slip a de tongue.

RAM. Well dat's alright he knows.

ARNOLD. So he knows why Una left me, is dat what yer been trying ter say?

RAM. Yes he does.

ARNOLD. Well le' we ask him.

RAM. Well that's what we have ter do but he will let you know through yourself. The truth will come ter you from him, that's how he works.

ARNOLD. Well if dat's how he works why don't we ask him an' save a lot of trouble.

RAM. When it's time fer you to know he will tell you.

ARNOLD. But a want ter know now. Dat's what a come ter see yer fer. Yer mean a come at de wrong time.

RAM. Well something like that but then again there's no right time or wrong time, dere's just his time, yer see.

ARNOLD. Well, brother Ram, a go trust you because it look funny ter me.

*Voice from the back.*

BATEE. Is alright if a put on de vegetables now?

RAM (*shouts*). Yes yes but mind yer wash dem an' watch how much salt yer put in it.

BATEE. I know how much salt ter put, a only ask if de time was right.

RAM. Yes, yes, go ahead.

ARNOLD. So, brother Ram, how long yer been doing this kinda ting?

RAM. Since last year. People coming ter see me.

ARNOLD. So I en de first.

RAM. No.

ARNOLD. Or is just de way Alfred sound I thought I was de first.

RAM. A tell yer dat Alfred was up ter something.

ARNOLD. So what kinda a people yer does get? We people or yer does get some English people. Because a know a lot a dem people does have dey troubles too. Yer does get any a dem?

RAM. Yes, a get a few of them but the ones who really seem interested in what I have ter say is de hippies.

ARNOLD. Who's de hippies? O yer mean dem long hair people who does wear den funny kinda clothes. I like de girls an' dem. I like ter see dem when dey en wearing no bra an' dey nice breast showing. A hope a not upsetting a holy man like you talking 'bout these things but you know what a mean after all, de man put dat on dis earth too, so it must be alright, is dat true, brother Ram?

RAM. Yes a know what yer mean. I had a few but a carn't talk about it de wife might hear and a have enough trouble wit' she without adding a few more but *boy* dey really go fer dis holy ting.

ARNOLD. Is dat a fact. A better open a church too.

RAM. No it's not something you must use for base motives.

ARNOLD. What brother Ram?

RAM. I mean you must do it to help people.

ARNOLD. But I is people an' a helping me an' a sure a helping dem. No man must be never trow a good booto on dem. A catch one in de pub once when a give she de whole ting, she nearly pass out.

RAM. Yes, brother, but dat is in de past we've gone beyond those kind of things.

ARNOLD. Brother Ram, when I go past those kinda tings a go be really beyond.

RAM. I see.

ARNOLD. An' dat's another thing since Una left me. I en get a good night's sleep yet, an' when I see me brother in de morning he happy going ter work just like I used ter be. A carn't understand it.

RAM. Well that's what we are going to do try and understand it.

ARNOLD. Brother Ram, a mean you couldn't get one a dem hippies fer me?

RAM. I carn't do dat. I am not in dat business. If it so happens dat you get one well go ahead, but for me to know, brother Arnold, it's out of the question.

ARNOLD. But is alright fer you to get one.

RAM. It's different. One or two came to me for help and help takes different forms.

ARNOLD. Or a think a see what yer mean but if yer know any a dem who looking for a place ter stay give dem my address.

RAM. Well come ter think about it some a dem especially de young girls does need special treatment and it would be nice ter have somewhere away from familiar objects, they distract de mind a lot, but that is only in special cases.

ARNOLD. A know what yer mean, brother Ram. A know just what you mean, brother Ram. Una use ter say de same ting. She need ter get out an' see different people but de only different people she used ter see was me brother.

BATEE (*from the kitchen*). I en saying notting but I think is time somebody look at de vegetables, you know they looking soft, soft, an' me do like no soft vegetables yer know. I en eating no squashy, squashy food, dat is fer babies, me is a big woman yer know.

RAM. Yes, yes, coming, let's have a look, boy dis woman, a comin'.

RAM *goes back*.

BATEE. Yer get de ten pounds?

RAM. Hush ner not so loud he go hear yer. I en get it yet but it coming. I car jest say gimme ten pounds, there are ways of doing these tings.

BATEE. Well if you 'fraid ter ask him, le' me come an' ask him.

RAM. Who say anyting 'bout 'fraid. I en say a 'fraid. A say yer have ter wait fer de right moment dat's all.

BATEE. I en say yer 'fraid I say it look like yer 'fraid.

RAM. Look, woman, yer causing ter much trouble yer know.

BATEE. You better make sure yer get dis ten pounds or else den yer go see what trouble really is. Yer done get me mouth running fer chicken an' don't let him fool you, dem guards does make good money yer know.

RAM. Ssshhhh, keep yer voice down.

BATEE. A warning yer if dis time yer en get no money de next time any a dem come in here a go trow de baby pot all over dem.

RAM. What wrong wit yer, woman? Like yer don't hear. If a tell yer it coming it coming, so what's all de fuss about.

BATEE. Well yer better make sure dat's all.

RAM *returns.*

ARNOLD. Like de woman giving yer some trouble, brother Ram.

RAM. Boy trouble is she middle name. Soon as she open she eyes in de morning she start an' is only when she lie down ter sleep she close down. She worst dan de BBC.

ARNOLD. A know just what yer mean. Una was de same ting, she used ter start on me mother an' work she way down de whole family tree an' de funny ting is she used ter say how me brother, de same one she living wit, she use ter say how me brother was dirty an' en have no shame living wi' all dem girls an' how he even went wit' de dirty white girls, but now she living wit' him so how yer work dat out, brother Ram?

RAM. Well dat's what we have ter do together, brother Arnold. We have ter get on de right track, on de right plane as it were and then de answer will evolve from within.

ARNOLD. Yer mean like a belch, brother Ram?

RAM. Yes something like dat.

ARNOLD. A carn't wait but it taking a long time, brother Ram.

RAM. It will come, it will come, give it time. I'm going ter go into a little trance ter see if anyting coming, ter see if a getting anyting but a must warn yer if yer see a do anyting funny just keep still and quiet because yer mustn't break de train of thought and something else don't be frighten if yer see anyting strange.

ARNOLD. Why, why what go happen? (*Getting up, anxious.*)

RAM. Nothing go happen just be calm.

RAM *assumes a Yoga position, changes to another starts humming and constricting and breathing heavily.* ARNOLD *looks about anxiously.*

ARNOLD. You alright, brother Ram? Brother Ram, answer me, brother Ram.

RAM. A thought a tell yer not to bodder me, eh?

ARNOLD. But, brother Ram, I was scared I thought something happen ter yer.

RAM. Alright a go try again and dis time don't worry me. I trying ter help yer. How a go get de message if yer start ter stop me?

ARNOLD. A sorry, brother Ram, a sorry, go ahead I en go say nothing.

RAM. Right.

RAM *goes into his trance again. He is deep in trance.* ARNOLD *gets up and walks around him curiously, making sure he is gone.* ARNOLD *gets a pin and sticks it in* RAM.

Oh God! Wha' yer do dat for? Dat hurt yer know. Look a bleeding now. A go get blood all over me white kuta.

ARNOLD. But, brother Ram, I always hear when somebody in a trance dey carn't feel nothing, an' yer look really gone. Anyhow yer get anyting, yer get anyting, any message?

RAM. How a go get message when you sticking kina ting in me?

ARNOLD. But, brother Ram, dem Indians in India does stick all kinda tings in dem and still get messages.

RAM. Well dem different, man, dis is Britain, dis en India.

ARNOLD. Ar a see, is de cold.

RAM. Yes well dat have something ter do wit' it.

ARNOLD. Well try again ner.

RAM. Nar twice is enough and if I en get notting den I en go get notting. Now, an' me en want yer stabbing me soon as a close me eyes, is bad enough me woman in de back giving me hell plus you trying ter kill me.

ARNOLD. A sorry, brother Ram, a really sorry. So what we go do, brother Ram? How we go find out why she left me?

RAM. Well I think we better try what we decide. Dat you get a message ter she. Tell she am, dat somebody who know she father just come up from Trinidad and she father tell me ter look she up, a have some news for she, a present fer she. Yea dat's it. A have a present fer she, from she father. A could always give she one a me bracelets. Right yer got dat?

ARNOLD. Loud an' clear, brother Ram. Dat go work, a have a feeling dat go work.

RAM. Well you do your part I go do mine and de forces going come together like hog an' grass.

ARNOLD. No, brother Ram, like hog an' mud.

RAM. Yes, yes, like hog and mud, dat's what a said, so how much do you give the bookies ev'ry week?

ARNOLD. Well sometimes I give dem five, sometimes dey give me five. Is hard ter say a do keep a check but I on top.

RAM. Dat's a lot a money ter trow away every week. Why yer don't come an' see me before yer bet? I get numbers too yer know especially for de Derby an' dem big race.

ARNOLD. I didn't know dat.

RAM. Yes, man, but anyhow le' we fix up dis matter first den we go work on de horses.

ARNOLD. So yer could really pick winner, brother Ram?

RAM. Pick dem, a more dan pick dem, a could even give yer second an' third.

ARNOLD. But how come Alfred never say notting 'bout dat?

RAM. Well a tell yer he was up ter something but he en want anybody else backing de winners, de price go come down.

ARNOLD. But he worst dan me, brother Ram, he don't back no winners at all.

RAM. But a mean just in case he back dem, he en want de price ter be low, yer see?

ARNOLD. Yes a see what yer mean, yer carn't trust nobody dese days.

RAM. But Alfred's still a nice guy yer know. He just en have he t's crossed, but he alright. Anyhow a better go an' see 'bout de food, she keeping too quiet an' dat is a bad sign. Alfred tell yer about me rates?

ARNOLD. No he didn't say notting 'bout dat.

RAM. Well he must be forget but a does charge a small fee fer me expenses an' so.

BATEE *from inside*.

BATEE. De child crying again yer know. Yer carn't hear de child cry? Wha' happen yer deaf or what? Well if you car hear she I telling yer now.

RAM (*shouts*). A coming, a coming, yes expenses you know, overheads an' books and charts and instruments.

ARNOLD. I see, an' how much is dat den?

BATEE (*from inside*). De child still crying yer know.

RAM. A coming, a coming. Well for a full sitting like dis say ten.

ARNOLD. Pounds?

RAM. Yes. Well a don't only mean for this sitting a mean fer seeing Una an' getting her to come back an' all dat.

BATEE (*from inside*). So what am I supposed ter do, stuff paper in she mouth? I trying ter read yer know an' a carn't read wit' de child crying yer know, so make up yer mind.

ARNOLD. But, brother Ram, a only have thirty bob.

BATEE (*from inside*). Well make up yer mind, yer coming or yer en coming?

RAM. Well give me de thirty bob an' bring de rest next time yer come.

ARNOLD. Dis woman costing me a lota money.

RAM. Well she worth it.

ARNOLD. A only hope so, brother.

RAM *shows* ARNOLD *to the door*.

RAM. Well you will see, she is as time goes by, you will see right, you get de message ter her an yer give me de green light.

ARNOLD. Right, brother Ram.

RAM. Right sita, ram, whale come salam, shalom, peace, ciao, via con Dios, mind how yer go.

BATEE (*from inside*). When yer done wit' dat damn foolishness maybe yer could see 'bout de child.

RAM. Alright, alright, what wrong wit de child?

BATEE. She stop crying now but she hungry, where de money? Yer get de money? How much yer get?

RAM. A get thirty bob.

BATEE. Thirty bob, dat's all yer get, a big man like you, yer sit down here all night an' all yer get is thirty bob. So where I go get a chicken for thirty bob? Gimme de damn money anyway. (*Grabs it and stalks off.*)

RAM *holds his head and looks up.*


## Scene Two

*The next day. Doorbell rings.*

RAM. Ram, Ram, oh, hi, man hi, come in, come in, how are you?

LUCILLE. Hello, hi, fine, fine, how are you?

MARK. Hello, hi man, how are you doing?

RAM. I'm doing well, still holding strain you know, up and down you know how it goes, don't tell nobody but a think I'm winning.

MARK. Wow that's good, you must be on a good buzz, boy. I'm just trying to level off.

RAM. So how are you, Lucille?

LUCILLE. I'm fine I had a fantastic day yesterday.

RAM. Yea what did you do?

LUCILLE. Well, I went shopping and that was nice and in the afternoon I met a friend and we took the kids to the park and that was nice and they enjoyed it and we dug it and it was nice.

RAM. That's nice I had a fantastic yesterday too.

MARK. Yea.

LUCILLE. Yea what did you do?

RAM. I saw a real, natural cat from back home you know, pure soul very simple and unspoilt, really beautiful, you know and he turned me on.

MARK. Yea what does he do?

RAM. He works on the underground.

MARK. Yea.

LUCILLE. Yea.

RAM. Yea, it's funny and he had a real human problem you know, like we used to have before.

MARK. Yea.

LUCILLE. Yea.

RAM. Well he's got them, boy has he got them but it was nice to relate with him you know clear and simple it seems when you're away from it and it was so beautiful man, I was able to see things so clearly man, I don't know where I got the power from, but I got it.

MARK. Yea.

LUCILLE. Yea.

MARK. So what was wrong with him?

RAM. Well his wife left him.

MARK. Yea.

RAM. An' dig this, she's living with his brother.

LUCILLE. Wow, his brother.

MARK. Wow, yea.

RAM. Yes, I know his brother, to you it might seem strange but it's a very West Indian thing it might not seem like a lot but to him it's a very real problem.

MARK. Yea, I know it's funny, how some people seem unable to observe a situation from a detached point of view when in fact that's the only way to do it.

RAM. Yea.

LUCILLE. Well I don't know so much he probably loves her very much.

MARK. Yea, I'm not saying he doesn't but she obviously digs his brother more, so, he should learn to relate within that reality.

LUCILLE. Yea, I know that, you know that, but does he know that?

MARK. I don't know.

LUCILLE. Right, he obviously doesn't so all he can think about is his woman and how to get her back, right.

MARK. I suppose so.

LUCILLE. Right, what did you tell him?

RAM. Well, I didn't tell him anything definite, I tried to show him where the problem comes from and he should, you know what we were talking about last week, see it in a greater sense.

MARK. Yea, I mean, if he goes on like that he'll have one problem after another, right?

LUCILLE. Right. Was he able to grasp the meaning?

RAM. Well I don't know if I managed to show him everything but I did manage to show him to make him change his direction a little.

MARK. Well, that can't be bad but you must be careful you know you mustn't let other people slow down your evolution.

RAM. No, I got that well in hand but still the more credits one can pick up along the way the better.

LUCILLE. Yea, so what did you tell him?

RAM. Well, I told him to get her to come and see me and I'll talk to her.

MARK. Yea.

LUCILLE. That's a good move you're still within your scene. You think she'll come?

RAM. Well he thinks she'll come but yer see if she comes that's cool, if she doesn't come that's cool too.

MARK. Yea.

RAM. Dig this, you know how he'll get her to come. He's going to get a message to her that I have a present for her from her father.

LUCILLE. Wow, yea, so she going to come here not expecting anything. Wow, what a buzz.

MARK. Who's the chick, what does she do?

RAM. I think she works at Lyons.

MARK. Yea.

RAM. Here make that up, ner.

LUCILLE. Wow, yes, I was wondering what was keeping you.

RAM. Well I thought I'd keep you in suspense for a while, do a Hitchcock.

MARK. Yea, is it new?

RAM. Like a baby, it just came over yesterday and I just came and handed me an ounce, just like that.

MARK. Wow, yea, how's your wife, still uptight?

RAM. Yea, she'll never learn.

LUCILLE. Have you tried to tell her?

RAM. Yea I tried, I tried to tell her but she carn't see so I just leave her, I do my bit. I carn't do more than that.

LUCILLE. Yea.

RAM. But it's hard for her you know she came straight from a small village to London.

MARK. Yea.

RAM. You can imagine the contrast.

LUCILLE. Yea.

RAM. I was lucky, I could adapt but it's different with her, she carn't change, so I just leave her.

LUCILLE. Yea, we brought a sound over for you to hear. (*To* MARK.) Put it on.

MARK. OK. (*Goes. Heavy sound.*)

RAM. Yea, that's nice.

LUCILLE. You like it?

RAM. Yea, it's nice, who is it?

LUCILLE. Santana.

RAM. Yea, is it The Lion?

MARK. No it's the one after but you can still hear bits of The Lion.

LUCILLE. Yea.

BATEE (*from kitchen*). Yer wouldn't mind turning down that noise de child trying to sleep yer know.

RAM. Turn it down, turn it down.

MARK *goes*.

LUCILLE. Shall I go and see how she is?

MARK. Yea.

LUCILLE *goes into kitchen*.

LUCILLE. How's the baby?

BATEE. The baby's fine, she's sleeping now.

LUCILLE. What's her name?

BATEE. Her name's Sharma.

LUCILLE. Oh, yes, Sharma, I hope we didn't wake her.

BATEE. No you didn't wake her but the music was too loud.

LUCILLE. Why don't you come inside and sit down.

BATEE. No I like it here.

LUCILLE. Oh, well, see you then, 'bye.

BATEE. Yes, 'bye.

*Outside*.

RAM. How is she?

LUCILLE. She's alright.

MARK. Good, here, this is good.

LUCILLE. Yea.

MARK. So when is this chick coming to see you?

RAM. I don't know, anytime.

LUCILLE. You must let us know how it turns out.

MARK. Yea.

RAM. Well we'll see.

*All three silent for five or ten minutes, stoned, staring into space.*

MARK. Ha! Ha! Ha! Ha! Ha!

LUCILLE. What, what are you laughing at? What's so funny?

MARK. I was thinking about that cat and his brother, it must be a strange relationship.

LUCILLE. Yea, come to think of it it is, I mean, your best friend, or someone on the same scene, but not his brother, I can't see it.

MARK. What does he do?

RAM. He works on the buses.

MARK. Yea, too much.

RAM. Yes, it's the underground versus the buses.

LUCILLE. I think the buses will win.

MARK. Why?

LUCILLE. Well it's healthier, fitter, more sunshine, better vibes.

MARK. Yea, but the underground, it's heavier, more soulful, more power.

LUCILLE. Well, we'll see.

MARK. So, when she comes here what are you going to tell her? How are you going to do it?

RAM. I don't know, I'll just play it by ear and hope I find the right note.

MARK. Yea, that's interesting.

LUCILLE. Can we come and hide and maybe listen, that would be a groove.

RAM. No, I don't think so.

LUCILLE. No, we can't do that, that wouldn't be fair. I'd like to though.

MARK. How about a tape recorder?

RAM. No, no, I'll forget to turn it on . . . I'll tell you.

MARK. Right.

LUCILLE. Great, when did you say she was coming?

RAM. I don't know, maybe tomorrow.

LUCILLE. I see, so if we come on Saturday you'll know by then.

RAM. Yea, should.

MARK. Good we were coming on Saturday anyway so now we have something special to come for, great.

LUCILLE. If the buses win I'll buy you a nice curry.

MARK. And if the underground wins I'll buy you a Chinese, so you can't lose.

RAM. That's nice.

MARK. We shouldn't have told him that because if he feels like eating curry he'll make the buses win.

LUCILLE. No he wouldn't do that.

RAM. No I wouldn't do that.

MARK. Right that's settled then.

LUCILLE. Is she always there.

MARK. Who?

LUCILLE. In there.

RAM. Sometimes.

LUCILLE. Doesn't she ever come in?

RAM. Not when people's here.

LUCILLE. I see, well it's your scene, you know how to handle it.

*A stoned silence again, lasting as long as necessary.*

MARK. Right we better see about splitting.

LUCILLE. Right.

RAM. Yea, yer going.

MARK. Yea, hey, man, how about scoring some off you.

RAM. You know I don't believe in selling, I'll give you some here.

MARK. Right, beautiful.

LUCILLE. Right I'm ready, should I go and say goodbye?

RAM. No I'll tell her you did.

LUCILLE. Right, till Saturday then.

MARK. 'Bye.

RAM. Peace.

*BATEE comes in.*

BATEE. Dey gone?

RAM. Yes.

BATEE. Phew, dis place stink a drugs, an' look at the ashes all over the place. If yer think I going clean it yer lie.

RAM. Is alright, I'll clean it, I'll clean it. (*Pause.*) Well, a suppose Gandhi swept.

## ACT TWO

### Scene One

*Next day. Bell rings.*

RAM. Ram, Ram, Ram, come in welcome to the house of truth, come in.

UNA. Thank you.

RAM. I am Ram.

UNA. My name is Una, Mister Ram.

RAM. There is no need for the mister, just Ram would do.

UNA. Alright, Ram.

RAM. How are you then?

UNA. I am fine am, I came to pick up the, am.

RAM. Oh yes, yes yer come fer yer present, I've got it somewhere, here. (*Looks.*) Yer in any hurry, I know I've got it here somewhere.

UNA. No, no hurry.

RAM. Well when it's ready to turn up it will, these tings have a funny way of happening, would you like something ter drink?

UNA. Yes, thanks.

RAM (*shouts*). Batee, bring two drinks, a orange.

BATEE. De orange is fer de child, yer know me en buy no orange fer you.

RAM. Never mind all that, bring two orange.

BATEE. Right, right. (*Brings drinks. To* UNA.) Hello. (*To* RAM.) Dis en no cafe yer know.

UNA. Hello.

RAM. Alright, alright.

BATEE *goes*.

Right, dat looks nice.

UNA. Yes.

RAM. Is it alright?

UNA. Yes it is.

RAM. It could do wit' some bitters though.

UNA. Yer mean ter say yer have bitters?

RAM. No I en have none but it could do wit' some.

UNA. Yes it could do wit' some rum too.

RAM. Yer mean ter say yer have rum?

UNA. No, I en have no, but it could do wit some.

RAM. Or a see. It go turn up just now, I'll have another look in a minute. (*Looks.*) Ar, here it is, a tell yer it would turn up. (*Picks up bracelet.*)

UNA. Yes it's nice, it's nice, he didn't send no letter wit' it?

RAM. No no letter, a suppose he thought de present was so nice dat he didn't tink you'd want a letter too.

UNA. Yes dat's true, a must write an' thank 'im.

RAM. Oh, it's nothing, it's nothing . . . Who?

UNA. Oh, my father.

RAM. Oh yes, write him but don't mention de bracelet, dey opening de letters an' dem back home, an' if dem postman get ter find out people sending yer jewels dey go look out fer yer letters, an' open dem up.

UNA. Oh yes.

RAM. Yes. But anyway, yer go be able ter thank him personally soon.

UNA. Why, he coming up.

RAM. No, but you and Arnold must be making a trip back home pretty soon.

UNA. I don't live wit' Arnold no more, I left he long time ago and besides de underground don't go to de West Indies, a know a lot a English people think so but it don't.

RAM. Oh, I see, I didn't know you left him. Well he going ter have ter go by he self.

UNA. A tell yer de underground don't go dere, how he going go?

RAM. Or, a see so, you don't know.

UNA. Don't know what? What a don't know?

RAM. Oh yes dat's true, it must have happened right after you and him split up.

UNA. What happen? What happen after we split?

RAM. Well I don't know if a should tell yer, a mean, a don't know if it's my place ter tell yer but a suppose now yer left him yer just like anybody else, anyhow it carn't do no harm.

UNA. What carn't do no harm?

RAM. So you don't know Arnold had a win on de pools, a third dividend a tink dey call it.

UNA. He, win money, on de pools, well a never, dat man, dat bobo, I carn't believe it.

RAM. Yes, a not saying he win a fortune but as far as I hear is enough.

UNA. But, wait, my, husband, win money, my husband.

RAM. Yes, yer husband Arnold but a mean now dat yer left him yer carn't really do anything about it. By the way why did you leave him?

UNA (*thinking*). Oh, I left him because he never take off de damn uniform, he take mey to de pictures, he in de uniform an' as we going he say 'Mind de doors' – dat is he idea of a joke. Yer see wat I had ter put up wit'?

RAM. Yes, a see.

UNA. But I saw him on Sunday an' he still look de same ter me. He en look no richer, yer sure he win money? An' he still wearing dat uniform.

RAM. Well dat's why, he's such a genuine guy, although he win all dat money he still living de same way and doing de same kind a job an' yer carn't see no sign a money. He en showing off as some people does do. When dem win a lot a money he still don't offer nobody he cigarettes, a mean how sincere can a man get? A mean even me, living my kinda life, if I won de pools, is bound ter make some difference, if only de slightest but wit' him no difference at all. Maybe he should be sitting here talking ter people.

UNA. Really.

RAM. Yes no sign at all.

UNA. Yes come ter tink of it he was always sneaky wit' money.

RAM. Yer see he was practising all this time.

UNA. Yes.

RAM. But anyhow is too late now yer miss yer chance.

UNA. Too late fer what?

RAM. Ter enjoy de money an' maybe even make a trip back home ter see yer father.

UNA. It en too late, I is still he wife, he legal wife, I en divorce him, an' he en divorce me, so what too late.

RAM. No, I was just thinking, you've left him and started a new life of your own, you don't want ter go back to all dat.

UNA. Who carn't go back, if I go back now he bound ter take me.

RAM. Well, I'm not so sure, he.

UNA. He what, he have another woman, I know dem woman yer know, soon as dey hear a man have some money dey after him like a shot an' he so foolish he going believe anything dey tell him.

RAM. No, he ken have no woman.

UNA. Dat's good, he better now, am, a suppose he move now buy a new house an' ting, eh?

RAM. No, he still living de same place, a tell yer he en change.

UNA. Oh.

RAM. Yer going ter see him?

UNA. Well, I is he wife, isn't I he wife, an' if I don't look out fer him, who going protect him from all dem blood sucking woman, dat's what a wife is for, ter look after she man.

RAM. Alright but a warning yer, if yer go there don't expect ter see any money don't mention money or even look fer it because he go think dat's what yer come back for, an' remember yer left him so it's going ter take a long time fer him ter place he trust in your hands again.

UNA. I know I'm prepared.

RAM. Right now what about de fella yer living wit'?

UNA. Well dat's another problem, is he brother.

RAM. He brother? Who Arnold's brother?

UNA. Yes de one on de buses.

RAM. Lord yer really get yerself in a mess day.

UNA. Yes he's another one always in de damn uniform too an everywhere we go always saying 'Hold tight' and 'No standing on top'. Dat's he idea of a joke too. What a go do, brother Ram? He very jealous, he go beat me up, a know he go beat me up, a know.

RAM. What about Arnold? Yer not worried about Arnold?

UNA. He is alright, Arnold is he brother, is me he go beat.

RAM. Let us think. I know what, tell him yes tell him yer father sick an' dying because he hear he favourite daughter left she husband and living wit' he brother an' de only way ter give him back he will ter live is fer you ter go back ter yer husband, but yer en really want ter, but yer have ter fer yer father sake, how dat sound?

UNA. Dat sound good, Mister Ram. Dat could work, dat could work. Right I'll go an' see him now, thanks, Mister Ram.

RAM. Dat's alright, my child, dat's alright, my child, an' when yer see Arnold tell him I say don't forget de balance.

UNA. What balance?

RAM. He go know what I mean, 'bye then.

UNA. 'Bye.

*Sound of child crying.*

RAM. Batee, Batee, de child crying, Batee, Batee, de child crying.

BATEE. Batee gone out, Batee in a restaurant in a mink coat having dinner wit' a tall good-looking man an' he Rolls Royce park outside, dat's where Batee is.

**Scene Two**

*The next day.* RAM *is sitting reading newspapers.* BATEE
*comes in and sits down.*

RAM. A see Boysee get married.

BATEE. Boysee, Boysee Ramcharan, wha yer see he get
married?

RAM. It here in de papers.

BATEE. Who he marry?

RAM. Some girl from Couva.

BATEE. I didn't know Couva had any girls ter get married, wha
is she name?

RAM. Rita Narinesingh.

BATEE. Rita Narinesingh, Rita Narinesingh get married?

RAM. Yes, it right here look.

BATEE. Yes, is she, well look at my crosses. Rita Narinesingh
get married, if any body had tell me Rita Narinesingh had get
married a woulda a tell dem de lie.

RAM. But how yer could say dat?

BATEE. Yer know Rita Narinesingh?

RAM. No.

BATEE. Well shut yer mouth. A must write Ivy an find out how
de wedding went.

RAM. All dese letters yer writing a hope yer have money fer de
stamps, anyhow de same time ask Mousa what is de chances
of opening a church down dere.

BATEE. Who yer tink yer is – Winston Churchill?

RAM. Alright, alright, do bodder.

BATEE. Who was dat just now, dat was a white girl, I don't want no white girls coming into my house yer know, they too dirty, I have ter clean dis house yer know.

RAM. Alright, alright, she gone, it was just Robert, he brought a friend around.

BATEE. Dat Robert, next time a see him a go tell him, not ter bring he dirty white woman he pick up in de street here.

RAM. Alright, next time you see him, you tell him.

BATEE. A go tell him we, yer tink a 'fraid a Robert, I don't owe Robert notting, yer know, Robert en holding no secret fer me.

RAM. He en holding no secret fer me neither, so what yer talking bout, anyhow yer making a big ting outa notting.

BATEE. Notting yer call it, he bring dem dirty white woman in my nice clean house an' you call dat notting.

RAM. If you would only try ter see dat there is a lot of valuable work, ter be done in de Community, yer see dat nice girl, dat just left here, well she is doing more for black people dan you yer own people.

BATEE. Who, black, me en black yer en see I brown skin, yer colour blind or what.

RAM. Woman, yer head hard just like a coconut.

BATEE. Yes I know you go on worrying bout my head, is yer own head yer must worry about an' all de foolishness yer does get up too, I radder my head like a coconut dan like a toffee, de next time I en have no money a go take yer ter de sweet shop an' sell yer.

RAM. Yes, well dat's why yer will always be stupid, because yer always tink 'bout money, yer wouldn't get off yer ass an do someting an try an reach people, an' help dem, yer just tink everybody dirty, you dirtier dan all a dem, beauty is in de eye of de beholder an' so is dirt, yer see.

BATEE. Well if I dirty a glad, me en having notting ter be clean fer, dis is a dirty country. (*Baby starts to cry.*) Yer see what yer cause now, look de child crying.

RAM. Well go an' pick she up, ner.

BATEE. Who me pick she up I busy, you pick she up.

*Door bell rings.*

RAM. A wonder who dat could be.

BATEE. I don't know, must be one a yer children, yer have more children dan one a dem Sheiks.

*RAM goes to the door.*

RAM. Ram, Ram, salam whale come, shalom, hello, good evening, hi. Come in, welcome to the house of reality, truth and love. What you need I provide. What you provide I need. What you desire I recommend. What you recommend I desire. My thoughts are at your service. Come in.

ALBERT. Thanks, a have me little boy here.

RAM. My name is Ram. I am Ram. Ram is I.

ALBERT. Yes, my name is Albert.

RAM. Yes I know.

ALBERT. Well this is why a come ter see yer. (*Thumps son.*) Say 'good evening' ter Mr Ram. (*Thump.*)

SKIN HEAD. Watcher.

RAM. Hello.

ALBERT (*thump*). Watcher. What yer mean by watcher. Say good evening.

SKIN HEAD. Good evening.

ALBERT. You see, Mr Ram, dat what Albert come ter see yer for.

RAM. What? What's wrong wit' him?

ALBERT. What's wrong with him? Yer mean yer carn't see it. Me work hard fer ten years ter send fer me family right. A do' mind doing dat. Dat's wat a man have ter do but yer know what really hurt me. Dis one dis one him say, him is a skin head.

RAM. Yes I know.

ALBERT. So what a go do wit' him? A try all kinda ting. Him still a skin head, a mean it hurts ter see yer son go bad. Yer have any children, Mister Ram?

RAM. Yes I have one.

ALBERT. Well you much know what a talking 'bout.

RAM. How much yer have?

ALBERT. Fourteen, fourteen children I raise. Yer wouldn't believe dat would yer? Fourteen, thirteen a dem turn out good. De last one turn out a skin head. (*Thump*.) Sit down, sit down. A do' know where a went wrong wit' dis one.

SKIN HEAD. Roit, roit.

ALBERT (*thump*). Don't answer me. No roit, roit, say yes Dad. Tell me where a went wrong. He don't want ter join de army. He don't want ter come on de council wit' me. So wha' a go do wit' him, eh?

RAM. Well I'm not sure. I'll have ter tink about it.

ALBERT. Tink, dat en go help. I think about it all de time. Him still a skin head. Me ask him what is a skin head. Him say him don't know, so me ask him why him is a skin head. Him

say him don't know so what we go do? (*Thump.*) Tell Mr
Ram why yer is a skin head.

SKIN HEAD. Don't know do I.

ALBERT (*thump*). What's dis, 'do I' business? (*Thump.*)
Answer properly.

SKIN HEAD. I did, I did answer proper, don't know.

ALBERT. Well tell him. What is a skin head. Tell him.

SKIN HEAD. Don't know.

ALBERT. You see. A car get notting outa him. Do more a ask
de less a find out.

RAM. Well it's a tough one.

ALBERT. If he tough, dat's one ting he get from me, he
toughness.

RAM. Well what do yer want ter do?

SKIN HEAD. Don't know. I've seen you ain't I? I've seen you
shopping down the Portobello with dem hippies, that where I
get me Reggaes.

RAM. Yes I go out shopping sometimes.

SKIN HEAD. Yea I've seen you.

ALBERT. What does dat mean, you see him out shopping. An'
where you get money to buy records, eh? An what kinda
answer is dat, eh?

SKIN HEAD. Nofink, it don't mean nofink. It just means I've
seen him before. You know what I mean doncher?

RAM. Yes, I know.

SKIN HEAD. Well.

ALBERT. What dat have ter do wit' what yer go do wit' yerself.

SKIN HEAD. Nofink. It don't have nofink ter do wifit, nofink. I don't know what yer getting so excited about.

ALBERT (*thump*). Don't answer me back. What's all dis about yer carn't even talk properly.

RAM. Well I think you should let him to develop naturally. Dis skin head is just a phase.

ALBERT. A what?

RAM. A phase. Just something he's going tru and he'll grow out of it. Didn't you, at one stage of your existence think that your life was changing?

ALBERT. Not one stage, I had fourteen a them stages. Yer tink yer go grow out a it?

SKIN HEAD. Don't know do I?

RAM. Have you tried loving him?

ALBERT. Of course a love him. A wouldn't be worrying 'bout him if a didn't love him.

RAM. Well, maybe yes. Should try de other approach. My father used ter say 'spare de rod and spoil de child'.

ALBERT. Yer mean beat him. What beat me own child. Look wha' wrang wit' yer. I bring thirteen children, a never beat one a dem an' a en go start now. A tought you was supposed ter be a holy man, an' you tell me ter beat my child. Come le' we go, dis man en know what he talking 'bout. (*Thump*.) Hurry up.

SKIN HEAD. Yes, Dad, right, Dad.

ALBERT. Wait till a get me hands on dat Alfred a go' hit him such a last he go take ten years ter recover. Five years fer every pound he get off me.

RAM. Yer mean ter say yer give Alfred two pounds.

ALBERT. Then give him. He say dat was he commission.

RAM. Oh ho. Oh God dat Alfred.

ALBERT *and* SKIN HEAD *leave.*

BATEE. What yer making dat noise for?

RAM. Is Alfred.

BATEE. What wrong wit' him?

RAM. He stupid dat's what's wrong wit' him. He sending me de wrong kinda people dat's all.

BATEE. What kinda people yer want him ter send?

RAM. People wit' money.

BATEE. But Alfred en know people wit' money.


### Scene Three

*Doorbell rings.*

RAM. Oh it's you, hi, come in, come in.

MARK. Hi man, how you doing?

LUCILLE. Hi, how are you?

RAM. I'm fine, still winning.

MARK. That's a long buzz.

RAM. Yea the longer the better.

MARK. Yea.

LUCILLE. Yea.

RAM. So how are things with you all?

MARK. Oh we're fine.

LUCILLE. I had a fantastic day today. I went shopping and that was nice and I met a friend and we took the kids to the park and that was nice and they enjoyed it and we enjoyed it so it was nice.

RAM. That's nice.

MARK. Yea, so what's been happening with you?

RAM. Well I had a groovy day too. That chick came and she was really beautiful. You know real pure natural soul, really unspoilt like they say on the package 'Untouched by human hands'.

MARK. Yea what does she do?

RAM. A think she works at Lyons.

MARK. Oh yes.

LUCILLE. Yes and she was really groovy. What was wrong then, what caused the split?

RAM. Yer know how we used ter be, hang ups and likes and dislikes well these people are so beautiful and natural it's fantastic.

LUCILLE. Yea when I think back how we used to be before, it's a big joke, I can't imagine how we coulda been so blind.

MARK. Yea, anyhow what was her hang up?

RAM. Well she didn't really have a hang up as such. It's just that she wanted different things out of life.

LUCILLE. Ar wants, I want, she want, you want.

RAM. It's just that she couldn't relate with the guy.

LUCILLE. Why, did she leave him?

MARK. Yea.

RAM. She said something about the uniform and his sense of humour she didn't like.

LUCILLE. Ar likes, I like, she like, you like.

RAM. Well anyhow she didn't like the uniform.

MARK. That's crazy.

LUCILLE. Well I know it's crazy, you know it's crazy but to her it's not crazy, to her it's a real problem.

MARK. Still it's good to observe these things at a distance and not get involved.

RAM. Right.

LUCILLE. Yea by the way that grass was something else, we really enjoyed it.

RAM. Yea.

MARK. Yea we went home and really blew it. What's good about it is you don't need much. Is it all gone?

RAM. No I've still got some left, here.

LUCILLE. Wow yea, let's roll.

MARK. I must buy some before it disappears.

LUCILLE. How is she? Still uptight.

RAM. Yea you know, no change.

LUCILLE. You change, I change, Mark changes, you've got to change, doesn't she know that.

RAM. No I don't think so.

MARK. Have you tried to tell her?

RAM. Yes I try but I carn't do more than that.

LUCILLE. Yea that's true. We brought over a new sound for you to hear, put it on, Mark.

MARK. Right. (*Does.*)

RAM. Yea, yea, it's nice.

LUCILLE. You like it?

RAM. Yea, who is it?

MARK. It's Herbie Mann.

RAM. Right. Is it de Village Gate?

MARK. No it's the one after, Memphis Underground, but you can still hear traces of Village Gate on it.

LUCILLE. Right.

RAM. Yea. (*Stoned silence.*)

MARK. So what did you tell the chick?

RAM. Well I didn't tell her anything really I just, I couldn't tell her anything, I just, what I did was to redirect, all I did was to use one of her own hang ups to get her to go in a certain direction that's all.

LUCILLE. Right.

MARK. Yea, so you didn't try to show her reality?

RAM. No I couldn't.

MARK. Well that's cool.

LUCILLE. Well what did you do?

RAM. I just happen to let her know how lucky I think she and her husband was to have won some money.

MARK. Oh I see, you didn't know they were apart.

RAM. Dig?

LUCILLE. Right.

RAM. And how, they'll be going back home soon and yer know what reaction that creates.

MARK. Yea.

LUCILLE. Yea wow too much, what a shot.

MARK. Yea.

LUCILLE. Right that's a good move because you're still within your sphere of self because she's already on the bread trip.

RAM. Right but I carn't help feeling a little.

MARK. No, man, you're cool. By using her existing hang ups you haven't altered the structure of her line and don't forget the credits.

RAM. Right.

LUCILLE. Right so what you have to worry about?

RAM. Nothing.

*Voice from outside.*

BATEE. Alya trying ter deafen somebody or what?

MARK. What, what?

LUCILLE. What she.

RAM. No turn down the sound.

LUCILLE. Yea turn it down.

MARK *turns it down.*

MARK. What's wrong with her man?

LUCILLE. I'll go and see her. (*Goes.*) Hello, was it too loud?

BATEE. Yes I have a headache.

LUCILLE. Is it bad?

BATEE. Yer ever had a headache?

LUCILLE. Yes.

BATEE. Well yer know what's like then.

LUCILLE. Yea but whenever I get one I always lie down and do some exercises.

BATEE. What kinda exercises?

LUCILLE. Breathing exercises.

BATEE. Well I carn't do that, I have a cold.

LUCILLE. Yea, well I hope you're better soon.

BATEE. Oh nothing wrong wit' me.

LUCILLE. Yea how is the baby?

BATEE. Yer mean Sharma, she's sleeping, she's got a cold too.

LUCILLE. Have you tried hot lemon?

BATEE. No but a gey she two tablets and de doctor say dat should do de trick.

LUCILLE. Yea what were the tablets?

BATEE. Me en know, some green ones.

LUCILLE. Well at least it's nothing serious.

BATEE. No it's nothing serious. She should be alright tomorrow, God spare life.

LUCILLE. Yea well I hope she's better soon, 'bye then.

BATEE. Yes, 'bye.

LUCILLE *goes back in.*

MARK. Alright?

LUCILLE. Yea she just said the most fantastic thing.

RAM. What was that?

LUCILLE. She said something about God sparing life.

RAM. Oh that, dat is a old saying back home. All de old people used ter say that, she must be hear her grandmother say it.

MARK. Yea it sounds really turned on back there.

RAM. Yea well we have our way of doing it.

LUCILLE. Yea. (*Stoned silence.*)

MARK. Ha ha ha.

LUCILLE. What what, what's so funny? What are you laughing at?

MARK. I was just thinking of that chick coming here all unaware and leaving really turned on.

LUCILLE. Yea but is she really turned on? She turned onto a bread trip but is she really turned on?

MARK. No but she going back to him.

LUCILLE. Who says she's going back to him?

MARK. Well she obviously wants to go back, all that bread waiting for her.

LUCILLE. Well I don't know so much. I think she probably wanted to go back to him anyway, she just got the reason to do it that's all.

MARK. Yea maybe.

LUCILLE. Right.

RAM. Yea.

MARK. How is he supposed to have got the money anyway?

RAM. On the pools.

LUCILLE. Wow yea.

MARK. Yea yea that sounds possible.

RAM. Yea well it came easy. I only hope it works.

MARK. Yea if it works you're cool and if it don't work you're
still cool. Right?

RAM. Right let's roll another.

LUCILLE. Right.

MARK. Yea. So we're eating Chinese?

RAM. Let's have a compromise, although it should be Chinese
let's eat Indian right?

LUCILLE. Right.

MARK. Okay. I'm cool.

LUCILLE. Aren't we forgetting something?

MARK. What?

LUCILLE. What about the brother, the buses?

MARK. Yea what did you do about him?

RAM. Well I didn't do anything about him. Really again I used
or at least I think I used a hang up of his but I'm not sure
how that will turn out but mostly it depends on her, the chick
how she handles it.

LUCILLE. Yea so in fact you haven't imposed your karma on
the outcome, one way or another.

RAM. Right.

MARK. Yea but what, how is she going to get rid of him?

RAM. Well dat's just it. She's not going to get rid of him.

MARK. What then?

LUCILLE. How?

RAM. Well she's going to tell him that she got to ge' back to her husband.

LUCILLE. Yea but why?

MARK. Yea why, man?

RAM. Well her father's sick and dying yer see because he heard that his favourite daughter is living with her brother-in-law an' he don't want an old man's death on his hands or at least I'm counting on that, so.

LUCILLE. So, wow, one hit moving up the charts.

MARK. Right.

RAM. So, we're eating Chinese.

MARK. Right I told you, heavier, more power.

LUCILLE. Well I still think you get better vibes on the buses.

MARK. Yea maybe but vibes is vibes. It's not the vibes it's you. (*Stoned silence.*) Ha ha ha.

LUCILLE. What what's so funny?

MARK. No I was just thinking.

LUCILLE. What what?

MARK. No I was just thinking how funny it would be if the father was really sick and dying that would be too much.

LUCILLE. Yea what you think of that, Ram?

RAM. Dat's nothing. What if Arnold really won the pools, eh?

LUCILLE. Ha, ha, too much.

   *Door bell rings.*

RAM. A wonder who dat could be? Dis time a night. (*Goes.*)
Ram, Ram, salam whale come, shalom, peace, good evening,
come in, welcome to the house of truth.

*Inside.*

MARK. Oh oh we better split, let's go in the kitchen.

LUCILLE. Right.

BERTRAM. A sorry ter disturb yer at this late hour but Alfred
said a could come any time an' a just finish me shift, yer see a
do de late shift an' dat's from five ter twelve if a was on de
early shift a woulda come earlier.

RAM. Dat alright, take a seat.

BERTRAM. Well Alfred say yer was a brainy guy yer see an'
yer does solve people problem and them.

RAM. Well yes I do sometimes but first it depends on the
problem and second it depends on the outside forces.

BERTRAM. What outside forces?

RAM. We won't go into that at the moment but as time goes by
you will see.

BERTRAM. Oh yes a hope so.

RAM. Well hope is an important part of it too. Did Alfred say
anything else?

BERTRAM. No he only say yer does help out people wi'
problem.

RAM. Well what is your problem?

BERTRAM. Well it's not a problem really yer see, it's about a
woman.

RAM. What about her?

BERTRAM. Well yer see a living wit' this woman an' a want ter get rid a she but a don't know how. A try all kinds tings. A even wear me uniform all de time because a know she don't like it. She still stay. A even make de same joke dat de man she left used ter make. She still stay.

RAM. Why yer want ter get rid of her?

BERTRAM. Well yer see her is me brother wife an' me father sick and dying because he find out dat he favourite son living wit' he brother wife.

RAM. Oh I see, wow.

BERTRAM. An' yes a don't care how yer fix it an' how much it cost. A just had a little win on de pools.

RAM. Yea. Yer what? But dat's fantastic, man. Right you leave everything ter me. I go fix it fer you and send yer me bill.

BERTRAM. Dat's sound fine ter me.

MARK *and* LUCILLE *come out.*

MARK. Wow yea that's fantastic.

LUCILLE. Yea too much.

RAM. An' don't be surprised if things happen sooner dan yer expect.

BERTRAM. Yer mean yer does work so fast. Yer faster dan the number 28. Yer know it used to be number 31 but de 28 take over.

RAM. Yes, well sometimes, sometimes tings have a habit of happening dat way.

BERTRAM. But yer is a marvel man. Yer marvellous.

RAM. Well sometimes. By the way this is Mark and Lucille. Two friends of mine.

BERTRAM. Howdy.

MARK. Yea. Hi, man.

LUCILLE. Hi.

MARK. We were just about to go out for a meal. How about coming and celebrating with us?

BERTRAM. Well, if a not go be in de way.

MARK. No we don't mind.

LUCILLE. It's great.

BERTRAM. Well if you all don't mind then I'll even stand de bill.

LUCILLE. Great.

MARK. Right let's go then. By the way I hope you like curry.

BERTRAM. I don't mind.

LUCILLE. Great.

RAM (*shouts*). Batee, a going up de road. A coming back soon. Yer want anything?

BATEE. No I en want notting. Take yer time, no hurry.

   *They leave.*


**Scene Four**

ALFRED (*comes in*). Ram, brother Ram, yer dey.

RAM. Yes I here, who's dat?

ALFRED. Is me Alfred. A hear yer want ter see me an' look who a bring ter see yer, Thelma.

RAM. Thelma, is you Thelma. A carn't believe it.

THELMA. Ramsomair Narinesingh but boy yer change, yer really change.

RAM. But look at Thelma. Ner yer is de last person a expect ter see.

ALFRED. A tell yer he would be surprised.

RAM. Come in ner and have a seat. How long since yer come?

THELMA. I came over on Friday night, well Saturday morning.

RAM. Dat's fantastic, man, how long yer here for?

THELMA. I'm going back next week. I just came for a two week stay.

RAM. But dat's great. So how are you?

THELMA. I'm fine, I'm de cream and everybody home is fine. After you stopped writing we thought dat wit' yer bar exams keeping yer busy yer couldn't write and every year we look at de results and couldn't find yer name we thought yer had change yer name or something.

RAM. No I didn't. I just didn't think it was fair on pa ter go through all dem hard times fer me. What I'm doing is trying ter save myself an' do it on my own.

THELMA. Yer is still de cream yer know. Yer uncle Ramdass died, he entered a rum drinking competition and he win but is de last drink dat kill him. He drink five bottles an' de second finish up with four.

RAM. Yea, a carn't remember who it was but somebody wrote me and told me all about it. What about Sonny?

THELMA. Well he married an' have children now. One is nine de other is seven.

RAM. Sonny – things really change.

THELMA. An' yer Auntie Ruby say she still waiting on de

picture a Buckingham Palace yer promise she. She want one a
you an' one a de Queen so don't forget this time. Yer
remember she is de one who lend yer fifty dollars when yer
was coming over here.

RAM. Yes, yes. How is all de boys an' dem?

THELMA. Dey all fine. Some a dem get married, some a dem
still hanging about. Yer Uncle Leonard well he is a big shot
now wit' a American company, driving 'bout in a big car.

RAM. Uncle Leonard a big shot. A always know he would do
something. He was de only one I could relate with, he was de
only hip one. So what yer doing?

THELMA. I still single waiting for Mr Right but having a good
time till he comes along. What about you?

RAM. I married an' have a kid. My wife in de kitchen I'll go an'
get her in a minute, an' I'm sorry about.

THELMA. Ar, what yer sorry about, yer said yer woulda send
for me but after yer stop writing I say well yer must be meet
one a dem dolly birds we keep hearing about so I forget all
about that and we was too young for a start but yer is still de
cream, when yer going ter pay us a visit? Carnival is still de
cream yer know, everybody does play Mas even de Indians
an' all does play Mas.

RAM. Wow dat sound fantastic – I was thinking about it.

THELMA. I know yer mother an' Auntie's dying ter see yer.

RAM. Yea I could just imagine it, too much, yer put me on a
real home sick trip.

THELMA. Well carn't be bad. So when ter tell dem de could
expect yer?

RAM. Tell them when a pass me finals dey go see me. A go
come down an' buy everybody a drink.

THELMA. Yer ever come across what's his name, Peter Lutchmansingh, he was doing his bar exams too. A don't know what became of him.

RAM. No he wasn't in my class but a tink a know de name.

THELMA. Yer must remember him, man, his father an' he used ter carry dirt.

RAM. Oh yes, yes I remember he had some nice sisters.

THELMA. Yes dat's de one but dey all married now.

RAM. Yea so what yer think of England?

THELMA. It en bad.

ALFRED. So Ram a hear yer wanted ter see me.

RAM. Yes a want ter discuss some business wit' yer but no hurry. So Thelma how yer meet up with Alfred?

THELMA. Well believe it or not but he married to a cousin a mine an' a went ter look him up an' he tell me he know yer.

RAM. Oh a see.

THELMA. Go an' get yer wife ner, a dying ter meet her.

RAM. Alright.

RAM *goes into kitchen.* RAM *and* BATEE *come out.*

Batee, dis is a old friend of mine, Thelma dis is me wife, Batee.

THELMA. Hello.

BATEE. Hello, hello, Alfred.

ALFRED. Hello, Mrs Ram.

BATEE. Yer just come up?

THELMA. Yea.

BATEE. What yer tink of it?

THELMA. It en bad but yer car beat Trinidad. How you like it?

BATEE. I don't like it. I dying ter go back home, it too cold, de people don't like me, dey tink we is dirt an' de treat we like dirt, dey lazy an' dey say we lazy, dey dirty an' dey say we dirty, dey bad an' dey say we bad, how yer could like a place like dat?

THELMA. Well I heard a lot of stories but I only just came so I carn't say.

BATEE. Well take my word for it. Dat de way it is an' don't stay a minute longer dan yer have ter stay, is a evil kinda ting dat does rub off on yer if yer stay too long. You look like a nice girl, you go back home an' tell anybody who tinking a coming here dat. Tell dem do' bother it en worth it.

RAM. How you could say dat?

BATEE. Well is true everybody know it, you is de only one who carn't see it, yer could see everything else except dat an' it staring yer full in yer face everyday. Instead a assing around all day why don't take a look at dat.

RAM. Yer giving Thelma de wrong impression.

ALFRED. Ram, I think a better come back some other time.

RAM. No you stay it's nothing, it's alright.

BATEE. Better she get de wrong impression dan de right one, both a dem is de same. If we tink dey don't like we an' if dey don't like we is de same ting but I know it, but you is de only ass who carn't see it. I don't know what wrong wit' yer.

RAM. You don't know what yer talking 'bout you don't go anywhere she don't go anywhere. (*To them.*)

BATEE. Yer right a don't go anywhere. Dat's why a don't go anywhere because everywhere a go a see dem. A don't have ter go nowhere ter know dey don't like we, a could stay in me own home an' know it but one place dey carn't touch me is in my kitchen. Dat's de only place I safe because is mine.

RAM. She carn't understand. Do you all understand her? I don't.

BATEE. Yer don't. Yer don't want ter. You tell dem back home is a trap, a big trap, an' somebody have ter tell dem, somebody have ter say de truth, dat is a failure, de only want we over here ter work fer dem an' ter make dem feel superior, don't mind dem, Trinidad en much but is we own is a heaven compared to dis.

RAM. She don't know what she talking 'bout. Yer have ter get out an' meet people, get ter know dem, get ter understand dem. Oh what's de use. Look I have two nice friends, it's a pity yer carn't meet dem?

BATEE. Who Mark? and what she name, Lucille. She is such yer friend she carn't even remember yer own child name, everytime she come here a have ter tell she. Dem is de two most false people a ever meet. Dey carn't say notting sensible. All dey talk is foolishness. All de time. A never hear dem say one sensible ting.

RAM. Dat's where yer wrong yer see because Mark is a lecturer an' Lucille went ter university.

BATEE. Well he could be a doctor, he still foolish an' she, well, dey could keep dey university if dat is all dey teach she. A wouldn't like ter tell yer where ter put dat university.

THELMA. You really feel dat way about it?

BATEE. Look, child, is five years I here and every night a go ter bed a pray dat when a open me eyes in de morning a go see de sun shining, home. An' every morning a pray dat dis is me last day here, a pray dat something would come an' pick me up and take me.

THELMA. But you'd be surprised yer know, Trinidad's changed a lot, de Government.

BATEE. A don't care how much it a change a don't care if as soon as a land der de shoot me. I'd die happy, really happy. Not happy fer a minute because yer see something funny on de telly but happy all de time, here in yer heart even when yer en happy yer still happy in yer heart, a carn't describe it but is a feeling yer have inside.

RAM. I had no idea you felt like dat.

BATEE. Well yer never ask me. Yer just take it fer granted. Dat because you busy assing up yerself, everybody feel de same way, but now yer know.

THELMA. Well I better be going. A have a lot a people ter visit. A have more message dan de pony express.

RAM. Yea right. It was nice seeing yer, baby, yer looking well an' ting – an' a hope Mr Right comes along real soon.

THELMA. Yea he's not far. Yer is still de cream, Ram.

RAM. An' tell dem dey go see me real soon.

THELMA. Try an' make it. A hope a see you soon too, Batee.

BATEE. 'Bye, child, an' take care. Look after yerself.

THELMA. Yer coming, Alfred?

ALFRED. Yer wanted ter discuss someting, partner?

RAM. Boy, what a could tell yer.

ALFRED. Well leave it fer now, ner. (*Leaves.*)

BATEE. I going in my kitchen. (*Goes.*)

RAM *stays in front room.* (*From kitchen.*) Bringing in de sheep, bringing in de sheep.

RAM *gets up and goes in kitchen.*

RAM. Yer is a sheep here or wat? Wha' is all dis 'Bringing in de sheep'?

BATEE. If you could be a law student, I could be anyting.

RAM. Yer see you, dis is de last time I ever bring you out ter meet anybody. Yer really let me down, you does do it on purpose or what?

BATEE. Who do what? De girl ask me a simple question an' a answer she. What yer going on about?

RAM. De least you could a do was be civil.

BATEE. Well dat's where you wrong because dat's one ting I en go be.

RAM. Anyhow de next time anybody come you stay in yer kitchen.

BATEE. Dat's alright wit' me. When I ready ter move is only one place I going an' yer know where dat is.

RAM *leaves.* ALFRED *bursts in.*

ALFRED. Brother Ram, we back in business, Mr Clarkson say.

RAM. Who is Mr Clarkson?

ALFRED. De bookie.

RAM. Oh yes.

ALFRED. He say he want ter do a deal wit' yer. Fer every one a yer clients yer send ter back winners he go pay yer a pound.

RAM. Yea but supposing dey win.

ALFRED. Brother Ram! We could charge dem ten per cent of de winnings man.

RAM. Right, so that way we carn't lose.

ALFRED. Lose what?

RAM. But tell him I en only doing it for the money you know, tell him I still want de respect due to a holy man.

ALFRED. Right brother Ram I go take care of that (*Goes.*)

BATEE *comes in with bowl of rice.* RAM's *back is turned.*

BATEE. Dis is de rice fer de dinner, Mr Holy Man, would you like ter bless it?

RAM *spins around.*

*Nice* was first staged at the Almost Free Theatre, London, on 12 February 1973, with Stefan Kalipha as the MAN. The production was directed by the author. It was subsequently revived at Riverside Studios, Hammersmith, on 5 January 1980, with Norman Beaton, and was again directed by Mustapha Matura.

*A prison canteen (tables, chairs etc). In it a black man in uniform. He is thirty-five to forty years old. He is sweeping/wiping and speaks directly to the audience.*

MAN. Wen a come off de boat de customs man was nice ter me, so i was nice back ter him, but a friend a mine who come ter meet me say, boy yer shouldn't be nice ter dem, dey do' like we, but i say nar man it en so, it en so at all, wen people nice ter yer, you must be nice back ter dem, and if yer want people ter be nice ter you, you must be nice ter dem, but anyhow he say a was foolish an a go fine out, but a was nice ter he so de next day he carry me down ter de exchange dey call it, and de man dey was nice ter me too, so a was nice back ter him, so wen dey give me dis job sweeping out a office, i say tank you ter de man, an he say tank you back ter me, but me friend say, a shouldn't say tank you ter him, but i say de man say tank you ter me so i say tank you back ter him, an i tell him if yer want people ter say tank you ter you you have ter say tank you ter dem, but he say how a was wrong, but i say nar man, i en wrong i rite, den he say how i stupid, but anyhow a say tank you ter him, so de next night he carry me ter a night club, where dey had some girls dancing with coloured men, de first time a see white woman dance wit coloured man, and dey en dancing straight an back yer know, dey dancing wit dey bottom all over de place, so i say boy dis is de place fer me, so a went up an ask one a de girls nice fer a dance an she dance wit me an it was a good dance an we had a good time, but me friend pull me aside an say boy, how a go teach yer ter live in dis country wen yer do' listen ter me, yer mustn't be nice ter dem, dey do' want yer ter be nice ter dem, but i say nar man, dat en true because i was nice ter she an she was nice back ter me, but he say de same ting again dat i go fine out, so a miss a dance trying ter fine out, but a en fine out notting, so a went back an ask she ter dance an she say yes an we dance again, but a notice me friend wasn't dancing at all, so a say he must be en feel like

dancing or maybe he foot hurting him, so anyhow wen de
club start ter close me friend come pulling me saying le we go,
le we go, but i say nar man, i go ask de lady ter go home wit
she an see wha she say, but me friend say dey do' want we in
de house much less in dey bed, he say dey only like ter dance
wit we an get hot ter go an heat up de white boys, but i say
nar man, dat en true, because i know dat if you heat up
someting is you have ter eat it but he say i en know dese
woman an i en go get notting off she an dat if a go wit she, in
de morning she go cry out an say a hypnotise she an rape she,
but i say nar man, it en so if a woman heat you up she heat
you up fer a reason, an de reason is because she want you ter
burn she, but he say i is a idiot an a go fine out but anyhow a
ask she nicely ter come home wit she an she say yes, so a
leave me friend outside de club, an me an she went home an
had a nice time an in de morning she en cry out an bawl rape
or anyting she just say she have ter go ter work an if a does
go ter de club often, she go see me again, so i say yes a does
go sometimes an a hope a go see she again, an she say she
hope so too, so a went outside an a did'nt even know where a
was but a ask a policeman nice an he tell me how ter catch a
bus back ter me friend's house, boy wen a tell me friend wha
happen yer shoulda see de man, de man went mad, de man
start ter cuss me an call me all kinda names an tell me a
shouldn't ask no policeman notting dat if yer ask dem anyting
an dey fine out yer new dey go lock yer up fer someting, but i
say nar man, if yer want ter fine out anyting is a policeman
ter ask an if yer ask dem nice dey go answer yer back nice but
he say a go fine out, but i say how a go fine out he just say a
go fine out, but anyhow a was nice ter him so he take me ter
de pub wit him, so wen we get inside de pub, i say le me buy
de drinks, he say no, a mustn't buy drinks fer people, a must
le dem buy de own drinks if a buy drinks fer dem dey go tink
a stupid an drink up all me money, but i say nar man, it en
so, if yer buy people drink dey go buy yer back a drink, but
he say de same ting again how a foolish an how a go fine out,

an if a don't hear a go feel, so anyhow dey had a white man
stanning up next ter me so a buy him a drink an he buy me
back a drink, so a say well if he buy me back a drink, a have
ter buy he back a drink an so it go on until me friend say yer
see wha a tell yer de man go drink out all yer money but i say
nar man, dat en go happen, but anyhow he say he going next
door ter de betting shop an wen a ready ter go come fer him,
so wen time come fer de pub ter close de white man a tink he
name was Fred, Fred tell me he have a bet ter put on, dat he
get some tip from some horse's mouth an if a have any money
ter put it on it, so we went next door an put on de bet, a
notice me friend wasn't looking too happy, so a say wha
wrong man, he say he lost all he money, so i say well, look de
man just give me a tip an he say ter put all yer money on it,
but he say dey en go give no coloured man horse ter back on,
because dey en want ter see no coloured man win money, so i
say nar man, because he just put he own money on it, but he
say da is a trick ter fool me, but i say he fool he self because
he put more money dan me, anyhow de horse come twenty
ter one so i en do bad at all anyhow a give me friend a five
pound note an we went home wen we get dey who could be
waiting fer we but de girl from de club, de same girl a meet
last night, she say how she pass in ter see if a was going ter de
club later, a musta tell she where a was living, but i say well if
yer going ter de club ter night yer might as well stay here an
wen time come fer we ter go we could go together so she
come inside an me friend say dat if people see she come after
work dey go say dat she working fer me, but i say nar man,
dey car say dat, i only meet she last night how dey go say dat,
but he say a go fine out an dat he going an see a film round
de corner, now dat surprise me because i know he wasn't no
theatre man, but a say he must be feeling lonely so anyhow de
girl take off she shoes an start ter clean up de place, an wen
she done she say wha we have ter eat, i tell she notting, she
say not ter worry dat she go round de corner and get
someting, so i say da is awright wit me, so she went, wen she

come back de woman cook one food, pardner a never know
white woman could cook so, so a say dat dis woman is
someting boy, an den after we finish eat she take off all she
clothes an say she want de same dat a give she last night, so i
say awright an a give she it an we had a nice time man, wen
time come fer we ter go ter de club, she say she tired so i say
well le we stay here so she say right she is awright wit she, so
da is how we spend de night, i en even know what time me
friend come in, wen he come in i en even hear im a just feel
im trying ter pull de girl in he half a de bed, but she musta be
too heavy fer he, because he give up quick, but in de morning
a went ter work an leave she dey wit him so i en know wha
happen wen a come back home de night an tell de man wat a
nice foreman a had yer shoulda see de man go mad, just like
wid de policeman so ter change de subject, a ask him wha
bout de girl if she get out awright he say yes but a shouldn't
tink de foreman nice because dey en nice an dat he job is ter
make coloured people work hard, but i say nar man, dat en
true dem have ter work hard too, but he say is a different
kinda work, but i say work is work an if yer working
someplace wit people yer have ter be nice wit dem, but he say
how a go learn, an how de girl leave a message saying how
she go be at de club ter night an dat i must come, so a tell im
tank yer, but boy a was feeling so tired i say i en going ter no
club ternight he say, yer see how tired yer is, is because de
foreman working yer hard, but i know a was tired fer
someting else, but he say it was de foreman so i en say
notting, anyhow bout twelve a clock de door bell start ter
ring, who it could be but de girl, de same girl from de club,
de girl who come home here an cook me a meal, she say she
en see me in de club an she come ter see if anyting wrong wit
me, but i say nar man, nottin en wrong i just taking a rest da
is all, so a ask she if she want ter come in an stay, but she an
me friend say de same ting, she say she en want ter stay, an
me friend say he en want she ter stay, so a figure dey musta
have a row or someting anyhow a put on me clothes an went

round by she an we had a good time again, wen a come back from work dat night, me friend say boy, wha yer doing de woman go kill yer, i say nar man, she en go kill me, den he say dem white woman could take more man dan we know so den i ask him how he go feel, if a move out because is me an he was paying de rent, well boy de man went mad again, just like wit de policeman, an wit de foreman, he start ter cuss me an say how a ungrateful, an how is he who look after me wen a first come ter dis country, an is my people beg him ter look out ter fer me, an how now i want ter left him in a lurch, boy a never see a man go so crazy, an den he ask me if a moving in wit de girl, so i tell im a wasn't sure as yet but a was tinking of it, well is den he start ter cuss me, an buse me, well boy wha a could do, but say tank yer fer looking after me but i en want yer ter look after me no more, an a go pack up an leave by ter night, but yer see deep down inside i know he was a nice guy, because he en charge me no rent fer de four days a stay by he, anyhow a move in wit dis girl, well it was awright wen we first start, but den de woman start ter do all kinda a ting like tell me how a mustn't wear sock in bed, i tell she a cole, an how a mustn't wear me pajamas under me clothes, again a tell she it cole, but like she en hear an how i mustn't be nice ter de woman next door, an one set a i must do dis an i mustn't do dis, so i tell she nar man, dat en go happen because fer one ting wen it a cole me en want ter take off no pajamas is den yer go catch cole, but she en listen, she tell me i stupid and i en know bout dis country, an dat de woman next door go believe i after someting because i so nice ter her, but i tell she nar man it en so, is wen yer nice ter people dey go be nice ter you, but den she come like me friend she call me idiot an burke a was going an tell she me name wasn't burke but a was too tired, so anyhow one day wen a come home from work, just as a reach de top a de stairs, who should come outa she door but de woman from next door, so i give she a howdy like a does do anytime a does see she, anyhow dis time she ask me if a have a shilling

fer de meter, well a tell she i en have no shilling on me but a
have one inside on de mantlepiece, she say go in fer it, so i
say awright, an a open de door, soon as de woman come in
de room, de woman start ter get on, de woman start ter tell
me all kinda ting like how i so nice an she like me because i
so nice, so i tell she i tink she nice too, an yer no wat de next
ting a know is me an de woman having a nice time on de bed,
den de woman start ter bawl an groan like she never want ter
stop, so me en stop she, de next ting a know is de door bust
open an who should come in but, de girl who a living wit, de
same girl from de club, well boy a never jump so fast, but it
en me she go fer is de woman next door, both a dem start ter
cuss one another an row a never know white woman could
cuss so much, de girl tell de woman how she is a hoe, an de
woman tell de girl how she is a slut, an how she wouldn't
push me wit a barge pole, an how is me who pull she in de
room an give she a asprin an take advantage a she headache,
so boy yer could imagine de fix a in, so right dere an den a
say de best ting ter do is go, so whilst both a dem rowing a
pick up me bag an put me clothes in it, an as a hit de door, de
girl turn round an notice a going, she say wha yer going, a
say a going an stay wit me friend, boy de girl start ter cry an
break down an tell me all kinda ting like how she love me an
she car live witout me an how if a left she go kill she self, well
boy dat slow me down, but is wen she tell me she go do
anyting fer me den a stop, well by den de woman from next
door gone, after a tell she tank you fer coming in, an she tell
me tanks fer de shilling, so den de girl tell me how she go
look after me an make sure i en have ter work because she
know i en like ter go ter work in de cole, well she was right
dey, an another ting is she say she go bring enough money fer
both a we, well boy wha a could say ter dat, a tell she tanks
dat da is awright wit me, an she say awright too as long as a
do' leave, well a put down me bag an is den she start ter tell
me how she love me an how no man ever please she like how
i please she, so anyhow tings start ter go good a went in an

tell de foreman tank you fer de job an how a go be leaving
soon an he say well how he go miss me an how it was nice
having me work fer him, an ting, so pardner tings start ter get
good de girl start ter work so hard dat after a while a never
get ter see she, she go out ter work an wen she come back she
sleep, but i didn't mind so much because everytime she come
in she used ter bring in one set a five pound notes a never see
so much money in me life, boy a tell yer i'd go outside an
spend an spend an de money still wouldn't done, so after
awhile a start ter save it, anyhow a didn't mind not seeing she
so much because de woman from next door used ter cook me
food an bring it in an me an she use ter have a good time, so
a couldn't complain too much, now de next ting a know is
she too say she want ter go out an work fer me because she
could do better dan de girl, an how she have more contacts
an she could work harder, so i say awright den give it a try
no harm in trying an see if yer like it, so anyhow she look
happy wen a tell she dat, but de only ting was worrying me is
who go cook me food, because wit both a dem out a go
starve, but anyhow a say well if tings turn out so wha a go
do, but as soon as a say dat wat should happen but a knock
on de door, an who it could be but de landlady she say she
come ter collect some rent, so i tell she ter hold on a minute
an le me open de door well she come in de room ter collect
she rent but i feel she come in ter look around, so i en say
notting because is she place an if she want ter look around an
see wha going on she have a right ter do dat, anyhow we sit
down talking an de next ting a know is how she start ter tell
me bout she husband an how bad he does treat she an how
he do give she notting so i say well some man like dat an she
say how i nice an how i understand an how she feel she could
talk ter me, so i say tank you because if people feel dey could
talk ter you dey must be like you, so boy we sit down dey
talking, all morning an den she say well is lunch time an she
have ter go down an cook an how nice it was talking ter me
an she sorry how she take up all me time, but i tell she nar

man, it en so is awright i enjoy it so den she say how she go
make up fer it by bringing some lunch fer me so i say awright
den if da is what yer want ter do, do nottin else, so anyhow
she bring up de lunch and a must say she cooking wasn't so
hot but i tell she it taste nice an she like dat because de next
ting she do is ter give me a hug an a kiss, so i say well if yer
want ter give me a hug an kiss, i want ter give you a hug an
kiss too, well she say she would like dat because is a long
time no man hug she an kiss she, not because no man en
want ter do it but because she en want any kinda man ter do
it, de man she want ter do it must be a nice man, an he must
be a kind man an he must understand she well i tell she she
right ter want dat an anyhow me an she had a good time
man, everyday she used ter cook me food an come up an me
an she would have a good time until she husband come home
from work den a wouldn't see she but a would know she was
dey because sometimes she would start singing, i love you
baby, an i need you baby, an sometimes she would collect de
rent in de morning an put it back under de door in de
evening, so i know she was dere, anyhow one day me an she
husband was talking an he say how dat he always wanted ter
go ter de West Indies because de people always so happy an
nice so i tell im dat if he tink de people so nice over here he
should go down dere an he go see how nice dey really is an i
even tell him how if he go down dere he could stay with my
people an dem an he say how nice dat was an tank me an
ting, so after dat me an he was de best a friend an he used ter
ask me tings like he hope he wife singing do' bodder me an i
know how woman was, i say nar man, i do' mind i like she
singing an i glad ter hear people singing, because wen dey do
dat it mean dey happy, an i like ter know people happy, an is
a funny ting because den he used ter get serious but den he
would start smiling again, so he was awright an yer know
someting he never used ter take me ter he pub but everytime
he come back he used ter bring me a Guinness, yer could beat
dat everytime like de sun rise, but a never fine out wha he

used ter mean by do kill meself Guinness car kill, but anyhow
he was me mate, de first mate a ever had, anyhow yer see
how some people could be nice, so one day a buy one a dem
Jaguar cars an who a should see crossing de road in front a
me, right cross me bonnet but me friend, me same friend who
meet me off de boat, so i say wha happening man, how life
treating yer, he say not bad he still trying he luck wit de
horses an dem but it look like i doing awright, so i say nar
man, it might look so but i still paying rent an dat en so
good, but he say well a look like a doing better dan he, so a
telling him he must be backing de wrong horses, a tought i'd
give him a joke an cheer him up yer know, but anyhow he en
get no happier so a say i'd buy him a drink like old times,
anyhow dat brighten him up a bit, so we went in a pub, wen
we get inside de pub, de man start ter tell me he troubles how
he was living wit some woman an how de woman take all he
clothes an sell dem, an how he en have no money an no
where ter live, so i say well boy yer could come an stay by me
till tings get fer de better an he fine somewhere of he own,
well is den he get bright because de next ting a know is he en
finish he beer, de first time a ever see him en finish a whole
beer, but anyhow we go home by he an pick up he few tings
an a take him round by me, but it hit me dat my girl en like
him, so she en go want him sleeping wit we so what a go do,
anyhow a know de landlady had a room going spare so a
wasn't worried, anyhow wen a get dey a call she aside an
explain de position ter she an she say is awright if is a friend
a mine, but boy some people de more yer do ter help dem is
de more dey let yer down, no sooner dan de man get in de
house de man want ter know where all de meters is an wha
kinda locks dey have on dem, yer could beat dat, so i say well
look man, yer get a room, yer get a food, well take it easy,
rest yer body an see how tings go ner, but nar, he say i soft, i
en have no brains, i car see further dan me eye, an i en have
no business brains, so i say well if is meter yer looking ter teef
from he en have no brains, because if yer teef dey go lock yer

up, so better dan dey lock yer up, here look some money
from me wen yer get a job pay me back, well boy if yer see de
man grab de money, no sooner a take de money out me
pocket, it was in he hand, so he was awright but de next ting
a know is he trying ter pull de landlady in he room, one night
de same one who does sing i love you baby, an i need you
baby, she say she en give im no cause ter pull she in he room,
but i en so sure, yer do know how people does take tings, a
mean ter say he hear she singing i love you baby, i need you
baby, he must be tink is he she talking bout, yer car blame de
guy, so i say well look if is woman yer want why yer do ask
dem nice ter give yer a piece he say he do ask no woman fer
notten an he en asking no woman nice fer notten wat he want
he go take an wen he want a woman he go take she, so i say
look pardner it en so it go, dat if he ask he never ter know he
might get it, but anyhow he en listen, so de next ting a hear is
he go in de woman next ter me room an smelling up all she
panties, so i see him an a say ter him look ner man, if is a
woman yer want ask me an a go get one fer yer, he say he en
want no woman, woman is trouble, now dat start me tinkin
because one minute he pulling de landlady in he room an de
next he saying he en want no woman so wha he up to, so i
say well look here i go give yer some money go an look fer
yer own place de man start ter cry an beg me ter let him stay
saying i is de only friend he ever had an how i treat him so
good an how he shame he try ter take advantage a he position
wit me, so i say nar man da is awright, as long as yer behave
yer self an he say he go do dat so da was awright yer know
wat happen, yer know what de man do wen a tell yer some
man bad dey bad yer now, de man go down stairs an tell de
landlady husband how i an she carrying on but he en know i
an he was mate so he come an tell me an we had a good
laugh, but he en satisfy wit dat he go an tell de police how i
living off prostitute not one but two prostitute, an i living off
de immoral earnings, well anyhow wen de police come ter see
me, de police start ter laugh because he car see how a guy like

me could have not one but two woman on de road fer him an he sorry dat he had ter trouble me so much, so i say a sorry dat he had trouble too, because wen people nice ter you, you must be nice back ter dem, so de police leave but de man en satisfy wit dat yer know wha he do, i en know where he get de letter form from he write me modder an de woman a was living wit back home an tell dem, wait fer it, he tell dem how, boy some man malicious yer know, he tell dem how i doing well an how i making a lot a money, an how i have me own house an ting, well de next ting is dey write me after all yer car blame dem dey hear dey boy making money so dey bound ter write, well anyhow dey write me an say how as a doing so well if a could send fer dem, well wha a go do a say awright, as man, a have ter send fer dem, after all, a mean ter say so anyhow a went round de corner an buy a house, an a send fer dem, so all a dem come me modder de woman a was living wit an me four children, Clarice, Claudine, Clarissa an' Claude, move in ter de house round de corner, a used ter sleep dey nights an tell dem a had work ter do at de other house, so tings start ter go good, me modder start ter do some cleaning an me woman start ter take in some washing an make some plans ter open she own laundrette, so who could complain, but boy wen a tell yer dis life funny it funny yer know so tings start ter go good, wen de next ting a hear is me friend want ter see me so i say awright, but he round de corner, yer know, an he en a three penny bus ride away, nar man de man in Brixton Prison, so a get me forms ter visit wen a get dey, de first ting de man say is how a doing, so i say yer bring me all dis way ter ask me how a doing, but he say nar man, dat en what he want ter see me for, he say he want me ter pay a fine fer him, so i say well da is awright, how much it is, well he say is only twenty pounds, it turn out he break a meter an dey charge im twenty pounds an he couldn't pay so dey trow him inside, so i pay de fine an dey let im out, but dat en all de man want me find place fer him ter live, so i say awright, a go do dat a figure prison must a change him, put

some sense in him, so a give im a room in de house me
modder an dem was living in, a figure me modder could keep
an eye on him during de day an i could watch im during de
night, an a tell im, a say if a only catch yer near me meter, is
out yer going, friend or no friend, but he say nar man, dat en
go happen, he change, he en go do dat kinda ting again, how
he could do a ting lik dat ter me after a so nice ter him, an
how if people nice ter yer yer must be nice ter dem, so a
jump, but den a say he must be really change a mean ter say,
ter hear him say a ting like dat, an a have ter believe im, after
all is a ting i say meself, so a say well he really learn now, he
really get de message, well boy tings start ter go good, a get
me children in a school, me woman open she laundrette, an
de man en even going near me meters, if he want ter go ter de
WC in de back just not ter pass de meter, de man going
through de front door an going round, just not ter pass me
meters, da is ter tell yer how good de man get, an he get nice,
he get nice ter everybody, he start ter say tank you, ter
everybody, an smiling ter everybody, an dat en all he get a job
as a nightwatchman in a factory an he even come home an
say how nice de foreman is, yer could beat dat, well he beat
it, he even get a job fer me modder on de factory bench, so
wha a could say ter dat, a could only say well tings like, never
say die, an wonders never cease, an when mango ripe it go
fall, anyhow dat en all de man even start ter pay me back me
money, not in big pieces but a one here a one dere, but dat
was good dat shows he was trying, he heart was in de right
place, anyhow i stop tinking bout im, but an wen a say but a
mean but yer know, one day de man pay me back a five
pound note an when a look at de five pound note well a had
ter look yer know, because he never pay me back so much,
when a look at de five pound note, a see it was de same five
pound note a give me wife ter put in de bank fer me, so dat
hit me but a figure she must be change some money fer him,
so i en worry bout it, but an a say but again yer know, de
man start ter pay me back one set a five pound notes, an all a

dem is what a give she ter put in de bank so pardner a ask yer wha a go do, wha you woulda do if all de five pound note you give yer wife ter put in de bank yer see turning up in another man hand, an is a man yer help, i help de man yer know, tell me what you woulda do, (*Slight pause.*) yer can tink a notten, well i go tell yer what i do or wha i was going ter do, a was going ter go over ter de pub an buy im a Guinness an tell im do kill yer self, but yer know what happen, when a get in de pub, de man in de pub say dey do' serve black people in dis bar i have ter go round, so a hit im, an when a hit im, he fall against a whole pile a boxes an de whole bar mash up, so da is what a in dis prison for, well boy a really learn me lesson, da is de last time a go ever be nice anybody.

*A bell rings and the man gets up and walks out singing.*

I love you baby
I need you baby.

*Play Mas* was first performed at the Royal Court Theatre, London, on 16 July 1974, with the following cast:

| | |
|---|---|
| RAMJOHN GOOKOOL | Stefan Kalipha |
| SAMUEL | Rudolph Walker |
| MISS GOOKOOL | Mercia Mansfield |
| FRANK | Norman Beaton |
| MR McKAY | Charles Pemberton |
| DOCTOR | Tommy Eytle |
| MRS BANKS (Negro woman/Bishop) | Lucita Lijertwood |
| MR TATE (First Undertaker) | Frank Singuineau |
| MR LYLE (Second Undertaker) | Robert La Bassiere |
| SERGEANT | Trevor Thomas |
| MRS SAMUEL | Mona Hammond |
| CHUCK REYNOLDS | Ed Bishop |

*Directed by* Donald Howarth
*Designed by* Douglas Heap
*Costumes designed by* Peter Minshall
*Lighting by* Nick Chelton

Act One takes place in the Gookools' tailor shop in Port-of-Spain, Trinidad, before Independence.
Act Two takes place in the office of the Chief of Police in Trinidad, after Independence.

*To Franz Fanon
for his dedication in his struggle
to understand and overcome
black misery*

## ACT ONE

### Scene One

*Day time. A tailor shop made of bare wooden boards, in the middle one, a sewing machine, a wooden counter, a dummy in the corner, a wooden box on the floor.*

RAMJOHN *is dressed in a white T-shirt, khaki trousers,*
    *slippers. He is cutting some khaki fabric.*

RAMJOHN (*calling out*). Samuel, bring in de focking ting nar.

SAMUEL (*off*). Okay.

    SAMUEL *comes on dressed in a coloured T-shirt, shorts,*
    *barefoot, carrying a wooden box.*

RAMJOHN. Right good.

    *He holds it up to look at it.*

SAMUEl. Wha yer go do wit it?

RAMJOHN. I en' sure yet.

    *He puts it down, goes back to cutting.*

SAMUEL. I see yer just wanted me ter bring it.

RAMJOHN. Yes.

SAMUEL. Yer just like ter see me work. (*He sits down.*)

RAMJOHN. Yes.

SAMUEL. I see.

RAMJOHN. Go an bring de odder one.

SAMUEL. All right. What yer go do wit it? (*He gets up.*)

RAMJOHN. I en' sure yet, go an bring it.

SAMUEL. All right.

RAMJOHN *becomes involved with staring at the crate.*

SAMUEL *goes, returns. As he enters, interrupting*:

Here.

RAMJOHN. Shh, let see. Hmm. Yes maybe. Yes, a tinking a keeping some chickens, dis might do, yes a suppose so, yes okay, I'll have dis one.

SAMUEL. A could sit down, now?

RAMJOHN. Yes – no.

SAMUEL. Make up yer mind.

RAMJOHN. Yer better go an see if me modder want anyting.

SAMUEL. All right.

*He goes through to the yard, in it is MISS GOOKOOL, holding a shirt over a tub.*

SAMUEL. Miss Gookool, de boss send me ter see if yer want anyting?

MISS GOOKOOL. No, tell im, I en' want notting.

SAMUEL *turns.*

But wait, see if yer could reach up da shelf an get me a block a soap, a trying ter wash dis ting, but car' come out.

SAMUEL. All right.

*He reaches up, brings down some soap, gives it.*

MISS GOOKOOL. Tanks.

SAMUEL. Anyting else?

MISS GOOKOOL. No, but see if . . .

SAMUEL. Da is what a ask yer.

MISS GOOKOOL. What?

SAMUEL. If dere was anyting else.

MISS GOOKOOL. No, but if de iron off a want yer ter switch it on for me.

SAMUEL. All right. (*He does it.*) Anyting else?

MISS GOOKOOL. No, it was on?

SAMUEL. No, it was off.

MISS GOOKOOL. Yer switch it on?

SAMUEL. An da is wha yer tell me ter do.

MISS GOOKOOL. Yes, you do it?

SAMUEL. Yes.

MISS GOOKOOL. Well, yer better go an see if Mr Gookool want anyting.

SAMUEL. All right. (*He comes through.*)

RAMJOHN. Yer was a long time. What yer was doing?

SAMUEL. Notting. Miss Gookool wanted me ter reach she a piece a soap.

RAMJOHN. A see, yer reach it?

SAMUEL. Yes.

RAMJOHN. A hope yer didn't spend all morning doing it.

SAMUEL. No, yer wanted me for someting?

RAMJOHN. No, yer could sit down now.

SAMUEL. All right. (*He sits.*)

RAMJOHN. Here, take dose trousers an unpick de seams.

SAMUEL. All de seams? (*He takes the trousers, examines them.*)

RAMJOHN. No, just de inside leg, yer do' know how ter unpick a leg?

SAMUEL. Yes, I know but a was just asking.

RAMJOHN. Well, do' ask, just unpick de leg.

SAMUEL. All right.

*He begins to unpick with a finger nail.*

RAMJOHN. Yer know one day . . .

SAMUEL. One day what?

RAMJOHN. One day somebody go come in here an ask me ter build a double breasted eight buttoned wit vest an drape trousers. Yer go see how ter build suit.

SAMUEL. Yer mean yer never build a double breasted eight button before?

RAMJOHN. No, dat is what a say, one day somebody go come in an ask fer one, an is den a go build it.

SAMUEL. Or a see, how yer go build it?

RAMJOHN. Well, first a go start wid de shoulders – yer must start wid de shoulders.

SAMUEL. Yes.

RAMJOHN. Because if yer do' get de shoulders right, yer in trouble, de shoulders must be right, dey must be straight an broad.

SAMUEL. Den what?

RAMJOHN. De shoulders must be like de front of a boat, dey must make de room for de suit ter pass.

SAMUEL. Yes, den what?

RAMJOHN. Den de lapels, de lapels must lie down as if dey

sleeping forever, dey mustn't move at all, even wen yer take off de suit de lapel mustn't move.

SAMUEL. Den what?

RAMJOHN. Den de sleeves.

SAMUEL. What bout de sleeves?

RAMJOHN. De sleeves must bend like a piece a iron –

SAMUEL. Iron do' bend.

RAMJOHN. Yer not listening ter me or what?

SAMUEL. But iron do' bend.

RAMJOHN. What does bend?

SAMUEL. Steel, is steel does bend not iron.

RAMJOHN. All right, den de sleeves must bend like a piece a steel an whenever dey come back it must be like dey never move.

SAMUEL. A see.

RAMJOHN. Whey you fin out iron do' bend?

SAMUEL. I do' know, a just know it do' bend, it does break.

RAMJOHN. A see, anyhow yer does talk too much, well dat it all?

SAMUEL. How yer mean?

RAMJOHN. Yer tink a suit is just shoulders, an lapels an sleeve?

SAMUEL. No.

RAMJOHN. Yer do' want ter know bout de buttons, de vents, de waist, de linings, an all bout de seams, yer do' want ter know bout dem?

SAMUEL. Yes, but what bout de waist?

RAMJOHN. Well now yer talking . . . but no, yer have it wrong, de buttons is next.

SAMUEL. How much?

RAMJOHN. Eight, a tell yer eight.

SAMUEL. All right, eight.

RAMJOHN. Well dem eight buttons must be like eight people, dey must be like eight soldiers, dey must stand up straight an strong an all a dem must be ready ter do a job every one a dem must be ready ter take a strain, an den wen dey finish dey must pop back up like notting happen, but he ready ter go again.

SAMUEL. A see, an what bout de waist?

RAMJOHN. Not yet, not yet, yer is a rushin? We en' come ter de waist not yet. How a go teach yer ter build suit if yer do' listen?

SAMUEL. All right, what next?

RAMJOHN. Well you tell me, yer know so much bout iron do' bend, you tell me what next.

SAMUEL. De seams?

RAMJOHN. No de seams come last.

SAMUEL. De linings come last yer say.

RAMJOHN. Well a make a mistake, is de seams come last.

SAMUEL. Or a see.

RAMJOHN. What happen, yer give up?

SAMUEL. No.

RAMJOHN. De vents, what bout de vents (*He laughs.*) how yer go build a suit witout vents, is so you learn ter build suit, witout vents (*He laughs.*) da go be one funny looking suit boy.

SAMUEL (*laughs*). Yes, what bout de vents den?

RAMJOHN. Well de vents is someting else, de vents must be dere, but yer mustn't know dey dere, is only wen yer sit down, or bend down, yer must know de vents dere, dey must close back like a pair a scissors, yer see like . . . (*He does scissors.*) dat.

SAMUEL. Yes a see.

MISS GOOKOOL (*calls out*). Samuel.

RAMJOHN. Wat yer want im for?

MISS GOOKOOL. A want him for someting.

RAMJOHN. But I want him here.

MISS GOOKOOL. He en' go take long.

RAMJOHN. Yer better go an see what she want.

SAMUEL. All right. (*He goes through.*) Yes, Miss Gookool?

MISS GOOKOOL. A want yer ter tip da tub up outside, it too heavy for me.

SAMUEL. All right, dat is all?

MISS GOOKOOL. Yes.

SAMUEL *picks up the tub, empties it, puts it down, turns to go.*

Samuel, before yer go.

SAMUEL. What? (*He turns.*)

MISS GOOKOOL. A want yer ter wash it out for me.

SAMUEL. A thought yer say dat was all.

MISS GOOKOOL. Well a change me mind, go an wash it out.

SAMUEL. All right.

> SAMUEL *picks up the tub, goes out with it, comes back.*

> Here.

MISS GOOKOOL. Tanks.

SAMUEL. Dat is all?

MISS GOOKOOL. Yes.

SAMUEL. Yer sure?

MISS GOOKOOL. Of course a sure, a wouldn't tell you a was sure if a wasn't sure, what yer tink a is, yer better go an see if Mr Gookool want yer for anyting.

SAMUEL. All right. (*He comes through.*) A did it.

RAMJOHN. What she wanted?

SAMUEL. She wanted me ter empty she tub an wash it out fer she.

RAMJOHN. Yer did it?

SAMUEL. Yes.

RAMJOHN. Yer fill it?

SAMUEL. No, she didn't ask me ter fill it.

RAMJOHN. Well how she go wash again if yer en' fill it?

SAMUEL. I . . .

RAMJOHN. Yer better go back an fill it.

> SAMUEL *goes through, picks up the tub.*

MISS GOOKOOL. Samuel, what yer doing?

SAMUEL. A filling de tub.

MISS GOOKOOL. I ask yer ter fill it?

SAMUEL. No.

MISS GOOKOOL. Well, what yer filling de tub for?

SAMUEL. Mr Gookool say I must fill it.

MISS GOOKOOL (*calls out*). RamJohn . . .

RAMJOHN. Yes.

MISS GOOKOOL. You tell Samuel he must fill de tub?

RAMJOHN. Yes.

MISS GOOKOOL. Why?

RAMJOHN. Because yer go need it, ter do yer odder washing.

MISS GOOKOOL. But I finish my washing. I en' have no more washing to do.

RAMJOHN. Well, I didn't know dat, how I go know dat, come Samuel.

MISS GOOKOOL. Samuel, yer better go.

SAMUEL. So yer want me ter throw out de water?

MISS GOOKOOL. No, as much as yer have it, a go do some more.

SAMUEL. All right.

SAMUEL *puts down the tub, comes through.*

RAMJOHN. Yer do it?

SAMUEL. What?

RAMJOHN. Trow out de water?

SAMUEL. No.

RAMJOHN. A tought she tell yer ter trow it out.

SAMUEL. No, she say as much as a have de water she go use it.

RAMJOHN. What she go use it for?

SAMUEL. I do' know, she say she have more washing ter do.

RAMJOHN. But a tought she say she finish washing.

SAMUEL. She finish but she had some more ter do.

RAMJOHN. How she could finish an still have more ter do?

SAMUEL. I do' know, she had more ter do, but she had finish.

RAMJOHN. A see, yer better sit down an finish unpicking dem trousers.

SAMUEL (*sits*). All right.

RAMJOHN. So wey a was?

SAMUEL. Yer was on de vents.

RAMJOHN. A finish de vents man, now we come ter de waist, a man waist different ter a woman waist yer know, so yer have ter be careful, de waist must be like a smooth piece a glass, yer mustn't know where de waist begin an de hip end, de waist must be dere but yer mustn't see it, not like dem Saga Boy tailors, dey do' know where ter put a waist, dey tink dat because is a waist it must be dere, but no de waist must start from here (*Shows.*) under de arms an come down, like dis yer see.

SAMUEL. Yes.

RAMJOHN. So don't forget dat.

SAMUEL. Den what?

RAMJOHN. Den we come ter de linings of course, how yer go have a suit witout no linings, it go stick.

SAMUEL. Yes, what about de linings?

RAMJOHN. De linings must be de inside of de suit.

SAMUEL. Yes.

RAMJOHN. De linings must make sure de suit is dere, because witout de linings yer en' have no suit, so yer have ter make sure dat wen yer put in a lining it stay, but de lining have ter do everything de suit do, it must follow, but it mustn't lead, an when de suit say stop, de linings must stop, an wen de suit say go, de linings must go, dey must be like brodder and sister, yer see wat a mean.

SAMUEL. Yes. What next?

RAMJOHN. Well next is de seams, small ting like de seams nobody tink de seams important but de seams is de most important part a de whole suit, people do' notice de seams, dey say boy dat is nice suit you wearing, or dat is a terrific suit yer wearing. But I see Robert Mitchum in a suit once an it was de seams, all a could see was de seams, pure seams, seams galore, de man had seams all over de place and wen de man grab (*Shows.*) Jane Russell yer tink is de suit grab she, nar, is de seams, is de seams grab she, because yer know Mitchum en' no actor.

SAMUEL. Yes.

RAMJOHN. Yes, man, Mitchum en' no actor, is de seams does act for him.

SAMUEL. Yes.

RAMJOHN. Dat is why whenever yer see Mitchum, he in seams but a sure he do' realise how important de seams is, is de tailor should get fame, he is de real star, Mitchum tailor.

SAMUEL. What is he name?

RAMJOHN. I do' know, I do' know he name, yer feel I is a dictionary?

SAMUEL. No.

RAMJOHN. I only know Mitchum name.

SAMUEL. A see.

RAMJOHN. But a know de seams play a important part, how de suit go stan up if it en' have no seams, eh?

SAMUEL. I do' know.

RAMJOHN. Well dat is it, no seams no suit – but do' tink de seams is just dere ter hold up de suit yer know, nar, de seams is dere ter say slim, long, short, fat, broad, all dem kinda tings de seams does say, yer see dey does even say French, Italian, English an Yankee, all dem kinda tings de seams does say so yer have ter learn ter place yer seams an ter let dem say what yer want ter say, yer seams can say fat, wen dey is on a tin man, yer know, dat is why I could always tell wen a man borrow a suit.

MISS GOOKOOL (*calls out*). Samuel.

RAMJOHN. Yer better go an see what Miss Gookool want, wen yer come back a go give yer de rest, she must be wanting yer ter empty out de odder water.

SAMUEL *gets up*.

SAMUEL. All right a going. (*He goes through, picks up the tub*.) Yer want me ter empty de water, Miss Gookool?

MISS GOOKOOL. No, I want yer ter unplug de iron, it shocking.

SAMUEL. An you want me ter unplug it?

MISS GOOKOOL. Yes, but be careful.

SAMUEL (*does it*). All right.

MISS GOOKOOL. As yer here yer might as well empty de tub an wash it out.

SAMUEL (*picks up the tub*). All right, yer do' want me ter fill it?

MISS GOOKOOL. Fill it for what?

SAMUEL. I do' know.

MISS GOOKOOL. If a wanted yer ter fill it, a woulda ask yer ter fill it, a ask yer ter empty it and wash it, dat is all.

SAMUEL. All right a go do dat.

MISS GOOKOOL. Wen yer finish go an see if Mr Gookool want yer fer anyting.

SAMUEL (*empties the tub*). All right. (*He returns.*) Right dat's it.

MISS GOOKOOL. It clean.

SAMUEL. Yes, yer tell me ter wash it, an a wash it.

MISS GOOKOOL. All right den yer could go.

SAMUEL. All right.

MISS GOOKOOL. Samuel!

SAMUEL. Yes.

MISS GOOKOOL. Tell Mr Gookool lunch go be ready in a little while.

SAMUEL (*turns*). All right.

MISS GOOKOOL. Samuel.

SAMUEL. Yes.

MISS GOOKOOL. What job Mr Gookool working on?

SAMUEL. He doing de khaki pants job, Miss Gookool.

MISS GOOKOOL. Okay, Samuel, go on.

SAMUEL. All right – yer want me fer anyting? (*He goes through.*)

RAMJOHN. No I just want yer ter finish unpicking dem trousers.

SAMUEL (*sits*). All right.

RAMJOHN. What she wanted yer fer?

SAMUEL. She wanted me ter unplug de iron.

RAMJOHN. She didn't want yer ter empty de tub den.

SAMUEL. Yes, but a empty it.

RAMJOHN. A see she car' unplug a iron by she self, she do know I need yer here.

SAMUEL. It was shocking.

RAMJOHN. It shock yer.

SAMUEL. No.

RAMJOHN. Well finish doing de trousers.

SAMUEL. She say lunch go be ready soon.

RAMJOHN. All right sit down, a have ter tell yer how ter make de vest.

SAMUEL. Yes, oh yes, someting else, she wanted ter know what job yer working on.

RAMJOHN. Why she want ter know dat, she know I doing de khaki pants.

SAMUEL. I do' know.

RAMJOHN. What yer tell she?

SAMUEL. I tell she yer doing de khaki – de vest.

RAMJOHN. All right – wait – yes de vest, now de difference

between a suit wit a vest an a suit wit no vest is de man, a man does wear a suit but a gentleman go wear a suit an a vest, you see what a getting at?

SAMUEL. Yes.

RAMJOHN. What a getting at?

SAMUEL. Dat a gentleman en' go wear a suit wit no vest.

RAMJOHN. All right, just checking, now a vest mustn't surprise yer or shock yer it must be dere, but only when yer want it an only when yer move back de jacket, yer see wat a mean.

SAMUEL. Yes.

RAMJOHN. Yer see how de jacket must fit de shoulders.

SAMUEL. Yes.

RAMJOHN. Well de same way de vest must fit de chest, it must hold de chest like a pair a hands, an open an close like dat. (*Demonstrates.*) Wit de breathing, as de chest rise, de hand open, as de chest fall de hands close, yer see.

SAMUEL. Yes.

RAMJOHN. So when yer see a man in a vest an he turn right, an he vest go left dat en' no vest dat is a cradle, man. (*He laughs.*)

SAMUEL (*laughs*). Yes, Mr Gookool?

RAMJOHN. Yes what?

SAMUEL. Yer feel yer go ever build one a dem suits?

RAMJOHN. How yer mean?

SAMUEL. A mean if yer feel yer go ever get ter build one a dem eight button suits?

RAMJOHN. Why not, a could do it. What yer feel a been telling yer de whole morning?

SAMUEL. Yes, a know, but yer feel anybody go ever want yer ter build one?

RAMJOHN. Of course, why not, a could do it, is only because de weather hot.

SAMUEL. Dat is what a mean.

RAMJOHN. Dat people does wear khaki pants all de time, but dat do' mean ter say everybody is de same, not because you wear khaki mean I have ter wear khaki pants too, so you feel nobody does wear suit, you feel I only make it up.

SAMUEL. No.

RAMJOHN. Man, look, I tell yer I see Robert Mitchum in about ten flims an in all ten he wears suit, so what yer telling me, a car' see?

SAMUEL. No.

RAMJOHN. Allyer Trinidadian really foolish, all allyer does go theatre for is ter see one set a man fighting an hugging wid woman an kissing dem, allyer do' go ter see de world, ter see what de outside world like different people an different customs, all allyer want ter see is a man beating up another man an dat is a good flim, an some girl telling him not ter do it, yer do' want ter see notting good.

SAMUEL. What is a good —

RAMJOHN. Man, I could call so much good flim, flim dat you never see, flim you never dream about.

SAMUEL. Yer, well call one, call one, a tell yer if a see it.

RAMJOHN. *How Green Was My Valley*, yer see dat?

SAMUEL. No.

RAMJOHN. Yer see what a tell yer?

SAMUEL. Who was in dat?

RAMJOHN. A go tell yer who was in dat, a go tell yer —

SAMUEL. Who, Robert Mitchum?

RAMJOHN. No, Mitchum didn't make dat one, a tell yer who it was, it was Donald Crisp, and Freddie Bartholomew, a bet yer never even hear bout dem, dey do' beat up no women, dem does act.

SAMUEL. Freddie who?

RAMJOHN. Bartholomew, Freddie Bartholomew.

SAMUEL. A see, what bout de gal, who was de gal?

RAMJOHN. Maureen O'Hara, it was Maureen O'Hara.

SAMUEL. A didn't see dat one.

RAMJOHN. I know yer en' see it, it too good, dat is why.

SAMUEL. Call anodder, give me anodder one.

RAMJOHN. Why, yer en' go know it, what is de use, yer go only open yer eye big like yer know someting but —

SAMUEL. Well try me, try me an see.

RAMJOHN. No, you try me, you call a good flim an I go tell yer if a see it.

SAMUEL. All right yer ever see a flim call *Five Graves ter Cairo*?

RAMJOHN. Dat a war flim?

SAMUEL. Yes.

RAMJOHN. Yes, it wasn't bad.

SAMUEL. Who was in it, who was in it?

RAMJOHN. Wait, a go tell yer – (*Pause.*) A car' remember.

SAMUEL (*laughs*). Yer see.

RAMJOHN. Yes, but dat was a war flim, dat didn't have notting in it, one set, a tank an bomb, an machine-gun firing all over de place.

SAMUEL. Well a go tell yer someting, dat is one a de best war flim dey ever make, yer see.

RAMJOHN. Yes I know dat, give me anodder but no war flim an a go tell yer if is a good flim.

SAMUEL. Yer ever see a flim call *Hurricane*?

RAMJOHN. Wid who, John Hall an Dorothy Lamour?

SAMUEL. Yes, dat was a good flim.

RAMJOHN. Dat wasn't no flim, man, all dat had was one set a breeze blowing an rain, an in de end dat is what get John Hall out a jail an safe de hurricane was de star, you call dat flim, you like dat?

SAMUEL. Yes.

RAMJOHN. Yer like star boy ting?

SAMUEL. Yes.

RAMJOHN. Well dat en' no flim, man, I go tell yer what is flim, yer ever see a flim call *Passage ter Marseille*?

SAMUEL. Yes I see dat.

RAMJOHN. Yer see it?

SAMUEL. Yes, dat was a good flim.

RAMJOHN. Dat wasn't no flim, man.

SAMUEL. A go tell yer it was Humphry Bogart, Sidney Greenstreet an Peter Lorre.

RAMJOHN. Who else, who was de girl?

SAMUEL. I do' – Maureen O'Hara?

RAMJOHN. It was Michelle Morgan, a bet yer never remember
– she was de girl in de car.

SAMUEL. Oh, yes.

RAMJOHN. Oh, yes. Oh yes, yer see how yer eye open big, oh
yes (*Mimicking.*) who else, who else, who else was in it?

SAMUEL. I do' know, tell me.

RAMJOHN. Ye ever hear bout Helmut Dantine?

SAMUEL. No.

RAMJOHN. Well he was in it, an yer remember de young boy
in it, he get shot on de boat.

SAMUEL. Oh, yes.

RAMJOHN. Oh, yes (*Mimicking.*) an yer remember compere
. . . ?

SAMUEL. What was he name?

RAMJOHN. A donno he name, but a know he was good, de
old man who give up he place on de boat.

SAMUEL. Oh yes, he was good.

RAMJOHN. He was good.

SAMUEL. He used ter catch de butterflies.

RAMJOHN. Dat's him.

SAMUEL. Yes I remember, I remember good flim.

RAMJOHN. A tell yer.

SAMUEL. So wat bout de trousers?

RAMJOHN. De trousers could wait te we finish de flims, you

just like me modder inside, all she want ter see me doing is make one set a khaki trousers, she en' want ter see me build no suit, but she do' know people does wear suit too.

SAMUEL. Yes.

MISS GOOKOOL (*calls out*). Samuel.

SAMUEL. Yes.

RAMJOHN. Go an see what she want.

SAMUEL. All right. (*He goes through.*) Yer want ter see me, Miss Gookool?

MISS GOOKOOL. Of course a want yer if a didn't want yer a wouldna call, here take dis.

MISS GOOKOOL *hands him two plates of food.*

SAMUEL. Tanks.

MISS GOOKOOL. What was all dat noise about?

SAMUEL. Me an Mr Gookool was just having an argument about some flims.

MISS GOOKOOL. Ah yer suppose ter be working, what allyer doing talking bout flims?

SAMUEL. It was just a nice argument –

MISS GOOKOOL. Dat boy, he always arguing, a do' know what wrong wit dat boy, is time he get married yer know, since de boy father dead, all he doing is arguing, arguing, arguing, all de time. Go take de food, it go get cold.

SAMUEL. Yes, Miss Gookool. (*He goes through.*) Here.

RAMJOHN. Tanks.

*They sit and eat.*

SAMUEL. Yer modder say is time yer get married.

RAMJOHN. Why?

SAMUEL. I do' know, she just say is time yer get married.

RAMJOHN. I see.

SAMUEL. She say yer always arguing.

RAMJOHN. I do' argue.

SAMUEL. Dat is what she say.

RAMJOHN. She could say what she like, yer ever seem a flim call *Rancho Notorious*?

SAMUEL. No, why?

RAMJOHN. Well it was a western, but is de first western dat didn't have a lota shooting in it.

SAMUEL. Or, dis food nice.

RAMJOHN. It en' bad.

SAMUEL. Wat yer go do, yer go get married?

RAMJOHN. What wrong wit yer, man, yer feel is just so yer does get married?

SAMUEL. No, but yer modder say.

RAMJOHN. Le' she say what she like.

SAMUEL. All right.

RAMJOHN. Wen is Carnival?

SAMUEL. Next month.

RAMJOHN. A know is next month, what time next month?

SAMUEL. De first Monday an Tuesday.

RAMJOHN. Yer playing Mas?

SAMUEL. Of course a playing Mas, an I is a Trinidadian a

bound ter play Mas, de only ting could stop me is if a get me foot break, an den a go still play wit one foot.

RAMJOHN. Who yer playing wid?

SAMUEL. Desperado Steel Band.

RAMJOHN. What dey playing?

SAMUEL. Sands of Iwo Jima.

RAMJOHN. Wat yer playing?

SAMUEL. A playing a marine, yer ever see de flim?

RAMJOHN. A tell you I do' see bad flim, man.

SAMUEL. Yer want ter play, why you do' play, we could have a good time.

RAMJOHN. I do' play Mas, dat is fer idiots, dat is for people who have money ter trow away, I en' have no money ter trow away so I go watch on.

SAMUEL. You have more money dan me.

RAMJOHN. A still en' have it ter trow away.

SAMUEL. It en' trowing it away, yer does enjoy it.

RAMJOHN. Enjoy what, jumping up all day an getting tired an drinking a lota rum, an fighting, yer call dat enjoying yerself?

SAMUEL. I do' get tired.

RAMJOHN. How much it does cost you?

SAMUEL. My Mas costing me fifty dollars.

RAMJOHN. So you spenning fifty dollars ter have a good time?

SAMUEL. Dat en' notting, some guys does spen three hundred dollars.

RAMJOHN. A know, dat is why dey is idiots.

SAMUEL. Yer modder tink yer want a woman.

RAMJOHN. I do' want no woman, wen time come fer me ter get a woman I go get one.

SAMUEL. Supposing yer modder get one fer yer, what yer go do?

RAMJOHN. She car' do dat.

SAMUEL. All yer Indian have ter do what allyer modder tell allyer ter do, an is Indian custom ter fix up a wedding, a bet if yer modder get some nice Indian girl fer yer, yer en' go say no.

RAMJOHN. Not me, man, I en' no Indian.

SAMUEL. What yer is?

RAMJOHN. I is a Trinidadian.

SAMUEL. You en' no Trinidadian, man if you is a Trinidadian how come yer do' play Mas, eh how come?

RAMJOHN. Not because I do' play Mas, mean I en' a Trinidadian, plenty Trinidadian do' play Mas.

SAMUEL. Well dem en' real Trinidadian man, dey might en' play it, but dey like it.

RAMJOHN. Well I do' like it.

FRANK (*off*). Hey, what happenin?

RAMJOHN *waves to someone passing in the street, calls out.*

RAMJOHN. All right, easy, like yer going up de road?

FRANK (*voice offstage*). Yes a going ter look up a neighbour.

RAMJOHN. All right den.

FRANK. All right.

SAMUEL. Who was dat?

RAMJOHN. Dat was Frank, de star boy.

SAMUEL. What make him a star boy?

RAMJOHN. He going up de road by a woman, he does go up dere every lunch time, she husband does work.

SAMUEL. How long dat going on?

RAMJOHN. Bout two years now, he does go up dere every day, de husband never catch him, dat is how he's a star boy, yer see dem pants he wearing, he still owe me a dollar fer dem.

SAMUEL. Well at least yer pants getting some fame.

RAMJOHN. What fame good for, I want me dollar, but is all right de pair falling off im, he go want anodder pair, den a go collect me dollar.

SAMUEL. Yer should do like him.

RAMJOHN. How yer mean?

SAMUEL. Get a woman.

RAMJOHN. Waste my time on a woman yer mean, dat is what he doing he do' work, he car' work, all he does do is catch he arse an go an see dat woman, hand ter mouth dat is what he is, an a bet yer he have anodder one fer de night, so how he go work, he too tired, dat is why I car' get my dollar.

SAMUEL. So what yer go do wit all dis money yer go make?

RAMJOHN. What make you tink I go make money?

SAMUEL. Well if you do' play Mas, an yer en' going an get married, yer bound ter make money.

RAMJOHN. I go save it, dat is what I go do wit it, yer feel I want ter make khaki pants all de days a my life?

SAMUEL. No, what yer go do?

RAMJOHN. I going ter open de biggest tailor shop dat Trinidad ever see.

SAMUEL. Yes.

RAMJOHN. It go have one section fer lightweight clothes, anodder section fer heavy weight an anodder section fer pants cutters, de best yer know.

SAMUEL. Yes.

RAMJOHN. An anodder one fer jacket cutters an anodder one fer waistcoat cutters an I go be running de whole ting.

SAMUEL. Yer dat sound like someting.

RAMJOHN. Wen people come in I go be at de door ter greet dem, an fine out wat dey want an take dem ter de section dat deals wit dem, yer see, no two by two, but *big*.

SAMUEL. Yer, dat sound.

RAMJOHN. So yer see I en' no dreamer, I have plans, big plans, so le' me put back dis ting an get back ter work.

SAMUEL. Yes, Mr Gookool.

RAMJOHN. Here.

*He gives* SAMUEL *his plate*. SAMUEL *takes it, goes through.*

SAMUEL. Tanks, Miss Gookool, de food was nice.

MISS GOOKOOL. It was too nice, allyer take a long time ter eat it.

SAMUEL. Me and Mr Gookool was having a discussion.

MISS GOOKOOL. What he discussing for, he always want ter discuss someting, me mind make up yer know he want a woman, da is what he want.

SAMUEL. I tell him dat.

MISS GOOKOOL. You tell him dat?

SAMUEL. Yes.

MISS GOOKOOL. What he say?

SAMUEL. He say he have plans.

MISS GOOKOOL. What kinda plans?

SAMUEL. He en' say, all he say is he have plans.

MISS GOOKOOL. Well a glad ter hear dat, good, all right do'
stan up dere, go back an do yer work.

SAMUEL. All right. (*He turns to go.*)

MISS GOOKOOL. He definitely say he have plans?

SAMUEL. Yes, big plans.

MISS GOOKOOL. He say big?

SAMUEL. Yes.

MISS GOOKOOL. All right go on.

SAMUEL. All right. (*He goes through.*)

RAMJOHN. Finish doing dem trousers.

SAMUEL. What bout de trousers?

RAMJOHN. Finish doing dem, yer was unpicking dem.

SAMUEL. No, a mean what bout de suit trousers.

RAMJOHN. Or a see, all right a go come to dat.

SAMUEL. Yer modder say she glad.

RAMJOHN. What she glad for?

SAMUEL. She say she glad you have plans.

RAMJOHN. You tell she bout my plans?

SAMUEL. Yes.

RAMJOHN. An what she say?

SAMUEL. She say she glad.

RAMJOHN. She really say she glad?

SAMUEL. Yes.

RAMJOHN. Dat's good.

SAMUEL. What bout de trousers?

RAMJOHN. Right de trousers, now de trousers en' like some guys tink separate from de jacket, yer know de trousers is wat complete de suit, some guys tink de trousers different because dey want ter wear de trousers by dem self, but dat en' right. I could always tell a suit trousers, a suit trousers must fit wid de jacket, wenever Mitchum take off he jacket I could tell, yer does see he trousers stanning up on he own.

SAMUEL. Yes.

RAMJOHN. An do' let nobody fool yer, a suit trouser witout a jacket is like talking a language nobody don't understand, de jacket must say someting bout de trousers an de trousers must say someting bout de jacket, yer see what a mean?

SAMUEL. Yes.

RAMJOHN. Why you tell she my business?

SAMUEL. She ask me, we was discussing someting an she ask me.

RAMJOHN. So she glad?

SAMUEL. Yes, man.

RAMJOHN. Dat's good.

SAMUEL. Dat is what I say.

RAMJOHN. A go still do it.

SAMUEL. What?

RAMJOHN. A go still go ahead wit my plans.

SAMUEL. Dat is what she want.

RAMJOHN. Dat is what she say she want, but dat is a trick, she know I does always go against she, so she say she glad, ter make me drop dem, but a go still go ahead.

SAMUEL. Yes.

RAMJOHN. It might en' work out yer know.

SAMUEL. Yes, I tink so, what picture Mitchum take off he trousers in?

RAMJOHN (*laughs*). Yer mean what picture Mitchum take off he jacket in?

SAMUEL. Yes.

RAMJOHN. Someting call *His Kinda Woman* dat was funny.

SAMUEL. Yes.

RAMJOHN. It was a complicated flim bout gangsters an ting, but he take off he jacket.

SAMUEL. What he trousers look like?

RAMJOHN. Fantastic, great man, yer know he big.

SAMUEL. Yes.

RAMJOHN. Well wen he take off he jacket, man, all yer could see is trousers, trousers all over de place, trousers up ter he waist, trouser down ter he shoes, an de cutting man, dey start big at he waist an dey end small, small at he shoes, an pleats, talk about pleats, de pleats so sharp yer could cut a nail on dem.

SAMUEL. Yes.

RAMJOHN. Dat tailor shoulda get a Academy Award.

SAMUEL. Yeah, Mitchum get one.

RAMJOHN. Nar man, a tell yer Mitchum en' no actor.

SAMUEL. Or.

RAMJOHN. All he does do is push out he belly an close he eye.

SAMUEL. Yes dat is true, Mr Gookool.

RAMJOHN. Yes.

SAMUEL. Yer feel I could build one a dem suit?

RAMJOHN. Ye'd like too eh?

SAMUEL. Yes, man, it should really happen sometime, a would really enjoy dat, man.

RAMJOHN. Well yer have to work hard an listen, an do what a tell yer ter do, an get de experience an den yer could build one.

SAMUEL. Well dat is what a here for, ter learn.

RAMJOHN. All right. Aa, look who here.

FRANK *enters pushing a bicycle, leans it against the shop.*

FRANK. What happening, RamJohn?

RAMJOHN. Boy a day wit dem, still trying ter make a penny, wen yer go pay me dat dollar yer owe me?

FRANK. Well dat is what a come ter see yer for, a want yer ter make me anodder pair a dem pants, and wen a pay yer for dem a go pay yer for de odder one.

RAMJOHN. All right, what material yer want it in, de same?

FRANK. Yes, boy, dose is me lucky pants, everytime a wear

dem someting does happen, but a wear dem so much, dey tearing.

SAMUEL. Dat's good one, man.

RAMJOHN. Same size.

FRANK. Yes I en' get fat.

RAMJOHN. All right den what happening, how come yer only trow a quick one ter day, yer en' have de time or what?

FRANK. What yer mean?

RAMJOHN. A mean up de road.

FRANK. Or, yer know bout dat.

RAMJOHN. Well nobody en' tell me notting, if dat is what yer worried bout.

FRANK. I en' worried, man, red flag flying.

RAMJOHN. A see, yer friend coming home fer lunch now.

FRANK. Yes, boy.

RAMJOHN. Yer have ter watch out.

FRANK. Yes.

RAMJOHN. He catch yer.

FRANK. Nar a hear 'im, in he come through de front an I move through de back.

RAMJOHN. A see, we better measure yer anyhow.

FRANK. All right.

RAMJOHN. Samuel take he measurement.

SAMUEL. How a go do dat?

RAMJOHN. Take de tape measure an do it, an write it down in de book, yer go see he name under Frank.

SAMUEL. All right. (*He picks up the tape, opens the book and begins to measure* FRANK.)

FRANK. All yer going ter de meeting ter night?

RAMJOHN. What meeting is dat?

FRANK. PNM having a meeting ter night in Woodford Square, it go have one set a woman down dere, dey going ter hear de Doc, de man making a lot a sense yer know, he say is time we get our independence, an start getting more money from de oil fields, yer know de oil companies does get seventy-five percent a de profits, an we does only get twenty-five.

SAMUEL. No.

FRANK. Well I didn't know dat either, is de Doc who let me know.

SAMUEL. Yes.

RAMJOHN. So what dat good for, what is de use a knowing dat yer car' do notting bout it, de oil companies have agreements signed for about ninety-nine years, how yer go change dat?

FRANK. Well de Doc say dat if PNM come ter power, he go negotiate a new agreement, he go get seventy-five percent and dey go get de twenty-five percent.

SAMUEL. Yes dat sound like de right way.

RAMJOHN. So you feel de oil companies go just do what he tell dem ter do?

FRANK. Dey have to he en' no idiot yer know like Albert Gomes, he is a PhD an he know bout economics, an de man write books too.

SAMUEL. Yes, how much books he write?

FRANK. Plenty, a tink two, one on slavery an one on Trinidad.

SAMUEL. He sound like really someting, man.

FRANK. An he used ter teach in a university in de States too.

RAMJOHN. Dat en' notting, university in de States come like private school here, anybody does go ter university in de States an get a degree, people does get degree for pole vaulting, but it do' mean anyting, if yer say Oxford or Cambridge den yer saying someting.

FRANK. Look, man, you is a DLP all yer Indian bound ter say dem kinda ting, all yer just want ter see black people foolish an working fer allyer, an Indian driving bout in big car, well dem days done, dis man is a Trinidadian who come ter help we, an who come ter tell we how ter better we selves, all yer Indian all right allyer en' need no help, all yer children go be lawyers or doctor, while we beg for shit, so do' tell me bout notting.

MISS GOOKOOL (*calls out*). RamJohn I do' want no argument in my shop.

RAMJOHN. Ma.

MISS GOOKOOL *comes through dressed in a sari.*

MISS GOOKOOL. A don't care, a say a don't want no argument in my shop an a mean it, dis is a tailor shop, if he want a pair a pants let him get measure an build it, but dis en' Woodford Square, if he want ter argue politics let him go down dere.

RAMJOHN. But, Ma –

MISS GOOKOOL. A don't care, a say what a say, an what bout de dollar he owe we?

RAMJOHN. All right, yer want a pants, we go make yer a pants but yer have ter pay a dollar first.

FRANK (*pulls away from* SAMUEL). I en' want no focking pants man, a change me mind.

MISS GOOKOOL. Well go den, yer en' even have money ter buy pants, an yer arguing politics, allyer nigger do' want ter work, all allyer want ter do is drink rum and fight an run after woman, but allyer do' like hard work, yer car' take it, it does kill yer out so go on talk yer politics somewhere else, yer ever see Doctor Williams wid a hole in he pants?

SAMUEL *laughs*.

Because he work hard, he do' sit on no ass all day, instead a you go an look fer work, yer hiding an peeping behind man woman, yer waiting fer de man ter go ter work for you ter go up behind he woman, what yer give she, what yer ever give she, de man should get a cutlass an chop off yer neck, get outa me shop now, get out.

FRANK. All right a going but allyer Indian better watch out.

MISS GOOKOOL. Is you better watch out de man do' catch you, look, a kiss de cross, next time a see him a go tell him yer going by he woman.

FRANK. Is de woman want me, is me de woman want, she love me.

MISS GOOKOOL. Well marry she den if she love yer, but nar, yer wouldn't do dat, dat mean yer have ter look after she, an dat is hard work an dat go kill yer, so go, get outa me shop, we do' want no worthless people in dis shop.

SAMUEL *laughs*.

MISS GOOKOOL. Samuel, you get back ter what yer was doing.

SAMUEL. Yes, Miss Gookool.

MISS GOOKOOL. RamJohn, I want yer ter get on wid de work, and I do' want no politics going on in dis shop, yer hear me?

RAMJOHN. All right.

MISS GOOKOOL. All right den.

MISS GOOKOOL *goes through to the kitchen.*

SAMUEL *and* RAMJOHN *begin to work. Pause.*

SAMUEL. Yer modder make de man look foolish, she make him leave wit he tail between he legs.

RAMJOHN. She don't understand dese tings, man.

SAMUEL. Yer do' tink she was right?

RAMJOHN. She wasn't right ter interfere, man, I is a big man, I could take care a myself, man, she see big man talking she mustn't interfere.

SAMUEL. Yer tink Frank was right?

RAMJOHN. Right bout what?

SAMUEL. Right bout what de Doc go do.

RAMJOHN. Well dat is what I wanted ter argue wit him but he couldn't stan facts.

SAMUEL. Yer going ter hear de Doc talk, I going.

RAMJOHN. You going.

SAMUEL. Well if what Frank say is true he sound like a man ter listen to, he sound like de kinda man we need, de kinda man we could do wid.

RAMJOHN. But what you know bout politics?

SAMUEL. Notting, dat is why a tinking a going.

RAMJOHN. All yer go hear is one set a lies.

SAMUEL. It might still be good, a might learn someting, who know, you coming?

RAMJOHN. A might, a might, a want yer ter finish unpicking dem trousers.

SAMUEL. All right.

RAMJOHN. De old lady surprise me, man.

SAMUEL. Yes she surprise Frank too.

RAMJOHN. Yes.

SAMUEL. You is a DLP?

RAMJOHN. I is a businessman.

SAMUEL. But you is a Indian, an DLP is a Indian party.

RAMJOHN. A tell yer I en' no DLP I is a businessman, dat is all, an I en' no Indian, I is a Trinidadian.

SAMUEL. But yer is a Trinidadian Indian.

RAMJOHN. You is a African.

SAMUEL (*stands up*). No, I do' live in a tree an wear no bush clothes an paint up my face, I is a Trinidadian, I look like a African ter you, I born an bred in Trinidad, you car' call me no African, a do' like dat, a do' like dat at all.

RAMJOHN. All right yer see, de same way you en' an African, I en' a Indian.

SAMUEL. But you is a Indian, you have Indian name, I en' have no African name, my name en' Aba Abadaba.

RAMJOHN. What kinda name yer have?

SAMUEL. I have a Trinidadian name.

RAMJOHN. Yer have a English name.

SAMUEL. Yes, Trinidadian, we does talk English.

RAMJOHN. But you en' English.

SAMUEL. Of course I is English, I does talk English, so I is English, we is English, all a we is English, man.

RAMJOHN. A tought yer was Trinidadian.

SAMUEL. Yes, but Trinidad is English, man.

RAMJOHN. All right, Mister Englishman, wen yer finish unpicking dem trousers a want yer ter sweep up dem scraps on de floor, Mr McKay from de oil fields coming an de place must look tidy.

SAMUEL. All right.

MISS GOOKOOL (*calls out*). RamJohn what time Mister McKay coming?

RAMJOHN (*to* SAMUEL). She was listening. (*He calls out.*) He said after lunch.

MISS GOOKOOL. Why yer didn't tell me sooner, yer know every time he come he like ter taste me roti.

RAMJOHN. I didn't tinka it.

MISS GOOKOOL. Well a go have ter do it quickly.

RAMJOHN. Go an see what she want.

SAMUEL. What bout de sweepings?

RAMJOHN. Do dat after she.

SAMUEL. All right. (*He goes through.*) Yes, Miss Gookool.

MISS GOOKOOL. Do' give me no yes, Miss Gookool, just pick up dat coal pot an light it, yer go find some coals outside.

SAMUEL. Yes.

MISS GOOKOOL. An hurry up.

SAMUEL. Yes, Miss Gookool.

MISS GOOKOOL. All right, Samuel.

*He picks up the coal pot and goes out. MISS GOOKOOL pours flour on the table, pours water on it, begins to mix.*

SAMUEL *comes back with the coal pot.*

SAMUEL. All right, Miss Gookool, anyting else?

MISS GOOKOOL. Yer could make roti?

SAMUEL. No, Miss Gookool.

MISS GOOKOOL. Well what yer asking me if dere's anyting else for?

SAMUEL. All right den. (*He goes through.*)

RAMJOHN. What she wanted?

SAMUEL. She wanted me ter light de coal pot for she.

RAMJOHN. She making roti?

SAMUEL. Yes.

RAMJOHN. Well finish sweeping up.

SAMUEL. All right. (*A beat.*) a going ter dat meeting yer know.

RAMJOHN. Go nar.

SAMUEL. Yes a going, a going ter hear what he have ter say.

RAMJOHN. Yes, well go.

SAMUEL. Yes a going.

MR McKAY *comes into the shop. He is dressed in a short-sleeved white shirt, khaki shorts, knee socks and shoes.*

RAMJOHN. Afternoon, Mr McKay.

MR McKAY. Good afternoon, Gookool, afternoon, Samuel.

SAMUEL. Afternoon, Mr McKay.

RAMJOHN. How are you, Mr McKay?

MR McKAY. I'm fine, Gookool, I've brought some orders for you and I want to have a look at those you've done so far.

RAMJOHN. Yes, Mr McKay, you'd like ter have a seat, Samuel dust dat chair fer Mr McKay.

MR McKAY. No thank you it's too hot for me, if I sit down I fall asleep.

RAMJOHN. Samuel, get down two overalls. (*He calls out.*) Ma, Mr McKay here.

SAMUEL *goes to a shelf.* MISS GOOKOOL *comes out wiping her hands on an apron.*

MISS GOOKOOL. Oh, Mr McKay, how nice ter see yer.

*They shake hands.*

MR McKAY. Hallo, Miss Gookool, how are those rotis?

MISS GOOKOOL. De rotis still nice I just doing some.

MR McKAY. Splendid, splendid.

MISS GOOKOOL. Dey should be ready soon, I'll put a few in a paper bag feryer, you'd like dat.

MR McKAY. Very much, very much, my wife looks forward to eating your rotis, and even the children now are getting to like them.

MISS GOOKOOL. Dat's nice, I'll put two extra in de bag den.

MR McKAY. That's very kind of you, most kind.

MISS GOOKOOL. Not at all, not at all, a won't be long. (*She goes through.*)

RAMJOHN *takes an overall from* SAMUEL *and shows it to* MR McKAY.

RAMJOHN. Yer see Mr McKay, a put de side pockets more in front like yer tell me so notting can catch on dem.

MR McKAY. Yes, very good. (*He examines the overall.*)

RAMJOHN. And Mr McKay, a put extra stitchings like yer tell me ter strengthen de pockets, so de men could put any kinda spanner in dem and de pocket go still hold.

MR McKAY. Yes, very good, very good.

MISS GOOKOOL. Samuel.

SAMUEL. Yes, Miss Gookool.

MISS GOOKOOL. Come a want yer.

SAMUEL. Yes, coming. (*He goes through.*) Yes, Miss Gookool.

MISS GOOKOOL. Go next door an ask de Chinese man for a big paper bag, an come back quick.

SAMUEL. Yes, Miss Gookool. (*He turns to go.*)

MISS GOOKOOL. Run, quick.

SAMUEL (*going out*). Yes, Miss Gookool. (*He goes.*)

   *Inside.*

RAMJOHN. An yer see, Mr McKay, a put de back pockets right at de back ter make sure wen de men reach ter de back, dey go fine it.

MR McKAY. Yes, yes, very good.

   MISS GOOKOOL *comes through.*

MISS GOOKOOL. De rotis won't be long, Mr McKay, a just send Samuel ter get some paper bags.

MR McKAY. You shouldn't go to so much trouble.

MISS GOOKOOL. Is no trouble, no trouble at all.

MR McKAY. You're much too kind.

MISS GOOKOOL. What keeping im, he should be back by now, he so foolish.

MR McKAY. Well, Gookool, I must say these look fine to me, very tough and hardwearing.

RAMJOHN. Yes, Mr McKay, dey tough an hardwearing, dey could take any kinda pressure yer give dem, a ask yer ter test dem, give dem a test yer see how strong dey is.

MR McKAY. All right, that's fine then, I'll take these two with me and I'll let you know how they stand up to our conditions.

RAMJOHN. Yes, Mr McKay, yes, Mr McKay.

*SAMUEL runs in, out of breath, holding two paper bags.*

SAMUEL. Here, Miss Gookool, de Chinese man next door didn't have no big ones so a had ter run down ter de corner ter get some.

MISS GOOKOOL. Give me dem.

*She snatches the bags from SAMUEL, and goes through.*

MR McKAY. And here are the orders for two dozen more pairs.

MISS GOOKOOL (*from inside*). Two dozen, dat's a lot, tanks, Mr McKay, and here are de rotis.

*MISS GOOKOOL comes out, hands the bags to MR McKAY. RAMJOHN puts the orders in his pocket.*

RAMJOHN. Tanks, Mr McKay, a should finish dese by de end a de month.

MR McKAY. Fine, fine, I'll have the van pick them up.

RAMJOHN. No need, a could get Samuel ter bring dem up ter you.

MR McKAY. That's settled then, good afternoon and thank you for the lovely rotis, Miss Gookool.

*MR McKAY walks out, SAMUEL, RAMJOHN and MISS GOOKOOL stand looking at him go, the sound of the car starting, they wave, the car drives off.*

MISS GOOKOOL. Goodbye, Mr McKay. What a nice man, he's a real gentleman.

SAMUEL. Yes.

MISS GOOKOOL *(turns)*. All right, all yer get back ter work now.

SAMUEL *(to RAMJOHN)*. Yer want me ter finish sweeping?

RAMJOHN. Nar, do' bodder.

MISS GOOKOOL. Yes finish it, de place still have ter look clean yer know.

SAMUEL. But, Miss Gookool, a want ter go ter dis meeting an if I do' leave now a en' go catch de bus going ter town.

MISS GOOKOOL. I do' *care*.

SAMUEL. Mr Gookool, you –

RAMJOHN. Yer know me modder is de boss.

MISS GOOKOOL. Samuel, if yer do' finish sweeping dat floor, yer not working here no more.

SAMUEL. I going ter me meeting, a want ter go, a have ter go. *(Leaning the broom against the wall, turns to go.)*

MISS GOOKOOL *(to SAMUEL as he leaves)*. Go den. Go ter yer meeting, yer sacked. See if dey go feed yer, yer go starve, yer tief.

SAMUEL. Tief? *(He goes.)*

RAMJOHN. Why yer do dat? I have two dozen overall ter finish before Carnival, who go help me?

MISS GOOKOOL. Do' worry, Mr McKay go understand. He is gentleman. But dat Samuel have ter learn, wen he get hungry he come back. You do' know how ter treat dem nigger yer know, you tink dey is human, dey en' human, dey is dog, feed dem and dey happy. But do' worry he go come back.

MISS GOOKOOL *goes through.*


**Scene Two**

*Some weeks later. Daytime. The tailor's shop.*

RAMJOHN *is at the counter sorting overalls into stacks. Consulting order, ticking.*

*In the distance is the sound of Carnival celebrations, people shouting, laughing, singing, and music, steel band, brass band.*

*A figure appears crouching from behind the scenery. The figure is* SAMUEL *dressed in US Marine combat outfit with sunglasses, cigar in mouth. He is carrying a sub-machine gun. When he gets to the doorway he stands pointing the gun at* RAMJOHN.

SAMUEL (*speaks all through the confrontation sequence with an American accent*). Right, Indian, yer time's come. Say yer prayers.

RAMJOHN (*looks up startled*). Samuel, no. (*He puts up his hands.*) What yer doing, man?

SAMUEL. A come ter get yer.

RAMJOHN. But, man . . .

SAMUEL. Say yer prayers.

MISS GOOKOOL *rushes through, puts her hands up.*

RAMJOHN. Why yer doing dis, man?

MISS GOOKOOL. Samuel, Samuel, a beg yer. After all we do fer yer, yer car' do dis, Samuel yer car' . . .

RAMJOHN. Me modder right, Samuel, yer car' do it ter me, not me. We treat yer like family, yer come like one a we, man, yer car' do it.

SAMUEL. I have my orders ter destroy de occupant at dis place, orders is orders.

RAMJOHN. Who give dat? We en' against nobody. We always get on wit everybody an if anybody need help or hungry we feed dem.

MISS GOOKOOL. Yer know how much people we feed, yer know how much life we save, you young yer know, you car' remember but if yer modder was alive terday she would tell yer plenty tings, wen tings was bad, she came an ask me fer help, an we help she, when yer was a little boy an yer was sick is we who give she rice and food ter keep yer alive, dat is . . . why yer car' do dis ter me, Samuel. Oh, God, a beg, do' do it.

SAMUEL. I have my orders.

RAMJOHN. Well, Samuel, at least tell me who give de orders, at least tell we who ter see, man. We could fix up someting. Tell me who ter se, man. I do so much fer yer, we is brodders, tell me, man, I could soon make sure you all right too. Man, anyting yer want, just tell me. Look, we talk about it, at least just listen.

SAMUEL. All right, but I still have my orders.

MISS GOOKOOL. All right, Samuel, do' listen ter me, I old fashion, I do' know notting, but listen ter RamJohn. You an he get along. I must be treat yer bad, but RamJohn always look out fer yer, is he who beg me ter let yer come an work here, is he who spend the time trying ter teach yer trade, listen ter him, RamJohn, you tell him.

RAMJOHN. Look, Samuel, I could go ter de bank. De bank en' close yet, I could run down dere, keep me modder here as hostage if a do' come back.

SAMUEL. My orders said notting bout hostages.

MISS GOOKOOL. Oh, God, Samuel, listen ter de boy, nar.

SAMUEL. All right, I'm listening.

RAMJOHN. I could go ter de bank an come back here in ten minutes, an give you anyting yer want, an enough fer de man who give yer de orders. What yer say ter dat, eh, how dat sound?

SAMUEL. Man, yer do' understand, orders is orders, say yer prayers.

MISS GOOKOOL. Oh, God, Samuel!

SAMUEL *pulls the trigger and sprays them; it is a toy gun.* SAMUEL *laughs.*

MISS GOOKOOL *collapses.* RAMJOHN *picks her up, helps her to a seat. She sits leaning on the counter.*

SAMUEL (*back to a Trinidadian accent*). I get all yer, yer see, dat is Mas, all yer do' know how to play Mas, dat is Mas, yer see.

RAMJOHN. Samuel, how yer could do a ting like dat, man yer nearly kill me modder. (*He faces* SAMUEL, *shocked.*) Yer all right, Ma?

SAMUEL. Dat is Mas, man, all yer Indian do' know how ter play Mas is we Trinidadian know how ter play Mas, we know bout Mas. I was a real marine, nobody en' tell me what ter say yer know, I just make it up, a get yer, a know a get yer, here, have a drink.

*He takes a water bottle out of his belt, hands it to* RAMJOHN, *sits down, takes off his helmet.*

RAMJOHN. No, I en' want no drink, no tanks.

SAMUEL. Is Carnival, man, yer must have a drink, man, everybody must have a drink Carnival time.

RAMJOHN. A do' want no (*He pushes the bottle away.*) drink.

SAMUEL (*drinks*). Look a sorry, a didn't mean ter frighten all yer (*To* MISS GOOKOOL.) Miss Gookool, a sorry, it was only . . . a, have a drink. (*He pleads.*)

RAMJOHN. No, man, a tell yer (*He again pushes.*) I en' want no drink.

SAMUEL (*drinks*). A ferget is against yer religion. But dis is Carnival, man.

RAMJOHN. A do' care.

SAMUEL. A get yer, eh (*He laughs.*) admit it, yer really believe I was a marine come ter get yer, yer see how ter play Mas.

RAMJOHN (*sits down*). Yes. Samuel, yer get me, yer get me.

SAMUEL. I leave de band down de road, a say a go come up here an show yer me Mas, if yer see de band, man, we have generals, admirals, nurses, doctors, pilots, tanks, planes, landing craft, an about two tousand marines, we bound ter win band a de year dis year, if we do' win it dere go be big trouble, de only competition we have is Bobby Ammow, he playing *Flowers a de Universe*, but dem white people do' know how ter play Mas. (*He drinks.*) Is we Trinidadian know how ter play Mas. We invent Mas, an is we who know how ter play it . . .

RAMJOHN. Yes.

MISS GOOKOOL *gets up, staggers, holding her head.*
RAMJOHN *gets up, helps her.*

MISS GOOKOOL. I going inside ter lie down (*To* SAMUEL.) A
do' want yer in my shop no more, yer hear.

SAMUEL. But, Miss Gookool, I . . .

MISS GOOKOOL. A do' care, Mas or no Mas, a do' want yer
round here no more.

RAMJOHN. All right, Ma take it easy.

MISS GOOKOOL. Samuel, a never ferget yer.

RAMJOHN *takes her through.* SAMUEL *drinks.* RAMJOHN
*comes back out.*

SAMUEL. So how yer like me, eh, a come good, eh?

RAMJOHN. Yes, yer come good.

SAMUEL. A look real, a look like de real ting?

RAMJOHN. Yes, yer look real.

SAMUEL. Yer ever see *Sands of Iwo Jima*?

RAMJOHN. No, a never see it.

SAMUEL. Well, dat is how we coming, yer tink a come good?

RAMJOHN. Yes, man, yer come good, yer get we.

SAMUEL. So yer tink I was (*He laughs.*) really goin ter . . . (*He
laughs.*)

RAMJOHN. Yes, man, yer play Mas so real, I tought yer was a
real . . .

SAMUEL (*laughs*). A car' believe dat.

RAMJOHN. Yes, man, yer really know how ter play Mas, dat
is plenty Mas yer playing.

SAMUEL. So yer really tink I would a . . . (*He laughs.*) Nar, man, I wouldn't do a ting like dat ter allyer. I grateful ter you an yer modder.

RAMJOHN. How yer mean?

SAMUEL. How yer tink I get money ter play Mas, since I leave here I doing well.

RAMJOHN. How yer mean?

SAMUEL. Since I leave here I is a king.

RAMJOHN. How yer mean, man?

SAMUEL. Well, yer know de meeting a wanted ter go ter dat evening?

RAMJOHN. Yes.

SAMUEL. Well, a didn't really want ter go, if yer know wat a mean, but a wanted ter go, yer modder . . .

RAMJOHN. I know.

SAMUEL. Is yer modder make me go, she get me so vex . . .

RAMJOHN. I know.

SAMUEL. Well, anyhow, a went, an man wen de Doc start ter talk de whole place change, man, yer know de ole political meetings people only used ter go ter see one anodder an ter talk an look fer women, but dis time de place change, people get serious, nobody en' heckling an laughing, people start ter listen man, an wen he finish dey jump up and cheer like Carnival, de man had de people, man.

RAMJOHN. Yes.

SAMUEL. An dey start ter pass around application form an ting, an a join, an a go ter all de meeting now.

RAMJOHN. Yes.

SAMUEL. Yes, an dat en' all, dey ask me ter open a branch in my area an ter represent it, so I doing well.

RAMJOHN. How yer . . .

SAMUEL. Well I in charge a my area now, I is a big man in my area, I does go ter all de business man in my area, an tell dem dat if dey do' give funds ter de party, wen we come ter power, we go take dem over, yer see.

RAMJOHN. Yes.

*The sound of a band, people, music getting nearer.*

SAMUEL. It easy. So I is a boss now.

RAMJOHN. Yes.

SAMUEL. But do' worry, you is me friend, if anybody trouble you, you just tell me, I go fix dem, dat Mister McKay, how he treating yer, he treating yer all right?

RAMJOHN. Yes, he's . . .

SAMUEL. I go have a word wit 'im, do' worry, I go make 'im give yer all de overalls ter make, wait yer go see, I go fix it.

*Someone in the band hollers,* Samuel let we go.

RAMJOHN. Yes.

*The band arrives outside.*

SAMUEL *gets up, puts on his helmet, picks up the gun.*

SAMUEL. All right! Boy, wen we come ter power we go change dis whole island, upside down, we go make all dem people who was taking advantage a we, suffer, we go make dem bawl, yer go see, de band coming, so a have ter go, see yer, RamJohn.

(*shouting*). Play Mas, Play Mas, PNM, PNM, *Sands of IwoJima. Sands of IwoJima.* Vote PNM. Vote PNM.

Wen a ask de people what party dey voting dey shouted out PNM, de young, de old, an all little children shouted out PNM.

SAMUEL *goes out firing the gun, dancing to music.*

RAMJOHN *stands watching the band pass.*

RAMJOHN. Yer all right, Ma? How yer feeling now?

MISS GOOKOOL. I en' feeling too well. (*Weakly.*) Yer better send fer de doctor.

RAMJOHN. Yes, Ma.

RAMJOHN *runs out, runs back in, goes through.*

Ma, I go have ter go fer de doctor meself, everybody playing Mas, yer go be all right?

MISS GOOKOOL. You go, son, I go be all right, just look after yerself.

RAMJOHN. Ma, a en' go be long, a come back right away wit de doctor.

MISS GOOKOOL. Yes, son, you go an take care.

RAMJOHN *rushes out.*

*Carnival celebrations in the background.* Shouts of PNM. *Faint strains of* God Save the Queen.

RAMJOHN (*off stage*). In here, doctor, she in here.

RAMJOHN *and the* DOCTOR *come in. The* DOCTOR *is wearing glasses and is dressed in a bush skirt and his body is painted with African symbols. He is carrying a bag.*

DOCTOR. Is a good ting yer catch me, yer know, a was just going ter meet me band, is Carnival, yer know.

RAMJOHN. Yes, doctor. (*He holds aside the curtain.*) In here.

> RAMJOHN *and the* DOCTOR *go through. The* DOCTOR *takes a stethoscope from the bag, examines* MISS GOOKOOL'*s, chest, takes her pulse, drops her hand.*

DOCTOR. She dead. Dis woman is dead. You bring me here ter examine a dead woman. If it is a certificate yer wanted . . .

RAMJOHN. I didn't know she was dead, doctor . . .

DOCTOR. Yes, she dead, I would say de heart.

RAMJOHN. But yer had to examine she.

DOCTOR. I coulda do dat Ash Wednesday, man, yer coulda come ter me office, dis is Carnival, man.

RAMJOHN. Yes, doctor, sorry . . . she collapse.

DOCTOR. Yes, de heart. (*They come through.*) Car' stand too much pressure, yer know, an she wasn't a young woman, but she work hard.

RAMJOHN. Yes, doctor.

DOCTOR. So how yer like me Mas, a come good, yer like how a come?

RAMJOHN. Yes.

DOCTOR. Yes, man is Ashanti, genuine Ashanti, yer know, (*Holding his beads.*) yer like de designs?

RAMJOHN. Yes, doctor.

DOCTOR. Taken from a genuine photograph, man, we bound ter win band a de year.

RAMJOHN. Yes, doctor.

DOCTOR. An if yer see de rest a de band, man, we have every tribe in Africa, tribe yer never even hear about, we go win it, we bound ter win it.

RAMJOHN. Yes, doctor.

*The sound of a band getting nearer. African shouts, chants, to music.*

DOCTOR. Dat sound like me band coming; a have ter go, a go send yer me bill.

RAMJOHN. What bout . . . ?

DOCTOR. Or yer want ter bury she?

RAMJOHN. Yes, doctor.

DOCTOR. Well, look, come ter me office an a go give yer de certificate.

RAMJOHN. Termorrow?

DOCTOR. Nar, man termorrow is Carnival. Tuesday I en' working, come Ash Wednesday morning.

RAMJOHN. But a want ter bury her by Ash Wednesday, is Hindu law . . .

DOCTOR. Well, make de arrangements, man, I go have de certificate ready.

RAMJOHN. All right, doctor.

DOCTOR. A have ter go now. A sorry bout yer old lady, she was a good woman.

*The band arrives, the* DOCTOR *picks up his bag.*

RAMJOHN. Yes, doctor.

*The* DOCTOR *goes out chanting, dancing in time to music. The band passes.*

RAMJOHN *slowly goes back to the counter, stacking overalls.*

*The sound of whistles blowing in the distance. A figure comes*

*into the shop blowing a whistle. The figure is dressed in an
all-black cowboy outfit, with a gunbelt. In one hand is a gun;
in the other is a small coffin with a coinslot.*

ROBBER. Halt, quick, quick, quick. I mustn't be late. I have to
be at de Robber's Gate by half past eight, so give, or your
soul will be for ever calling the call of the speechless. I have
climbed mountains, and walked over burning deserts, stop,
stop, stop, you mocking pretender, I am from de House of
Wisa, wen I walk, de earth tremble and de lion has growled
and averted my gaze. Wen I speak, lightning has flashed an
thunder has flowed from my mouth. I have eaten the heads of
ten viper snakes to get here, the Mighty Zocoppo has taken
me into the Forest of Darkness and showed me the hundred
and one trees to build the coffin without nails. So stop, stop,
stop and give I mustn't be late, I must be at de Robber's Gate
by half past eight.

*RAMJOHN puts a coin in the coffin.*

You have given to Tamaroo, your mighty soul will see the
crown of vestments and the black mule of tomorrow will kick
de dust from your path wherever you go, an you will sit at de
feet of my sister, de destroyer of all rascals.

*The ROBBER takes off his mask. It is FRANK.*

FRANK. RamJohn is me.

RAMJOHN (*smiling*). Yes, man.

FRANK. How a come, how a come?

RAMJOHN. Yer come good. (*Smiling.*) Yer come good.

FRANK. Here, have a drink.

 *FRANK takes a bottle out of a bag slung over his shoulder.
 RAMJOHN takes the bottle, has a drink.*

RAMJOHN. De old lady dead, yer know.

FRANK. Wen she dead?

RAMJOHN. Dis morning, she had a attack.

FRANK. A sorry ter hear dat, man, she was a nice old lady, although me an she didn't get on, a sorry ter hear dat, man. A know how yer feel, a leave de bottle. (*He puts the bottle on the counter.*) Have a drink, I have more in here. (*Patting his bag.*)

*A WHISTLER arrives. FRANK puts on his mask, blows a whistle.*

Quick, quick, quick, I mustn't be late I have to be at de Robber's Gate by half past eight.

*FRANK goes, blowing the whistle. A band passes.*

*RAMJOHN sits down drinking from the bottle. The sound of music approaching.*

*A NEGRO WOMAN dressed in bishop's attire carrying a staff in one hand and a collection tin in the other comes in dancing, her face painted white, cheeks red.*

BISHOP. My son, bless you, give to the Lord an he will give to you. Le' me hear de rustle of paper. (*Spells it.*) P.A.P.E.R. (*RAMJOHN puts coins in the tin.*) Coins make too much noise. May de Lord shine his light on you, peace be wit you, my son, peace be wit you. Band a de year, band a de year.

*Music getting nearer.*

*She dances out.*

*The band passes.*

*RAMJOHN drinks.*

*Two UNDERTAKERS come in dressed in long black coats. FIRST UNDERTAKER takes his hat off, holds it out.*

FIRST UNDERTAKER. We come fer de body, accept our sympathies.

SECOND UNDERTAKER. Yes, we come fer de body. Accept our condolences.

RAMJOHN *gets up, staggers.*

RAMJOHN. What, what de ass.

FIRST UNDERTAKER. As you are now, so once was I . . . As I am now, so you will be.

SECOND UNDERTAKER. Prepare yourself to follow me.

RAMJOHN. What, no, no, get yer ass outa me shop, a don't care, Carnival or no Carnival, I is a Indian, I is a Indian.

FIRST UNDERTAKER. But we come fer de body, de doctor band pass we parlour an he tell we yer modder dead, and we come ter pick up de body.

RAMJOHN *(staggering).* A don't care, yer not taking she, dis is Carnival, man, nobody does work Carnival. Haul yer ass, get out, dis is Carnival. Play Mas, PNM, PNM. *(Dancing out, shouting.)*

FIRST UNDERTAKER. Play Mas *(Watching* RAMJOHN *go.)* Indian, play Mas . . .

*Mas characters enter dancing. All chant* Play Mas, Indian, play Mas.

## ACT TWO

### Scene One

SAMUEL's office, some years later. After Independence.

*Scene: An office, daytime. It is large; at one side there are filing cabinets; in the centre is a large desk. Behind the desk is a large window (barred). In front of the desk are some chairs. On the walls are photographs (political). On the desk are some trays, one white phone, one red, and an intercom. On another wall is a large full-length mirror.*

SAMUEL *is sitting at the desk, dressed in a different suit. The intercom buzzes.*

SAMUEL. Yes, sergeant.

SERGEANT (*intercom*). Yer wife is here, sir.

SAMUEL. Tell her – I en' in.

*His* WIFE *bursts in.*

WIFE. Samuel, a want yer ter lock up dat woman next door.

SAMUEL (*intercom*). Never mind. Who, Mrs Khan?

WIFE. Yes.

SAMUEL. But dat is de Minister a Agriculture wife, I car' lock she up.

WIFE. An you is de Chief a Police.

SAMUEL. Yes.

WIFE. Well dat is your job.

SAMUEL. But I just car' lock up people so, a must have cause.

WIFE. Well I have cause.

SAMUEL. Why, what she do?

WIFE. What she do, de woman, tell Mrs Montague, dat I en' suited for de job a wife a de Chief a Police, an dat at de last reception I wear a night dress an say is a evening gown, dat blue dress, de one a got in Paris, and dat I get drunk an fall down de stairs, dat en' true.

SAMUEL. I know it en' true, yer know how dem women does talk.

WIFE. I trip.

SAMUEL. I know yer trip. Everybody know yer trip . . . do' mind.

WIFE. But she telling everybody dis.

SAMUEL. I car' . . .

WIFE. What a go do?

SAMUEL. She – yer mustn't le' dem women upset –

WIFE. Who upset? Me en' upset, she car' upset me. I know better dan dat, ter le' she an people like she upset me.

SAMUEL. Who tell yer, Mrs Montague?

WIFE. No, Mrs Watson.

SAMUEL. Oh.

WIFE. Mrs Khan tell Mrs Montague, an Mrs Montague tell Mrs Watson.

SAMUEL. Well you tell Mrs Watson dat Mr Khan have a girl friend and he does go an see she every Friday night.

WIFE. How you know dat?

SAMUEL. An I is de Chief a Police?

WIFE. Yes.

SAMUEL. I know everything. Let Mrs Watson tell Mrs

Montague an Mrs Montague go tell Mrs Khan, an dat go fix she.

WIFE. Dat bitch, who is de girl?

SAMUEL. One o' de girls in he office, he carry she ter Venezuela with him, on de last mission.

WIFE. No, I didn't know dat.

SAMUEL. Yes.

WIFE. An she en' know, de wife?

SAMUEL. No.

WIFE. What de girl like?

SAMUEL. A tink she pregnant.

WIFE. No.

SAMUEL. Yes.

WIFE. How long it going on?

SAMUEL. Bout two years.

WIFE. No.

SAMUEL. Yes, yer see yer mustn't le' dem upset yer, yer know dem en' nobody, dey tink dey better dan we but dey worse, dey could pretend, dat is what dey could do, dat is what dey good at but dey car' fool me, I know nobody car' fool me, I know bout all a dem, I know what alla dem does get up to, an wen I ready ta fix dem I go fix all a dem.

WIFE. What else?

SAMUEL. What you mean?

WIFE. Bout de girl.

SAMUEL. He buy she a sports car.

WIFE. No.

SAMUEL. Yes, a MG.

WIFE. An she still driving a old Chrysler. (*She laughs.*)

SAMUEL. Yes.

WIFE. Dat is a real joke, dat really make me laugh, an it always stalling.

SAMUEL. Yes.

*The* WIFE *laughs.*

Dat is all yer wanted?

WIFE. No, a want to open a bazaar.

SAMUEL. Well go an open one nar.

WIFE. No, you have ter arrange it.

SAMUEL. I car'.

WIFE. Mrs Thompson open a bazaar, an she husband is only a junior minister so why I car' open one?

SAMUEL. I do' know.

WIFE. Well fine out, an arrange it, an yer is de Chief a Police?

SAMUEL. Yes.

WIFE. Well make dem make me open one.

SAMUEL. All right a go get a bazaar fer yer ter open.

WIFE. But I en' want no Boy Scout one yer know. I want one wit big people.

SAMUEL. What bout de Young Pioneers.

WIFE. How old dey is?

SAMUEL. Dey old, bout eighteen, nighteen.

WIFE. Yer call dat old.

SAMUEL. I . . .

WIFE. All right, dey go do.

SAMUEL. Right den, dat is all.

WIFE. No, a want a chauffeur.

SAMUEL. An yer could drive, what yer want a chauffeur for?

WIFE. I want a chauffeur fer wen I go shopping. I need somebody ter help me wid de packages, none a de odder women does drive dey self, why I must drive, I is a idiot?

SAMUEL. No.

WIFE. A want one in uniform, give me one a yer men, dey do' do notting, all dey does do is stan up by de corner all day doing notting.

SAMUEL. Dey do' do notting, dey looking fer terrorist.

WIFE. I is a terrorist?

SAMUEL. No.

WIFE. Well what dey stop me for, I do' like nobody stopping me an asking me one set a question yer know . . . and having to show me papers and . . .

SAMUEL. All right, all right, a go get yer a chauffeur, a should know better but . . . anyting else?

WIFE. No.

SERGEANT (*intercom*). A ready wid de recommendations for de awards, sir.

SAMUEL. Tanks Sergeant, bring dem in.

WIFE. What awards?

*The* SERGEANT *enters with a folder.*

SERGEANT. Here, sir.

SAMUEL. No, you read dem.

SERGEANT (*reading from the open folder*). To Mrs Maria Agostini, fer leading de first dustbin strike in de history of Trinidad you are awarded de Order a de Cus-Cus, First Class.

WIFE. What?

SERGEANT (*still reading*). After putting out her dustbin, one morning an not having it collected dis lady put it in de middle a de road an get a chair an she sit down dey fer . . .

WIFE. How long she sit down dey fer?

SERGEANT (*looking up*). Four hours.

WIFE. Four hours.

SERGEANT (*reading*). Whilst all de little children an even some a de big people threw stones an laughed an abused her, before de bin was finally removed.

SAMUEL. Dat was someting eh, just like Gary Cooper, a bet dem children give she a hard time, a know wen dey ready dey could really be someting.

WIFE. She getting honour fer dat?

SAMUEL. De lady is a nice lady.

WIFE. She en' no lady. What she do, she en' do notting, I does do more dan dat, how come I en' get no honour? I does . . .

SAMUEL. De lady.

WIFE. What?

SERGEANT (*reading*). As a result a dis lady's protest from dat day de dustbins have been collected every day.

WIFE. Why she couldn't empty she own bin, I does. She feel she too good ter empty she own dustbin, I does have ter . . .

SAMUEL. Yer do' understand, it was a great ting she do.

WIFE. Great what, she only wanted ter get she name in de papers, you does let dese people get away wid murder yer know.

SAMUEL. Who I does let get away wid murder, I do' let nobody get away wid anyting yer hear, nobody car' get away wid anyting wid me yer hear.

WIFE. All right but de next time yer giving out awards le' me know. I go tell yer who should get award.

SERGEANT. So on behalf a de government an people a Trinidad an Tobago, you are awarded de Order a de Cus-Cus, First Class.

SAMUEL (*taking the folder from the* SERGEANT). All right, Sergeant, who next?

SERGEANT. De boy.

SAMUEL. A fine it. Winston Green you are awarded de Order a de Cus-Cus, Third Class, fer pelting de first stone a de mango season . . .

SERGEANT. Dat boy pelt de first stone a de mango season an knock down six ripe mangoes.

WIFE. What kind a mango?

SERGEANT. Julie mango.

WIFE. I like Julie mango.

SAMUEL. All right. He knock down six mango wid one stone, de most I coulda ever get was two, how he get six?

SERGEANT. Well yer see it was six in a bunch, an he use a flat stone an wen he pelt it so (*Pelts.*) it just spin an cut clean through.

SAMUEL. So, a shoulda use a flat stone.

SERGEANT. Yes.

SAMUEL (*reading*). So, on behalf a de government a de people a Trinidad an Tobago, you are awarded de Order a de Cus-Cus, a go make dat First Class, all right, sergeant?

SERGEANT. Yes, sir.

SAMUEL. Is dat all, sergeant? (*Handing over the folder.*)

SERGEANT. Yes, sir. (*He leaves.*)

SAMUEL (*to his* WIFE). Yer going now?

WIFE. Yes, unless yer want me ter stay for something else.

SAMUEL. No. No.

WIFE. All right den what yer ask me for? (*She leaves.*)

SAMUEL *sits down at the desk and sighs. Pause. The intercom buzzes.*

SAMUEL. Yes, sergeant?

SERGEANT (*intercom*). Mr Gookool here to see you sir . . . sir . . . sir.

SAMUEL. Send him in, sergeant.

*The door opens.*

SERGEANT (*off*). This way, please, sir.

RAMJOHN (*off*). Tank you.

RAMJOHN *enters hesitantly, dressed in a shirt and tie, holding a hat.* SAMUEL *turns, goes to meet him, hand outstretched, brings* RAMJOHN *over to a chair.*

SAMUEL. A, a, RamJohn, sergeant, come in, man, long time no see, a have a bit of a hang-over, what a could do fer you, take a seat, take a seat.

RAMJOHN (*sits, smiling*). Tanks, yer was drinking last night?

SAMUEL. Yes, de Prime Minister gave a function last night an' I had ter be dere. Boy someting else . . . Yer like de office? Not bad, eh? A have two telephones (*Indicating the red one.*) dat one is a direct ter de PM.

RAMJOHN. Yes, yes, it nice. (*Looking around.*)

SAMUEL. So what a could (*Sitting behind the desk.*) do fer yer?

RAMJOHN (*takes a letter out of his shirt pocket*). Is you send fer me, a get dis letter . . .

SAMUEL. Oh, yes, yes, yes. How yer doing?

RAMJOHN. Not too bad.

SAMUEL. Yer still with shop, an ting?

RAMJOHN. Yes, still dere.

SAMUEL. An de old lady passed away?

RAMJOHN. Yes.

SAMUEL. A know you is a man who know bout dese kinda tings.

RAMJOHN. Yes.

SAMUEL. Yer like de suit? (*He turns.*)

RAMJOHN. Yes, yes, it nice.

SAMUEL. New York, yer know, New York, a went over last year an get it dere.

RAMJOHN. Yes.

SAMUEL. Dem Yankee know how ter make suit, boy.

RAMJOHN. Yes.

SAMUEL. Me wife say it too flashy. But she en' know bout dem kinda tings. So how tings up de Hill, still de same way?

RAMJOHN. Still de same.

SAMUEL. Boy, you should a go ter New York, if yer see de place, outa dis world . . . dey smoking any marijuana up dere?

RAMJOHN. I en' know, a suppose so.

SAMUEL. Boy, if yer see de equipment dey have in dat place, talk about hi-fi, a never see so much stereo in me life, fantastic equipment. Boy, a bring back two thousand dollars-worth a hi-fi. Me wife say it too flashy but she do' know bout dem kinda ting, but . . .

RAMJOHN. Yes, so yer like New York, eh?

SAMUEL. Yes, man, a could live dere tomorrow.

RAMJOHN. Yes.

SAMUEL. A like de place, man, as soon as a land a like de place, yer know, a like de feel a de place, yer know, de way dey do tings.

RAMJOHN. Yes.

SAMUEL. But me wife say dey too flashy, but she do' know bout dem kinda tings. (*He laughs.*)

RAMJOHN. Yes.

SAMUEL. Dey have any guns?

RAMJOHN. Where?

SAMUEL. Up de Hill.

RAMJOHN. Not dat I know of, I do' know.

SAMUEL. Yer see all dis is still one a de boys yer know, de same old Samuel, do' let dis fool yer, yer know.

RAMJOHN. I know.

SAMUEL. Is just dat I like ter know how people getting on an what people doing.

RAMJOHN. Yes, why yer do' come up . . . ?

SAMUEL. Too busy, too busy, man I would like ter come up and put on short pants an just sit down by de corner an old talk wit de boys, just talk shit, like we used to but a too busy. Man, too busy, but I still like ter know how de boys getting on an try and help dem if a could.

RAMJOHN. Yes.

SAMUEL. Yer know dat Mr McKay, boy dat was real bad luck, yer remember, I tell yer a woulda get him ter give yer all de overalls ter make . . .

RAMJOHN. Yes.

SAMUEL. Well, boy, de same morning he agree ter do dat, de night he driving home he had de accident, dey say he was drunk an run off de road. Hit a coconut tree. Bam! (*He hits his fist into the palm of his hand.*) Yer know how dem coconut tree tough. Head smashed in, yer see. Bad luck, but I try ter get him ter do it an he agreed, he agreed.

RAMJOHN. Well, dat is how it go.

SAMUEL. John, a tell yer. De position is dis we hear dey smoking a lot of marijuana up de Hill, we en' mind dat but we hear dey getting guns, from, some say Cuba, some say Venezuela, I en' know but a have ter find out, we en' want no trouble . . .

RAMJOHN. I en' . . .

SAMUEL. A know yer go say yer en' know. (*He gets up, comes around to the front.*) But listen, you live up dere an dey know you, an . . .

RAMJOHN. But I . . .

SAMUEL. Yer do' want ter help me?

RAMJOHN. I en' say dat, is just I do' hear notting.

SAMUEL. Look, just listen, a send one a me boys up dere, but dey find out who he was an give him a hard time. But he see uniforms, bandages, a field dressing station, an ammunition, an dynamite. A telling yer dese tings ter let yer know dat we know someting going on. I en' want no names or anyting, a just want yer ter tell me what going on, dat is all.

RAMJOHN. I en' know, man, I en' even know bout dem guns an tings dey do' tell me notting.

SAMUEL. So someting going on?

RAMJOHN. No, I do' know.

SAMUEL. Well, John boy, a sorry yer take dis attitude, after we know one anodder so long. A sorry yer feel dis way. I tought me an you was friends.

RAMJOHN. Yes, but I do' know, I do' know notting.

SAMUEL. All right, times change yer know. Well, at least a satisfied wit one ting.

RAMJOHN. What is dat?

SAMUEL. Dat notting en' going on, because if anyting was going on, a know you is de man who woulda know bout it, eh?

RAMJOHN. Not me, man, I do' mix wit dem, I does just make me pants an dat is it.

SAMUEL. Yes, man, you should really go ter New York, yer'd like it, yer'd like de flims, too. Flims all day an not only American flims, yer know, but Italian flims, an French flims. Flims wit no shooting or anyting, man, just talking an moving bout in one room, yer know, dem kinda flims.

RAMJOHN. Yes, a hear dey making dem kinda flims in England too.

SAMUEL. Nar, man, not England, dem do' know how ter make flims. Is France an Hungary an Czechoslovakia.

RAMJOHN. Yes.

SAMUEL. Yes, man, wit sub-titles, you know underneath de pictures.

RAMJOHN. Yes, a saw one.

SAMUEL. We went wit de ambassador ter de United Nations ter see one an dey had a reception afterwards. But de flim man, a know you woulda like it, I didn't tink it was too bad, but me wife didn't like it. She say . . . but anyhow she do' know bout dem kinda tings, an if you didn't tell me bout dem I wouldn't know what ter look for. Yer married?

RAMJOHN. No.

SAMUEL. Yer modder wanted yer ter get married, yer know.

RAMJOHN. Yes, a know, but I never bodder.

SAMUEL. So you see, boy, dat is how ting change. I was talking ter people in New York not ordinary people, but millionaires, man, an dey was asking me, man, dey was asking me, man dey have millions a dollars just waiting ter invest in Trinidad, but dey say de situation is too unstable, dey was asking me what tings are like, an how we controlling tings, if de guys up de Hill could only realise what dey holding up, man, if dey only realise how de Island could benefit from outside investment. Boy everybody could get work, everybody could get a piece o' cake instead o' just sitting down smoking marijuana an talking black power, yer see what a mean, I want ter help dem.

RAMJOHN. Yes.

SAMUEL. Dat is why a want somebody, somebody who dey know, somebody dey trust, ter tell dem, if I go up dere dey say I up to some trick, I up ter someting yet see dat is why a telling you all dis, a giving yer it straight, a need yer help.

RAMJOHN. Me?

SAMUEL. Yes, you. Dey trust you, you is one a dem, dey go listen ter you, you en' have notting ter lose, yer know me not against you, yer see.

RAMJOHN. Yes.

SAMUEL. Yer see de position I in? I want ter help dem, but a car' . . . All a we is Trinidadian now, yer know, we have ter help one anodder.

RAMJOHN. What in it fer me?

SAMUEL. Now yer talking. Dat is more like it. Dat is de business man talking now. Boy, everybody could get someting outa dis, yer know me forming a regiment.

RAMJOHN. Yes.

SAMUEL. Well, de Yankee have a lot a money ter spend, dey need guns, equipment an uniforms yer see. You could be making all de uniforms, dat is if yer en' making none already, yer see, dat is how it works.

RAMJOHN. Yes.

SAMUEL. Well, look, do' decide notting yet, tink about it an at least let me know an if ever yer do' want ter do it, let me know who a could talk ter an we could arrange a meeting or someting. I could come up or dey could come here or anyting. OK?

RAMJOHN. Yes, all right. (*He gets up.*)

SAMUEL. All right, den, le' me take yer out.

SAMUEL *buzzes the intercom.*

All right. All right den.

RAMJOHN *goes.*

Sergeant, get me Chuck Reynolds. About our plans on de Hill, yes well – notting specific ter report, just dat someting is about to happen an yer could tell your people in Washington dat . . . Not as yet, I don't know if dey is Cuban, dey might be. I will, I will, but as far as de other trip is concerned, I keep you informed. Yes, okay, I'll be at the Club.

SAMUEL *puts down the phone. The intercom buzzes. He answers it.*

Yes, sergeant?

SERGEANT (*intercom*). Dere's some people here ter see yer, sir.

SAMUEL. Dey have a appointment?

SERGEANT (*intercom*). Yes, sir, de delegation.

SAMUEL. Oh yes, yes, sen dem in.

*The door opens. They enter. SAMUEL goes to greet them, hand outstretched.*

NEGRO WOMAN/BISHOP/MRS BANKS *in a black lace dress, hat, gloves.*

FRANK/ROBBER *in a suit and* TWO UNDERTAKERS *as in Act One, Scene Two.*

SAMUEL. Come in, come in, Mrs Banks, it's nice ter see yer. (*They shake hands.*) Frank, how yer doing, man? Sergeant, get some chairs.

FRANK. A do' tink yer know dese two fellars.

SAMUEL. No.

FRANK. Dis is Mr Tate.

SAMUEL. Mr Tate.

FRANK. An dis is Mr Lyle.

SAMUEL. Mr Lyle.

*They shake hands.*

MR TATE. No, we never met, but our paths have crossed a
number of times.

SAMUEL. Yes.

MR LYLE. Yes, a number of times.

SAMUEL. Well take a seat, take a seat.

*They sit.*

SAMUEL *goes behind the desk and sits.*

Well, Mrs Banks, it's nice ter see you, and how is your
husband?

MRS BANKS. His Lordship is as well as can be expected.

SAMUEL. A catch a glimpse a him, de last opening a
parliament but he didn't see me, a gave him a hello, but a
don't tink he heard me.

MRS BANKS. Yes, His Lordship finds de office of bishop very
tiring.

SAMUEL. Yes, I find my office very tiring too, but de minister
say if yer en' tired yer en' working so a must be working, eh?

MRS BANKS. Yes.

SAMUEL. Well, is nice ter see allyer now – de last time tings
wasn't looking so good, as yer know we have tings under
control now.

MRS BANKS. Yes.

SAMUEL. Yes, completely under control, who woulda believe

tree weeks ago we had a riot in de streets eh, who woulda
believe dat eh, nobody dat's who, wen allyer come here an
tell me we have ter do someting about I know allyer was on
de right track, because we was trying ter do someting about it
too, so wen we decide a state a emergency was needed, I was
expecting allyer –

MRS BANKS. Mr Samuel, we came –

SAMUEL. I know allyer come ter find out how tings going if it
working.

FRANK. We come –

SAMUEL. Do' worry, man, it working, it working like a dream,
nobody en' gathering on no street corner, soon as dey stan up
ter talk we grab dem, nobody car' give no public speech or
criticise de Government, so who could beat dat eh, nobody
dat's who, eh?

MRS BANKS. Mr Samuel, I, we, are happy ter hear dat de
regulations working an dat tings getting back ter normal
but –

SAMUEL. I glad too.

MRS BANKS. An dat is why we come ter see yer.

SAMUEL. I tink de state a emergency is de best ting dat ever
happen ter Trinidad, fer de first time I could remember
nobody en' stanning up an talking ter nobody, some people
even getting jobs –

MRS BANKS. But it car' last.

SAMUEL. Who say it car' last, of course it could last, it could
last fer as long as we want it ter last, an nobody – Mrs Banks
tree week ago dey run into dey cathedral an trow one set a
black paint over de statues saying Christ is black, an saying
dey want a mass in African right, an you Frank dey was
looting up all yer stores, right.

FRANK. Yes.

SAMUEL. Well den, dat en' happening now, A do' know bout allyer two fellars but tings wasn't looking too good –

MR TATE. We coped.

MR LYLE. Yes, we coped.

SAMUEL. Well all a we coped, I coped, you coped an de battleship coped, if we didn't have dat American battleship an dat English battleship standing by outside de harbour a do' know what coulda happen, we have tings in control but, we got ter keep we eye open, so do' say it car' last, it go last, it have ter last.

MRS BANKS. Mr Samuel, we came here ter ask yer ter get de state a emergency lifted.

SAMUEL. Never, why?

FRANK. Carnival coming, man.

SAMUEL. What, what. What dat have ter do wit it?

MRS BANKS. Mr Samuel, de church has not benefited from the declaration of a state of emergency.

SAMUEL. Not, benefited, how?

MRS BANKS. More people are staying away from church now, an dey blaming de state a emergency fer it.

SAMUEL. How is dat?

MRS BANKS. Dey saying de church is a gathering an if dey come ter church dey go get arrested.

SAMUEL. But dat en' true.

MRS BANKS. I know it en' true, but dat is what dey saying an we car' do notting about it.

SAMUEL. But what about de statues?

MRS BANKS. We moving wit de times, somebody making some black ones fer we, an his Lordship taking Swahili lessons, so we need de Carnival now.

SAMUEL. But why –

MRS BANKS. People have ter play Carnival an have a good time an feel guilty, an den come ter church, if dey en' play no Carnival dey en' go feel guilty so –

SAMUEL. An you, Frank, what bout you, Frank?

FRANK. As Secretary a de Chamber a Commerce a have ter ask yer ter look a de tourist point a view, we have hotels ter fill, one time a de year we does fill dem an if we en' have no Carnival what we go do?

SAMUEL. But what bout yer stores?

FRANK. Dey was insured, man.

SAMUEL. But –

FRANK. Look, man, I have two warehouse full a uniform an beads, if nobody play Carnival what I go do wit dem, so de economy suffer too.

SAMUEL. An what bout allyer two fellers?

MR TATE. We agree wit de church, we fer people enjoying dey self, an giving vent ter dey feelings.

MR LYLE. We fer more enjoyment, we feel wit tings how it is we not expanding.

SAMUEL. De answer is no, no –

FRANK. Why, man?

SAMUEL. Security, man, dat's why, because security is security dat's why, an we car' change dat, dat is a fact, we just get tings under control an allyer want ter upset dem, we is a nation now yer, people looking at we an respecting we yer

know, so do' come here asking me bout no lifting, I en' lifting
notting, allyer want progress, we progressing, but Carnival
en' progress, Carnival is long time colonial ting, wen de white
man le' we dress up an look foolish ter take we mind off we
troubles, but dat en' what we want, we want buildings an
engineers an investments, dat is what we want, no, no, no
rum drinking, no fighting, no spending money on foolishness,
dat car' help nobody, allyer do' understand dis is de first
chance dis Island ever had ter break outa bad habit, an, an,
we go take de chance, dat is wa we go do.

FRANK. Samuel, Trinidad famous all over de world fer
Carnival, if we en' have no Carnival what go happen, nobody
en' go come here –

SAMUEL. A do' understand allyer people yer know, one minute
allyer want someting declared de next minute allyer want it
lifted, dat is de last time a go ever get anyting declared fer
allyer.

MRS BANKS (*gets up*). Well an dis is de last time we go ever
ask yer ter lift anyting fer we, yer mudder ass. (*She goes to
the door.*)

FRANK (*rises*). Keep yer focking state a emergency. (*He goes to
the door.*)

SAMUEL (*gets up*). Right a go do dat, a go do dat.

*The* TWO UNDERTAKERS *get up.*

MR TATE. We'll be in touch, Mr Samuel, we'll be in touch.

MR LYLE. We will.

SAMUEL *goes to the door.*

SAMUEL. Let dem out, let dem out. Allyer lucky I don't lock
allyer up for forming a gathering.

*The door opens. They leave.* SAMUEL *paces.*

Sergeant!

*The* SERGEANT *comes to the doorway.*

SERGEANT. Sir?

SAMUEL. What de doctor say bout cell number 7-12-43 – and 97?

SERGEANT. Dey recovering, sir.

SAMUEL. What bout 142 and 397?

SERGEANT. No word yet, sir.

SAMUEL. De drugs en' working?

SERGEANT. I do' know, sir, he didn't.

SAMUEL. All right, tell im a coming down. We have to find out where dey guns coming from.

SERGEANT. Yes, sir.

SAMUEL *takes off his jacket, gives it to the* SERGEANT. *The* SERGEANT *goes off with* SAMUEL's *jacket.* SAMUEL *takes the pistol out of his holster, puts the pistol in a drawer, takes a piece of rubber hose out of the drawer, rolls up his sleeves, goes to a filing cabinet, takes out a file, goes.*

## Scene Two

*Some weeks later.* SAMUEL *is standing in front of a mirror drawing a gun from a shoulder holster, replacing it and drawing it again. He does this three times. The intercom buzzes.* SAMUEL *answers it.*

SAMUEL. Yes, sergeant?

SERGEANT (*intercom*). Mr Gookool is here, sir.

SAMUEL. All right, sen im in, sen im in.

*The door opens, RAMJOHN enters.*

Come in, man, come in. Take a seat.

RAMJOHN. Yer look busy, boy.

SAMUEL. Take a seat, take a seat.

RAMJOHN. Tanks, yer really have a nice office, man.

SAMUEL. Yes, yes. So how de boys on de Hill.

RAMJOHN (*half out of his chair, looking out of the window*).
Yes, man, yer have a good view too.

SAMUEL. Yes, yes.

RAMJOHN. Yes, man, life really treat yer good.

SAMUEL. Yes.

RAMJOHN. Yes, man, I remember Samuel, Samuel used ter
work fer me.

SAMUEL. Yes, yes, dose was good days.

RAMJOHN. Yes, man, yer remember de time me modder trew
Frank out? (*He laughs.*)

SAMUEL. Yes.

RAMJOHN. Boy, a never see Frank get so vex.

SAMUEL. Yes, yes, so . . .

RAMJOHN. De old lady was really tough, yer know.

SAMUEL. Yes, yes.

RAMJOHN. Boy, dem was good days, dey come not back, eh?
(*Sadly.*) Times really change.

SAMUEL. Yes.

RAMJOHN. So yer see New York, eh?

SAMUEL. Yes, I did.

RAMJOHN. Yer see de Empire State Building?

SAMUEL. Yes, I saw it.

RAMJOHN. It really dat tall?

SAMUEL. Yes, boy, yer can imagine it.

RAMJOHN. I could imagine . . . What about de Statue a
  Liberty, yer see dat too?

SAMUEL. Yes, a went up it.

RAMJOHN. How yer mean, yer went up, in a helicopter?

SAMUEL. No, it have a lift inside it, yer could go right up ter
  de top.

RAMJOHN. I didn't know dat.

SAMUEL. Yes, man, yer could see all over New York from
  dere. Hitchcock use it in a flim called *Sabotage* an Robert
  Cummings had ta grab a man from falling, but de man fall,
  he grab de man's sleeve but it rip at de shoulder so he fall. He
  didn't have a good tailor yer see.

RAMJOHN. A didn't see dat flim.

SAMUEL. It was a good one, plenty action.

RAMJOHN. Yes.

SAMUEL. But you do' like dem kinda flims, a ferget, so what is
  de position, yer decide anything?

RAMJOHN. Yes, I decide.

SAMUEL. Well, tell me nar, what yer decide, yer talk ter de
  boys?

RAMJOHN. Yes, we talk.

SAMUEL. I know yer woulda come good, you is a real businessman.

RAMJOHN. It en' have notting ter do wit business.

SAMUEL. What en' have notting ter do wit business – How yer mean, yer talk ter dem right?

RAMJOHN. Yes.

SAMUEL. Yer explain de position ter dem?

RAMJOHN. Yes.

SAMUEL. What dey say? How dey feel about de deal?

RAMJOHN. Well . . .

SAMUEL. Yes?

RAMJOHN. Well dey say . . .

SAMUEL. Yes?

RAMJOHN. Dey say dey do' want ter make anyting outa no deal.

*Enters* CHUCK REYNOLDS, *offers a cigarette and lights it for* RAMJOHN.

SAMUEL. How yer mean, how yer mean?

RAMJOHN. Dey do' want anyting outa it, dat is all.

SAMUEL. How yer mean, what dey want den, what dey want, dey want anyting?

RAMJOHN. Yes.

SAMUEL. Well tell me, tell me what dey want.

RAMJOHN. Dey say, if yer lift de state a emergency dey en' go cause no trouble.

SAMUEL. What? Dat is a trick. Dat is a trick. Dey up ter someting.

RAMJOHN. Dey want yer ter lift de state a emergency so dey could play Mas dey say, if yer do dat dey en' go cause no more trouble.

SAMUEL. No – de state a emergency stays, if dey want ter play Mas, tell dem go to Brazil.

RAMJOHN. Dat is what dey say. (*He gets up.*)

SAMUEL. Wait a minute. Wait a minute, le' me tink. Le' me see, you talk ter dem.

RAMJOHN. Yes.

SAMUEL. An dey en' want notting?

RAMJOHN. A tell yer no, dey say . . .

SAMUEL. A know, a know, what dey say, a just trying ter. (*He brightens.*) So dey just want ter play Mas?

RAMJOHN. Yes.

SAMUEL. Yer sure?

RAMJOHN. Yes, dey been worried dey do' know if wit de state a emergency if dey go have Carnival an dey do' know what ter do.

SAMUEL. I see all right. Yes, tell dem yes, tell dem I go lift de state a emergency an pass Carnival if dey do' cause trouble.

RAMJOHN. Okay, I go tell dem. (*He gets up.*) Is a deal.

SAMUEL. Yes, tell dem is a deal. Okay, den John. (*They shake hands.*) Tanks a lot fer fixing up de deal for me. Sorry bout de uniforms, boy, but de Americans want us to use deres. But you go get ter play Mas.

RAMJOHN. Yer ferget.

SAMUEL. What? Yer is a Indian?

RAMJOHN. No, a do' know how to . . . (*He goes.*)

SAMUEL. We're in business buddy, you can definitely give Washington the green light, as you say everyting is A okay, we have lift off.

CHUCK. Did we do a deal?

SAMUEL. Yes we did a deal, you won't understand it's a Trinidadianism, is someting, dat make we a uniquely fantastic people.

CHUCK. Did you find out who is supplying the arms.

SAMUEL. No, a didn't find out, it do' matter, you'll be seeing Carnival dat was de deal, I told you it was a Trinidadianism.

SAMUEL *goes to the door. The* SERGEANT *enters.* CHUCK *leaves. The* SERGEANT *leaves.*

## Scene Three

*Some weeks later. Carnival Day.* SAMUEL's *office, daytime. From the street there is the sound of Carnival celebrations.* SAMUEL's WIFE *is dancing. She is dressed in Elizabeth II Annigoni portrait dress. With her is* CHUCK REYNOLDS. *He is dancing out of time. Throughout this scene both are dancing.* CHUCK *is dressed in Hawaian shirt, Bermuda shorts.*

WIFE. Soon as a met yer I know yer was American yer know.

CHUCK. It must be the accent marm.

WIFE. No, is de Bermuda shorts. Wen we was in New York I saw a man in a pair just like dem.

CHUCK. Yes, marm.

WIFE. You do' have a accent.

CHUCK. Yes, marm, you know marm, this Carnival of yours is really out of this world.

WIFE. It en' bad, yer say yer from New York?

CHUCK. That's right marm.

WIFE. Yer know de Witfields?

CHUCK. No. Marm.

WIFE. Yer must know dem dey from America too.

CHUCK. No. Marm. (*Looking out of the window.*) The colours, those girls.

WIFE. Yes, dat's dem, dey have two nice daughters.

CHUCK. What, no marm, can't say. The music. What a beat.

WIFE. Yer must know dem, man. Tink. Witfield, dey light skin. Two nice daughters, de modder have a limp, an de husband always talking, yer must know dem man.

CHUCK. No . . . I can positively say that I don't.

WIFE (*to herself*). Well, dey tell me dey was from New York.

CHUCK. I sure like your costume marm.

WIFE. Yer don't think it's too flashy?

CHUCK. No, marm.

WIFE. Samuel thinks it's too flashy, but then he do' know about dese tings. Yer know how long it take we Trinidadian girls ter make dis?

CHUCK. No, marm.

WIFE. A week. It take we girls a week.

CHUCK. That's really something, marm.

WIFE. Once we make up we mind ter do someting, we does do it, yer know.

CHUCK. Yes, marm.

WIFE. We decide ter have Carnival an what happen?

CHUCK. Marm.

WIFE. We have it. Dat is what.

CHUCK. And how, it sure is something, marm. I wouldn't have missed it for anything.

WIFE. It used ter be better in de old days yer know. Yer sure yer en' know de Witfields?

CHUCK. I'm sure marm, I know a Withby.

WIFE. No. Dat en' dem.

CHUCK. Sorry.

WIFE. What yer sorry for? It en' your fault yer en' know dem.

CHUCK. No, marm. I can't wait to see Mister Samuel's costume. His must be something, huh? Did he make it himself?

WIFE. No, he get a tailor ter make it, some Indian friend a his.

CHUCK. It sure pays to have a good tailor.

*The door opens. SAMUEL enters dancing in time, dressed in a South American general's uniform, a large cigar in his mouth.*

SAMUEL. Hi, Chuck baby, like it?

CHUCK. Yea, it's great man.

SAMUEL. Tailored yer know. Ter fit.

CHUCK. Yea, man, it is. A feel like a peasant, man.

SAMUEL. No, man, yer mustn't say dem kinda tings. Dis is Carnival. Le' we have a drink, man.

SAMUEL *goes to the desk, pours drink, hands drink to* CHUCK.

Le' Castro come. He do' know how to play Mas.

WIFE. What bout me den.

SAMUEL *fixes a drink for* MRS SAMUEL *and takes it to her. The* SERGEANT *enters in full battlegear carrying a machine-gun.*

SERGEANT. Some people ter see yer, sir.

SAMUEL. Bring dem in, bring dem in, a like yer Mas sergeant.

SERGEANT. Tanks, sir, a like yours too.

MRS BANKS, FRANK, MR TATE *and* MR LYLE *enter.*

SAMUEL. Allyer come in, come in.

MRS BANKS. Samuel, de man, de man, Samuel.

SAMUEL. A like yer Mas.

MRS BANKS. You come good too. We come ter tank yer fer giving we Carnival. Man, an here, ter show yer how much we like yer a bring yer a present.

SAMUEL *takes the bible off the tray.*

SAMUEL. What it is?

MRS BANKS. Is a bible, a gold one. Me and Mr Banks choose it we self.

SAMUEL. Tanks.

MRS BANKS. Yer could read it, yer know.

SAMUEL. Tanks, tanks. An what bout you Frank, what you bring?

FRANK *steps forward with a casket.*

FRANK. Samuel, man, on behalf a de Chamber a Commerce, a come ter present yer wit de freedom a de city, man.

SAMUEL *takes the casket, opens it, takes out a scroll.*

SAMUEL. Tanks, man, you still going up the road?

MR TATE *and* MR LYLE *step forward.* MR TATE *opens a case.*

MR TATE. Mr Samuel, in recognition of you' services, please accept this . . .

SAMUEL *takes out a silver-plated pistol.*

SAMUEL. Now, dis is someting eh, Chuck look at dis.

CHUCK. It's a 357 Magnum, a real man stopper.

SAMUEL *points it at* CHUCK, *makes shooting sound, laughs.*

Easy man, easy.

MR LYLE. We took the trouble of loading it for you.

SAMUEL. Tanks, man, tanks, allyer have a drink man.

SAMUEL *puts the pistol in his holster.*

MR TATE. We don't.

MR LYLE. No, we don't.

MRS BANKS. Come Frank, le' we go an meet we band.

MRS BANKS. ⎫  Band a de year, band a
FRANK.      ⎬  de year.

*The delegation goes, dancing.*

SAMUEL (*as they cross to the balcony*). Come, Chuck, le' me

show you what Carnival is really like. Yer see how fantastic
we Trinidadians is.

CHUCK. Yea, man, what about our friends on the Hill, they
been quiet?

SAMUEL *joins him*, WIFE *follows*.

SAMUEL. Quiet, dey is de noisiest ting in town, yer hear dem,
all a dem down dere playing Mas.

CHUCK. Look at that headdress, man.

WIFE. Where, where?

CHUCK (*pointing*). That one.

SAMUEL (*pointing*). Dat one de one limping . . .

CHUCK. Yea.

SAMUEL. A release him last week.

CHUCK. He's still moving though. Go, man, go. The colours,
they're blinding, so artistic.

SAMUEL. An yer se dat one dere wit de bandages . . .

CHUCK. Yes, but . . .

SAMUEL. He en' no wounded soldier yer know, he get released
last week too.

CHUCK. And he's moving too. Yea, it's too much, man, too
goddam m . . . sorry marm.

WIFE. I do' mind.

SAMUEL. An yer see dose German storm troopers down dere.
Dose are my men. Dey go grab every terrorist, because we
know what Mas dey playing.

CHUCK. Yea, man, yea.

SAMUEL. An yer en' see notting yet, as Rita Hayworth say ter

Glen Ford. In a half hour we going ter hit de Hill wit a search party, den yer go see if yer guns is Cuban or what.

CHUCK. Crazy man, man, it's crazy.

SAMUEL. Right, sergeant.

SERGEANT. Right sir.

SAMUEL. Yer squad ready ter move?

SERGEANT. Yes sir.

SAMUEL. Well hit dem man. What you waiting fer? Go.

SERGEANT. Yes, sir. (*He salutes, goes.*)

SAMUEL *goes to the window.*

CHUCK. Crazy man, crazy.

SAMUEL. Play Mas, play Mas.

*The music gets nearer. The sound of machine-gun fire, explosions, all dancing play Mas.*

*Crowds enter, dance is interspersed with freezes during which we hear machine-gun fire.*

*Independence* was first performed at the Bush Theatre, London, on 15 February 1979 in a production by Foco Novo, with the following cast:

| | |
|---|---|
| DRAKES | Stefan Kalipha |
| ALLEN | Malcolm Fredericks |
| HARPER | Ewart James Walters |
| GERALD | Michael Howard |
| MARGARET | Mary Jones |
| YVONNE | Shope Shodeinde |

*Directed by* Roland Rees
*Designed by* Adrian Vaux
*Lighting by* Chris Ellis

The action takes place in Trinidad in 1978 at the pool bar of a former Grand Hotel.

## ACT ONE

*A pool bar at a hotel. Nearby a table, a large umbrella, chairs.*

*At the bar: an old barman, DRAKES (60–65) wearing black trousers, a white shirt, a black bow tie and a red jacket.*

*A young waiter, ALLEN (20–25) wearing black trousers, a white shirt, a bow tie.*

ALLEN. If a make 50 cents terday a go be lucky.

DRAKES. What bout if you make a dollar?

ALLEN. Dat go be a miracle.

DRAKES. What bout if you make five dollars?

ALLEN. Dat go be a nightmare.

DRAKES. Why?

ALLEN. Because it go mean de place full up.

DRAKES. All you young people is de same. All you never satisfied. You either give up hope or you hope for everything.

ALLEN. I en' give up hope. I have plenty hope as long as dey have termorrow I have hope.

DRAKES. In?

ALLEN. In anyting, everyting, I learn dat a long time. I believe in dat. What you believe, old people is all you who hold back tings because all you can see notting, all you believe notting can happen.

DRAKES. I believe in de past. I could see de past, dat's why, look at dis hotel.

ALLEN. A looking at it.

DRAKES. Yes, it old an run down now nobody do' come here.

ALLEN. Dey does come ter swim.

DRAKES. Yes, but I en' mean dat, dis hotel used ter be de best hotel in de whole a de West Indies, people used ter come here fer a night just ter boast dat dey had stay here.

ALLEN. Here.

DRAKES. Yes here, you do' know you was still a wish in yer modder head, but I tell yer, it had chefs from France and wine waiters in black. You do' know dey used ter have balls here, not parties wid everybody jumping up, but balls, wid gentlemen. A know dat is a word dat frighten you, but yes gentlemen in white linen jackets and ladies, yes ladies do' get frighten, ladies in tiaras, and de place had lights all around de grounds. It was like a Christmas tree, like magic. Man, people just shining an talking a say talking not shouting. Yer couldn't hear what dey was saying. It was just a tone, a hum if yer like, an laughter, sweet laughter, an we was happy too because it was nice.

ALLEN. How much a week you used ter get?

DRAKES. I know what yer getting at, but dat en' have notting ter do wid it, it was good.

ALLEN. Yer mean yer was happy slaves.

DRAKES. Dat is all you could tink bout.

ALLEN. No, dat en' all I could tink bout. A tell yer what I could tink bout, I could tink bout clean black earth, dats what, earth dat yer put a seed in an termorrow working wid only de dew for moisture de seed start ter grow.

DRAKES. You and you' farming.

ALLEN. Yes, me an me farming. I is a farmer an a proud of it, dat is life, dat is what, we have here de richest soil in de world an dat is what I want ter get away from dis stinking place for. Why I wasting my life here, when I could be growing tings with my hands? Instead I have ter use dem ter carry beers an rum punch.

DRAKES. You shoulda been here in de old days wen it was a pleasure ter serve drinks, ter see de pleasure on people's faces wen yer place de drink in front a dem an dey lips start ter run, wen dey come down fer de first cocktail a de evening, dey used ter spend all day looking forward ter dat.

ALLEN. Dey could afford ter.

DRAKES. Yes, an after a while yer get to know dem an dey didn't even have ter order, yer know what dey wanted before dey say Jack Robinson. An yer also know what time dey was coming, it was happiness in dose days. I had a head barman over me so I know who ter take orders from an he had a house manager over him so he knew who ter take orders from. Everybody had dey own territory, nowadays yer en' know what is what. Mabel in de kitchen have ter cook, wash-up an make she own food. We had boys just ter shine pans, yer hear, just ter shine pans.

ALLEN. Yes, a hear, give me a beer.

DRAKES *gets beer*.

ALLEN. Put it on my slate.

DRAKES. Nar do' worry nobody go check.

*He gives* ALLEN *a beer*.

A remember one time we had a new feller, his job was ter check de bar receipts. De first day he start, he taste every drink, we tell him he had ter, ter identify dem. He went home in a taxi, singing. De next one had ter sign paper saying he do' drink, but we break him in too, it was de only way we could make a profit. Yer see everybody had dey own territory an nobody cross over into nobody territory.

ALLEN. Yer mean yer was crooks.

DRAKES. No, not crooks. We understood each odder.

ALLEN. I see, well I say somebody should drop a bomb on it, a big bomb, what you say?

DRAKES. You want ter do it.

ALLEN. If a had one, make me a Molotov cocktail.

DRAKES. What is dat, I never hear bout dat one.

ALLEN. You, a big famous barman like you, a barman who boast he could make any drink widout looking in a book an you never hear bout a Molotov cocktail.

DRAKES. No, tell me then.

ALLEN. Is Russian.

DRAKES. A know dat, so it must have Vodka, but what else, tea?

ALLEN. No.

DRAKES. Bitters?

ALLEN. It have a bitter taste, but it do' have bitters.

DRAKES. What den, tell me then.

ALLEN. Look it up in yer book.

DRAKES. No.

ALLEN. Why not?

DRAKES. No.

ALLEN. Pride eh, pride go kill yer, but yer do' have ter worry, you en' number one barman no more. I hear bout a Indian feller . . .

DRAKES. Who? Ali, I teach Ali how ter mix. Wen Ali first come ter work here he didn't know what crush ice was, I had ter show him. Now because he start inventing drinks he get voted top barman, but all dem drinks he name, already had names, he just give dem new ones, I know dat.

ALLEN. Well everybody say he's de best.

DRAKES. What dey know, tell me what dis Molotov ting is then.

ALLEN. Pay me.

DRAKES. Pay yer what, a just give yer a beer, yer want more. Go jump in de pool.

ALLEN. A car' swim.

DRAKES. A know dat. A go throw de life saver.

ALLEN. It rotten.

DRAKES. A know dat too, yer know dis hotel was de first hotel in de West Indies ter have a swimming pool. All de odder hotels, all dey had was showers, an yes baths.

ALLEN. Baths.

DRAKES. Yes, baths, ter make der white people feel at home. But wen dat pool open it was a different story. Yer see dat piece of marble.

ALLEN. Which one?

DRAKES. De brown one.

ALLEN. All a it brown?

DRAKES. Yes, but if yer look good yer see a piece browner dan de odder.

ALLEN. Yes.

DRAKES. Well all de odders come from Italy on de last boat before war break out. De last boat.

ALLEN. An what bout dat one?

DRAKES. Dat one, come from a grave. Dey had one piece short an it cause a big gap right in de middle an de owner refuse ter open unless de gap fill.

ALLEN. So what happen.

DRAKES. Everybody beg him ter open, dey say nobody en' go notice. But he say no, it not right an somebody say I have a piece of marble, it en' the right shade but is marble. It was me father's grave stone. Take it. He take it, but he wasn't happy, he used ter walk by de pool every day, look at it an shake his head. If yer dive down dere now an turn it over yer go see somebody name on it saying 'Rest in Peace'.

ALLEN. Oh God Drakes, yer could lie.

DRAKES. I en' lying.

ALLEN. I tought I meet some big liars in my life, but you take de belt.

ALLEN *goes to undo his belt.*

DRAKES. I en' lying a tell yer.

ALLEN. Yer serious.

DRAKES. What is a Molotov cocktail?

ALLEN. Ah, a see.

DRAKES. Yer se what? He always used ter tell de pool men not ter clean dat slab, he wanted it brown like de odders.

ALLEN. Yer tink yer smart en'.

DRAKES. I en' smart, I is a old man, my brain is sawdust. How a old man like me could outsmart a young farmer like you? All yer farmers is de smartest ting in de world. Nobody can fool farmers, dem know everyting.

ALLEN. Like how ter make a Molotov cocktail.

DRAKES. Yes, if I make up my grave stone story, you make up yer Molotov cocktail.

ALLEN. But a Molotov cocktail is real.

DRAKES. Yes.

ALLEN. Yer do' believe me.

DRAKES. I en' say dat.

ALLEN. But yer hinting it.

DRAKES. I en' hinting notting.

ALLEN. All right, all right, a go tell you what it is.

DRAKES. I en' want yer sin yer soul fer me.

ALLEN. I en' sinning my soul for notting, but de only ting is . . .

DRAKES. What?

ALLEN. It en' a drink.

DRAKES. What it is den?

ALLEN. It en' a drink.

DRAKES. How it could be a cocktail an it en' a drink?

ALLEN. Is a bomb.

DRAKES. A what?

ALLEN. A bomb.

DRAKES. Yer really lying now.

ALLEN. No man, (*He laughs.*) is true.

DRAKES. Yer mean it does blow off yer head.

ALLEN. No, is something dey fight de Russians' tanks wid.

Wen dey invade dem dey put petrol in a bottle wid a piece of cloth, an light de cloth.

DRAKES. But dat is a flambeau.

ALLEN. Is a bomb too, it blow up de tanks, dats an what, yer see.

DRAKES. Why dey call it cocktail?

ALLEN. I en' know.

DRAKES. It en' right, it en' a drink, dat confuse people.

ALLEN. It do more dan dat.

DRAKES. You foolish, you could never make a farmer.

ALLEN. I could grow you, if I put you in de ground, you would grow – Drakes?

DRAKES. What.

ALLEN. Is true bout de grave stone?

DRAKES. Why yer do' dive down an find out?

ALLEN. A car' swim, man.

DRAKES. Well, how yer go know den, bring yer swimsuit one day an learn.

ALLEN. No tanks, I go stay on land, I know de land, I know what it could do an what it car' do, me. En' no fish, I is a worm.

DRAKES. Molotov cocktail.

ALLEN. A get yer en, admit it.

DRAKES. Yes you get me. But anybody hearing cocktail, the word cocktail mean drink. Anybody not only me would tink is a drink.

ALLEN. Yes, but a get yer.

DRAKES. No de word get me, you didn't get me, de word, not you.

ALLEN. All right.

DRAKES. Why he didn't call it soup or someting, or sauce?

ALLEN. Cocktail nicer, it have more sparkle.

DRAKES. What you know bout sparkle, yer do' know dey have black cocktail, dull cocktail, cocktail you could see through, cocktail yer car' see through, all kinds. I could make any kinda cocktail. I could make drinks change colour right before yer eyes an yer car' remember what it was before. I could put some nutmeg in a nog an you wouldn't know what yer tasting, an yer wouldn't see it either.

ALLEN. Make one den.

DRAKES. Ingredients, I en' have de ingredients. Dey take away all me ingredients an give me what? Beer, Coca Cola an rum punch, an ready-made rum punch at dat. If a had me ingredients I'd show yer what cocktail was all about. I'd hit yer wid so much cocktail, an every one different dat yer would feel like ye was de Prince a Wales. Yer want another beer?

ALLEN. Yes.

DRAKES. Man I would hit you a Rapid Rage.

ALLEN. Wha is dat?

DRAKES. Dat is white rum, wid brown rum, wid Coca Cola separating de sides, like de United Kingdom, an wen dey hit yer belly, is war yer see.

ALLEN. Yes.

DRAKES. If anybody come in here an a party already going an dey want ter catch up, I give dem a Rapid Rage, yer see den dey get in step.

ALLEN. Yes, what else?

DRAKES. Or if you want someting quiet but subtle, a long Planters Punch would do de trick.

ALLEN. What is dat?

DRAKES. You en' know what a Planters Punch is an you want ter be a farmer? Dat is what after yer ride all day over yer plantation yer man servant come an put before yer after he stable yer horse, man.

ALLEN. All right, all right, I go have tractor not horse.

DRAKES. Suit yerself, but is just rum, bitters, syrup, lime, an crush ice, yer know what dat is?

ALLEN. Yes.

DRAKES. Well a had ter ask yer know because some people do' know what crush ice is. I know a Indian feller . . .

ALLEN. All right, all right . . .

DRAKES. Well dat is Planters Punch, but is what yer do wid de lime is de secret. Yer shouldn't just taste rum an a lot a tings jumble up. It should be rum, wid a taste a lime an lime wid a taste a rum. An is de bitters dat does de subtlifying fer you. Dat is why barmen all over de world should get down on dey knees ter de man who invented bitters. Dat is a barman, bible, prayer book an commandments, he bandage an he plaster a Paris. Ask any barman, he would tell yer what I say, ask yer Mister Ali.

ALLEN. I en' know him.

DRAKES. You en' know him?

ALLEN. No.

DRAKES. I tought you an he was de best a friends. I tought you an he was like peas an rice, de way you rating him like he is number one boy, yer better be careful, you rating a man, an you en' know him. A have ter watch you, you is a interesting specimen.

ALLEN. All right Drakes.

DRAKES. I all right, is you I worried bout, so you working fer Ali, fer free, you doing all dis hard work for Ali fer notting. You should go an see him, an get pay for what you doing den you could go an buy yer piece a land an yer might even afford a tractor too. Fer de amount a work yer do what dey call you Public Relations Officer or Print Site Poster. We go have ter put you up by de roundabout.

ALLEN. All right Drakes, you is Number One, you is de best barman in Trinidad.

DRAKES. Only Trinidad? Trinidad is a small place.

ALLEN. De West Indies den.

DRAKES. De West Indies is also very small.

ALLEN. All right, de world den.

DRAKES. Now you getting warm.

ALLEN. All right.

DRAKES. An remember de word is barman, not barkeeper or bartender. Dem job is ter listen to people old talk or ter stop dem from fighting, or settle argument like who knock out Jersey Joe Walcott, or how much time Sugar Ray defend he title, an all a dem does keep book under dey counter ter tell yer so dey do' know anyway. No, my job is ter mix drinks, not make, dat is fer factory. Yer do' make drinks yer mix dem, dat is what a human being does. Yer hear, an do' forget dat.

ALLEN. Right.

DRAKES. Yer know what one a dem is?

ALLEN. What?

DRAKES. A human being.

ALLEN. Yes.

DRAKES. Good, yer know wen a finish wid you might even be half good, a might even make yer a good farmer an not just a planter of seeds.

ALLEN. All right, Drakes.

DRAKES. Anybody could do dat, yer know.

ALLEN. What?

DRAKES. Stick two seed in de ground an say mumbo jumbo an pour water on it.

ALLEN. No Mister Drakes, yer have it wrong. You watch too much Tarzan flims, farming is a science nowadays.

DRAKES. Dat's what it is.

ALLEN. Yes, it's ter do wit soil, oxygen, phosphates an sunlight, not de soap, but de ultra violet kinda. Yer get it, de same way you have ter mix up your drinks, de same way I have ter mix my soil.

DRAKES. But nobody do' drink what you grow.

ALLEN. Dey does do more dan dat dey does stay alive. If I was de Minister a Agriculture, Lands an Fisheries I would make dis island self-supporting. Nobody would work in no office. All dem stenotypist an Clerk Grade II an Grade III would be pulling plough.

DRAKES. A tought all yer using tractors nowadays.

ALLEN. Dat's how I would start dem off ter give dem a idea a de history a farming, have dem bare back in de fields.

DRAKES. De women too.

ALLEN. Yes.

DRAKES. Well you en' go get no field plough. Yer go have some happy workers but dat is all.

ALLEN. You could laugh, tell me someting seriously.

DRAKES. Seriously.

ALLEN. Yes.

DRAKES. I en' know notting seriously.

ALLEN. All right, tell me dis anyway, why you never wanted ter be a farmer.

DRAKES. Would Jokey do?

ALLEN. Anyting would do but just tell me an I go tell yer why not.

DRAKES. But if yer know already why a must tell yer, let me tell yer someting yer en' already know.

ALLEN. Tell me den. You fraid, you fraid a could be right, you fraid for once a might get you right.

DRAKES. No, all right a go tell yer but yer en' go like it.

ALLEN. Do worry bout me, I know, just tell me.

DRAKES. All right, because I always wanted ter be a barman.

ALLEN. What?

DRAKES. Yes, a tell yer yer wasn't going ter like it.

ALLEN. But why?

DRAKES. Ever since I was a little boy, I wanted ter be a barman.

ALLEN. But how man?

DRAKES. I went ter see a flim.

ALLEN. A tell yer is dem Tarzan flims.

DRAKES. No, dis wasn't no Tarzan flim man dis was a posh
flim in a city. Everybody in de flim was white except one
feller.

ALLEN. De barman.

DRAKES. Right, an everybody who walk into dis club, man an
woman, all a dem say, Hi Charlie, how yer doing, an he was
happy an smiling an shaking the cocktail all de time. Dat man
was de most popular man in de whole film, de police, de
crooks, everybody know Charlie, so I wanted ter be a
barman.

ALLEN. An dat is all?

DRAKES. Yes.

ALLEN. But Drakes yer still en' tell me why yer never wanted
ter be a farmer.

DRAKES. A tell yer.

ALLEN. No man, yer tell me what yer wanted ter be but not
what yer never wanted ter be.

DRAKES. But a never wanted ter be a policeman, or a fireman,
or a engineer, or a pilot.

ALLEN. Anyone but a farmer. Why not?

DRAKES. I do' know.

ALLEN. Yer see a told yer didn't know. I go tell yer, yer never
wanted ter grow yer own food an walk on a piece a land an
know it was yours.

DRAKES. No.

ALLEN. Yer never wanted ter walk an see yer crop sprouting
up he little head from de ground and de next day he get a
little bigger.

DRAKES. No.

ALLEN. An wen he ready yer pick him an eat him. All yours, all your own sweat an care.

DRAKES. No.

ALLEN. Yer see, I know why a go tell yer why, is de same reason black man fraid dogs.

DRAKES. What.

ALLEN. Slavery.

DRAKES. What.

ALLEN. Slavery. Black people fraid dog because dey used ter use dogs ter capture runaway slaves, dat's why dey fraid dogs.

DRAKES. But what dat have ter do wit farming?

ALLEN. Everyting, black people was beaten an chain ter plough all day ter farm people land, an dat's why dey do' want ter be farmers. All a dem want ter work in office.

DRAKES. A see.

ALLEN. But not me, I break dat hoodo, I going ter be a farmer. I going ter be de first black man ter break off dem chains an farm de land, my land, an en' feel no shame or hang-up. I go start a revolution.

DRAKES. But black people all over Africa does farm.

ALLEN. Because dey never leave dey home dat's why. But not in de West Indies, all a dem in office or driving truck, yer see. Yer see what a going ter do.

DRAKES. A wish yer luck.

ALLEN. Why you do' do more dan dat, an come an join me. We could work together. I know all de principles a farming.

DRAKES. But you en' have no farm.

ALLEN. A have a piece a land in mind, Drakes.

DRAKES. In mind, but dat en' on de ground.

ALLEN. Not yet, I need another thousand dollars an a could make a down payment.

DRAKES. A thousand dollars. Where you go get dat kinda money?

ALLEN. I go get it do' worry.

DRAKES. You go tief it.

ALLEN. No I go get it.

DRAKES. I en' have it if dat's what yer tink . . .

ALLEN. No, no, man, I en' doing dat, I want it, I need it, an dat's why I go get it because I want it so bad.

DRAKES. Well a tell yer a wish yer luck.

ALLEN. No man Drakes, I en' after yer money. I want yer ter see what I getting at man. My vision what I see man, how we rob we self a tings man, how we rob we self a pride, because a we own false pride, man.

DRAKES. Well a hope yer get it boy, but a thousand . . .

ALLEN. All right, all right do' worry, I go get it, I go get it.

DRAKES. So dat's why we fraid a dogs.

ALLEN. Yes.

DRAKES. I tought we fraid a dogs because dey might bite we.

ALLEN. All right, all right.

DRAKES. But a hope yer get what yer want son.

ALLEN. I go get it.

DRAKES. Yer en' go get it here.

ALLEN. I know dat but dey put me here an a have ter stay here in dis place de last relic a we glorious colonial past, de last.

DRAKES. Is only half left.

ALLEN. Half too much. Dey do it ter torture me, dat why, I could be doing my good work but look a me like some . . .

DRAKES. Barman in a flim.

ALLEN. No some robot waiting fer people ter come an activate me.

DRAKES. De Department put yer here an here yer have ter stay. If yer run away yer know what go happen.

ALLEN. I know, I have a friend who went ter one a dem Youth Training Camp, he say it worse dan de army.

DRAKES. All right.

ALLEN. Dey get de worse sergeant from de army ter run dem. Is get up a five in de morning, a cold shower, bread an tea fer breakfast an drill all day fer three weeks in de blazing sun. Dem sergeant say however difficult you is outside once you get in you go come out a responsible citizen, he had a hard time.

DRAKES. Dat's what it dere for.

ALLEN. Yes, but dey en' go get me.

DRAKES. Yer talk ter Harper.

ALLEN. I talk ter him but he can't help me he's just a pen-pusher in he grade three suit, an he grade three brain, all he want ter do is give orders.

DRAKES. He have pull in de Department.

ALLEN. Pull what, de only pull he have is if a give he a hundred dollars den he go pull someting.

DRAKES. Well do it.

ALLEN. Not me, a wouldn't beg dat frog fer a noise, not he.

DRAKES. Well dat is de only way yer get anything ter happen, notting en' change yer know. Is contact, is who yer know, before independence it was de same ting, who yer could ask for favour. You know how much people I get favour for, an wen a say favour I en' mean small favour yer know, I mean big favour.

ALLEN. Like what?

DRAKES. Like groundsman at de Oval, an head gardener at dem big house, dey didn't start off head gardeners but after dey get in as water boy dey move up, yes.

ALLEN. How?

DRAKES. All a dem used ter come here yer see, dey get ter know me an come ter rely on me, an tell me how de feller or cook or maid was getting on. I get plenty woman, dat way. Dat was de days wen servant was looking fer work not like terday wen if yer ask a girl ter work she want ter know if yer have Hoover an furniture spray. Now wid independence if yer have a good-looking sister yer could get any job, if you en' have dat, is how much yer could pay, it en' change.

ALLEN. I didn't . . .

DRAKES. Yer didn't know dat eh.

ALLEN. A didn't know it was so bad.

DRAKES. How you tink I get dis job? I had ter give de head barman ten dollars ter okay me an in dem days ten dollars was like a hundred. It go on all de time, all over de place.

ALLEN. A still en' begging Harper.

DRAKES. Yer want me beg him fer you.

ALLEN. No, I en' want . . .

DRAKES. All right, yer want me ask him fer you.

ALLEN. No.

DRAKES. I do him some favours.

ALLEN. Harper.

DRAKES. Yes. Why not, everybody have dey little favour dey want, you never know.

ALLEN. Dis place really corrupted. A could feel it, de walls, de paintwork, de whole town corrupted, a could . . .

DRAKES. It was always like dat.

ALLEN. Is de people not de land, de people make it so.

DRAKES. I do' know bout dat, dat's how I find it an dat's how I live in it. Anyhow put away yer bible, a trying ter help yer.

ALLEN. How?

DRAKES. Harper, a was telling yer bout Harper man. Soon after independence wen dey start allowing black people ter come in here as guest, Harper come ter see me.

ALLEN. Yes.

DRAKES. Well he come wid he big talk, yer know clearing he throat all de time, saying he's taking over de leisure side a de Department an he wants ter get ter know all he employees yer see. Employees, he employees.

ALLEN. Yes.

DRAKES. But it turn out de real story was dis, he clear he throat again an say 'Yes,' (DRAKES *clears his throat*.) 'I'm escorting a young lady to dinner ternight.' Yer get it, not bringing but escorting, man.

ALLEN. Yes.

DRAKES. So he escorting a young lady ter dinner here tonight an he want me ter look after him an greet him as though he's a regular.

ALLEN. No, yer do it?

DRAKES. Yes, of course a do it, a man who take over a head a yer Department ask yer for a favour an yer en' go do it. A more dan do it, a give him de works.

ALLEN. Wha yer do?

DRAKES. A go tell yer what a do. As soon as a spot him walking in a start ter mix him de best drink a had, a said good evening Mister Harper, loud, loud, so everybody could hear.

ALLEN. Dey hear.

DRAKES. Everybody turn around. He say, Hello Drakes. A say, The usual sir. He say, Yes, Drakes, but I'm getting bored with it an wen he come in termorrow night, we must decide on a new one.

ALLEN. What you say?

DRAKES. I say, Certainly, Sir, an he had a ball, yer see.

ALLEN. You is too much, Drakes.

DRAKES. No man, so yer en' see how he owe me a favour, an he en' do it once, he do it wid plenty woman, but what he en' work out is dat he was really a regular now, so let me ask him fer you.

ALLEN. No Drakes, a tank yer but I want ter do it my way.

DRAKES. All right, but I en' crude yer know, I en' go come out an say, Allen want a transfer.

ALLEN. I know.

DRAKES. A go suggest ter him in de interest a better manpower usage, dey like dem kinda big word bullshit, it would be in de interest of de efficiency of de Department if Allen went on a farm yer see.

ALLEN. A see, a see, but no I go do it my way.

DRAKES. All right but yer just have ter say de word.

ALLEN. I know, I know.

DRAKES. All right, yer want another beer?

ALLEN. Yes, you having one?

DRAKES. Yes.

ALLEN. All right.

DRAKES (*opening beers*). Right, two beers courtesy of the People's Republic, cheers old chap. (*They drink.*)

*The pool bar phone rings. DRAKES answers.*

Hello, pool bar – Yes, all right, tanks (*He puts the phone down.*) Harper coming, he just pass through reception.

DRAKES *snatches the beer from* ALLEN, *puts it with his own on the floor behind the bar.* ALLEN *grabs a tray, stands with the tray poised.*

HARPER *walks to the bar carrying a briefcase. He is 35–40, wears spectacles, a Mao type jacket, with short sleeves, matching trousers.*

HARPER. Good morning Brother Drakes, Brother Allen.

DRAKES. Morning, Mister Harper.

ALLEN. Morning, Mister Harper.

HARPER. Please Brothers, Brother Harper or Citizen Harper, surely you have heard of the Government's, your Government I might add, efforts to eradicate all traces of class distinctions.

DRAKES. Yes, Brother Harper.

HARPER. We are not ashamed of our colonial past, in fact they left us with some very sound institutions. The Civil Service for instance. But let us take the good an use it to our benefit, an the bad, like status and titles, let them proceed to the dustbins. Let us be progressive, an forward looking.

DRAKES. Yes, Brother Harper.

ALLEN. I agree, Brother Harper.

HARPER. No doubt you are surprised to see me.

ALLEN. Yes, Brother Harper.

HARPER. I believe you, Allen, if even you don't believe yourself, I used to work as well. I know how the grapevine operates when the boss appears, I used to jump and appear to be busy myself, but that is one of the old traditions I myself approve of. It has progressive qualities adhering to it. For instance, it is a sign of respect and respect is a good thing. Not respect of a boss or superior, but respect itself. If you have respect you respect yourself and it doesn't stop there, you also respect your job, and your country. So in with the good and out with the old, eh Brother Drakes.

DRAKES. Yes, Brother Harper.

HARPER. Good, now to the purpose of my visit. Contrary to your obvious suspicions, it is not to catch you out, sleeping or sunbathing. Both your records prove you are responsible and civic minded citizens. No, I have come here to inform you of the introduction of a new department policy that affects you and all who work at this establishment. Brother Allen where is your jacket?

ALLEN. I left it in de changing room, Sir – Brother.

HARPER. Why did you do that, Brother Allen?

ALLEN. It was hot, Brother Harper.

HARPER. It is always hot in this country, Brother Allen. It has always been hot in this country, Brother Allen. The temperature has not fluctuated more than a total of ten degrees, Brother Allen, and the People's Republic has gone to great expense to furnish you with a jacket, designed in London, to incorporate with the tone of this Leisure Centre and you have refused to wear it. Might I remind you the cost of your jacket equals a bag of cement, which in turn roughly equals the wall of a village school room. Do you not see Brother Drakes wearing his jacket?

ALLEN. Yes, Brother Harper.

HARPER. Do you in some way consider yourself to be inferior to Brother Drakes?

ALLEN. No, Brother Harper.

HARPER. Do you in some way consider yourself to be superior to Brother Drakes?

ALLEN. No, Brother Harper.

HARPER. Do you in some way consider yourself to be different from Brother Drakes?

ALLEN. No, Brother Harper.

HARPER. Good, you are progressing.

ALLEN. Yes, Brother Harper.

HARPER. Good, will you then go to the changing room an put on your jacket that the Republic has gone to so much expense to furnish you with.

ALLEN. Yes, Brother Harper (*He goes.*) a won't be long.

DRAKES. He's a good boy yer know, he just young.

HARPER. I am also young Brother, but you do' see me walking

bout wit my shirt outside my pants. We have ter set a
example for de young, ter follow, we wid experience.

DRAKES. I would vouch fer him yer know, Brother Harper,
he's a good boy. Is just dat he . . .

HARPER. Yes?

DRAKES. Well how a could put it?

HARPER. He's lazy, he objects to work.

DRAKES. No, no, notting like dat, sometimes I have ter tell him
slow down, he is a hard worker. He en' lazy at all in fact he
does work too hard an make everybody else look slow.

HARPER. What then, Brother Harper?

DRAKES. Maybe a using de wrong words but I car' use
language de way you use it, like a saxaphone to play . . . or
like Shakespeare . . .

HARPER. I never noticed you had any difficulty with words,
Brother Drakes.

DRAKES. Well, let me put it anodder way, yer see I alone could
run dis pool . . .

ALLEN *returns*.

HARPER. Ah good, you are now properly dressed, Brother
Allen. I will continue; as you may know this establishment
was taken over by the Republic to be used an enjoyed by the
citizens of the Republic, regardless of class, colour or riches.
We did it to show to the world and overseas visitors that with
independence we did not lose our happy, easy nature and
suddenly become dull and spartan, a common complaint of
many emerging nations. No, this establishment was to be our
People's Recreation Centre. It was a political as well as a
economic decision. However although the political decision
was morally right, the economic decision was incorrect. A

mistake was not made I remind you, insufficient data was available when the decision was made. Now we are in possession of sufficient data, a revised decision has been made. What has happened in fact is no one has used this establishment for months.

DRAKES. Yes.

HARPER. For what reasons we do not know. A proper public survey will have to be carried out, but I suspect we underestimated the anti-colonialist feelings of our good citizens. I say we, as a member of the decision making committee, I have to accept the collective responsibility of all decisions made by the said committee. Now I am to inform you of a further decision arrived at by a unanimous show of hands.

ALLEN. Yes, Brother Harper.

HARPER. And that is if by tomorrow evening at sunset, this establishment has not had one or more patrons, it will be closed.

DRAKES. What?

HARPER. Did you wish to say something, Brother Drakes.

DRAKES. No, Brother Harper.

HARPER. If you have a progressive suggestion to make, I will consider it and pass it on to my committee, Brother Drakes.

DRAKES. No, Brother Harper, I have no suggestion to make.

ALLEN. Brother Harper, I have a suggestion to make.

HARPER. Are you sure, Brother Allen, you want to add something to what a Government committee has already sat and deliberated for hours over?

ALLEN. Yes.

HARPER. Deliberation that involved precious man hours and the finest brains of the Department.

ALLEN. Yes, Brother Harper.

HARPER. Very well then, I will hear your suggestion.

ALLEN. I tink you right bout people not coming because it was a colonial place.

HARPER. Thank you, Brother Allen.

ALLEN. An I tink we should close it down now. Why wait fer termorrow at sunset, ter hell wit termorrow at sunset. Supposing some little boy run in for a Coca Cola, dat means he's a patron so what go happen?

HARPER. That precisely is what the committee considered, Brother Allen, and came to the decision it did. This establishment was opened for the needs of every citizen from a little boy to our pensioners. Whilst I admire your progressive outlook, I must insist that the terms of the committee's decision stand and that no attempt is made to conceal or deny access to citizens wishing to patronise this establishment until sunset tomorrow evening, do you understand, Brother Drakes?

DRAKES. Yes, Brother Harper.

HARPER. Do you understand, Brother Allen?

ALLEN. Yes, Brother Harper.

HARPER (*opening the briefcase, taking out a ledger*). Now Brother Drakes if you will be so kind I will take the weekly bar accounts.

DRAKES. Yes, Brother Harper. We have one case of Coca Cola, one case of beer, one bottle of rum punch.

HARPER. Before you go any further, Brother Drakes.

DRAKES. Dat is it, Brother Harper, dat is all we have.

HARPER. No, Brother Drakes, if you will be so kind as to let me complete my sentence, there are strict procedures laid down for the checking of the bar accounts of which I am sure you are aware.

DRAKES. Yes, Brother Harper.

HARPER. I would ask you to obey these procedures today as you have done on previous occasions.

DRAKES. Yes, Brother Harper.

HARPER. The recent decision in no way affects the smooth running of this establishment.

DRAKES. No, Brother Harper.

HARPER. Now, I will call out the individual items and you will inform me with a Yay or Nay or a number concerning each item and at the end of it you will hand me the paper roll from your cash register. Is that understood?

DRAKES. Yes, Brother Harper, understood.

HARPER. Brother Allen would you be so kind as to go and find all the other members of this establishment and have them assemble in the reception area and there to await my briefing.

ALLEN. Yes, Brother Harper. (*He goes.*)

HARPER. Good, then let us begin, Brother Drakes, today is the eighteenth of September, Nineteen Seventy-Eight, you agree?

DRAKES. Yes, Brother Harper.

HARPER. Good. Champagne. Bollinger RD.69.

DRAKES. None.

HARPER. Roederer Cristal Brut. 73.

DRAKES. None.

HARPER. Dom Ruinari Blanc de Blancs. 71.

DRAKES. None.

HARPER. Bollinger, 1973.

DRAKES. None.

HARPER. Veuve Clicquot Gold Label. 73.

*Lights begin slow fade.*

DRAKES. No.

HARPER. Lanson Red Label. 66.

DRAKES. No.

HARPER. Louis Roederer. 73.

DRAKES. No.

HARPER. Chaudron Fils. 73.

DRAKES. No.

## ACT TWO

*The next day – morning. The pool bar. The shutters are down.*

ALLEN *comes on in uniform, whistling, goes to the door. He tries to open it, it's locked. He goes and sits on a chair, takes out a newspaper, begins to read. He puts down the paper, looks at his watch, goes to the shutters, bangs on them.*

ALLEN. Drakesey – you dere, come on man a know yer in dere man. Come on. (*No reply.*) Come on man, Drakesey. Notting en' go happen, I know you in dere. I see de key missing from reception. Look man notting en' go happen. Look at me I come in laughing an happy, I brave, be like me and face it.

*The shutters slowly open. DRAKES is behind the bar, in uniform.*

DRAKES. You en' brave, you foolish.

ALLEN. What happen man.

DRAKES. Notting.

ALLEN. You sleep dere last night.

DRAKES. No, a was early dat's all.

ALLEN. Yer didn't hear me.

DRAKES. No.

ALLEN. I was making so much noise, I come in happy an singing man.

DRAKES. Why?

ALLEN. How yer mean why, because we closing down terday dat's why. Free paper burn.

DRAKES. How you know dat?

ALLEN. A know.

DRAKES. Somebody might come in fer someting an dat would be it. Yer hear what Harper say.

ALLEN. Yes, but nobody en' coming so what, but look at me I en' fraid, I taking de chance why yer do' be like me, man?

DRAKES. An do what?

ALLEN. Notting just look at it like a gamble.

DRAKES. Ter win what?

ALLEN. Notten, just a gamble. A excitement ter see what go happen, up ter de last ball see it like a cricket match. One ball ter go, one run needed ter win an de bowler running down de hill, de crowd tense, de wicket keeper crouching, de slip man pull dey trouser knees up an bendings.

DRAKES. I do' watch cricket.

ALLEN. Oh, shit man.

DRAKES. All right, all right, an den what?

ALLEN. Dat is it, an see what go happen.

DRAKES. Dat is it?

ALLEN. Yes.

DRAKES. Dat is why a do' watch cricket, notting does happen.

ALLEN. Dat en' true, de man does either get bowl out or he hit a four, yer see.

DRAKES. Yes all right, who bowling?

ALLEN. Me.

DRAKES. An I batting a suppose?

ALLEN. Yes an a bowling fast, yer know is a long run a taking like Charlie Griffiths.

DRAKES. Why not Prior Jones?

ALLEN. Who's he?

DRAKES. Do' worry.

ALLEN. Who he was, one a dem tie round yer waist cricketers.

DRAKES. Yes, but he was also one a de best fast bowlers dis
island ever produce.

ALLEN. One a dem old time gentleman.

DRAKES. Yes.

ALLEN. Not big Charlie, he was a real nigger. Once he bowl
Barrington a bouncer an nearly take off he head. De captain
ask him ter go an apologise in de dressing-room, Charlie say
no man, I en' doing dat an he have a bat in he hand dat's ter
hit de ball. He en' apologise an he get drop de next match but
he en' apologise, an dey had ter bring him back because he
was de best dat why he wasn't no gentleman.

DRAKES. No.

ALLEN. What you go do Drakesey?

DRAKES. How yer mean?

ALLEN. When we close down.

DRAKES. A tought we was waiting ter see what happen. Yer
mean a out already?

ALLEN. No, no, but yer must a tink about it.

DRAKES. I en' know.

ALLEN. Harper mention anyting different?

DRAKES. No, he say someting bout how my special skill is not
one dat is easy to use in a Developing Progressive Society.

ALLEN. What dat mean?

DRAKES. It mean a might en' get another job, dat's what, or

one a know how ter do. A might end up sweeping Frederick Street, or de market.

ALLEN. No man, do' say dat, dey have so much big hotel all over de place, you bound ter get one.

DRAKES. Two dat's all, an all a dem have young barman, an anybody could do what dey doing, even you. Pour drink from bottle into a glass an dat easy, all you do is hold de glass under de bottle an it switch off by itself, yer do' have ter do no measuring yerself. An he also drop a hint bout a man of my age, how difficult it is, everyting difficult. It was dat kinda hint what dey call a broad hint.

ALLEN. Yes.

DRAKES. Yer ever got one a dem?

ALLEN. Yes.

DRAKES. Yer know what a mean den.

ALLEN. Well a least yer go get a pension.

DRAKES. Pension what, I do' qualify.

ALLEN. How you mean?

DRAKES. I do' qualify, it came in after independence, right?

ALLEN. Yes.

DRAKES. Well I didn't make anough units, I started too late.

ALLEN. But yer have someting save up.

DRAKES. Not much, but I go manage, I go find someting anyhow. De ball en' bowl yet so what yer going on bout.

ALLEN. Yer right, yer right.

DRAKES. Yer still on yer run up.

ALLEN. Yes a tell yer it long man, a get greater swing dat way.

DRAKES. All right a have ter watch yer.

ALLEN. Soon as dis place close down ternight, I going ter de
Ministry a Agriculture termorrer morning ter make my
application, I en' going back in no hotel. Experience or no
experience, dey could say what dey want, but I going an clear
bush. I have me cutlass sharpen an ready, you should see it
man, it shining.

DRAKES. Why yer do' bring it an practice on de lawn?

ALLEN. No man, dat is gardening, I en' a gardener, I is a
farmer remember dat.

DRAKES. What is de difference?

ALLEN. All right, all right.

*A white couple enter, they are both elderly (60–65). He is
wearing a Panama hat, a cream linen suit, a regimental tie.
She is in a flowered print dress carrying a matching parasol.
They enter casually, looking around as if lost.*

Who is dem?

DRAKES. I do' know.

ALLEN. Dey can't be customers. Not . . .

DRAKES. No, dey must be get lost. I know dey tink is de
Botanical Gardens or . . . Go an tell dem.

ALLEN. Supposing dey want a drink!

DRAKES. Go an tell dem, man.

ALLEN. All right. (*He walks over.*) Excuse me, can I help you.
You looking fer . . .

MAN. Is this the Imperial? Isn't it, Hotel Imperial?

ALLEN. It used ter be but it close down, now is just de pool left
an dat's only fer swimming, so if yer want ter swim.

MAN (*to the* WOMAN). You see, I knew it, I told you it was here, you said it was the other side of the park. But I knew.

WOMAN. Yes dear, I remember it now. You were right, you always did . . .

ALLEN. Are you looking for somewhere?

MAN. Yes here, the Imperial, this is it.

ALLEN. But it close down now. We do' take any . . .

MAN. Yes, but it's still here, it hasn't changed. (*To the* WOMAN.) It hasn't changed one bit has it dear. It's all . . .

WOMAN. No it hasn't.

MAN. I don't remember those shrubs over there but that's about all.

WOMAN. Yes dear.

MAN. And the . . . Don't you have gardeners any more? It's all overgrown. All those wonderful hibiscus.

ALLEN. It's closed down now, sir.

MAN. I'm sorry we're keeping you, but we stayed here a long time ago, you see, a long time ago, and we thought . . .

ALLEN. Dis is just a pool bar now sir, wid a pool, an if yer want ter swim yer have ter . . .

MAN. Oh, a bar did you say, we'll have a drink then, then we can sit here an enjoy the old place. You'd like that wouldn't you dear?

WOMAN. Yes dear.

*The* MAN *and the* WOMAN *sit.*

MAN. It's all right to sit here isn't it?

ALLEN. Yes.

WOMAN. You must forgive my husband, you see we spent some time here when it was a hotel and they were wonderful times.

ALLEN. Yes.

MAN. We're keeping him, Margaret. Order the drinks.

WOMAN. I'm not keeping him, you order the drinks you always used to.

MAN. Well, we'll have two pink gins won't we. That's all right with you isn't it dear?

WOMAN. Yes, wonderful.

MAN. That's right, we'll have two large pink gins.

ALLEN. I'm sorry sir, we don't serve dose drinks.

MAN. But you said this was a bar, I'm sure I heard, didn't you hear . . .?

ALLEN. Yes sir, it's a bar, but it's a pool bar so we only serve rum punch, beer an coke.

MAN. Oh, I don't know, what do you say dear, beer's not really my cup of tea.

WOMAN. What ever you say dear. A rum punch sounds nice, I remember having one.

MAN. As you wish. We'll have two of your rum punches, I seem to remember they were quite strong. Let's not spoil a good day by fighting over drinks.

WOMAN. No dear, and it is a good day isn't it?

MAN. Wonderful.

ALLEN. So dat's two rum punches, eh. Yer sure?

WOMAN. Yes, thank you.

ALLEN *goes to the bar.*

MAN. There's something wrong.

WOMAN. What is it dear?

MAN. I don't know what it is but something's missing.

WOMAN. What is it dear?

MAN. Something's missing. Don't you see it?

WOMAN. I don't know dear, what?

MAN. Don't worry, it'll come to me.

ALLEN. Two rum punches.

DRAKES. What dey want?

ALLEN. You en' hear me, dey want two rum punches.

DRAKES. But who dey is?

ALLEN. I do' know dey say dey is some people who used ter come here an dey want two rum punch. Yer could beat dat de last focking day, de last focking minute dey want two rum punches, Drakes. Let me tell dem we en' have no rum punch, Drakes. I know dey en' go order notting else, Drakes an notting en' go show on de cash register.

DRAKES. No, man.

ALLEN. Drakes man, you do' know. Look, dey en' really want no drink, dey just want ter sit down an look bout de place so let we let dem, dey do' have ter have no drink, man. Dey only feel . . .

DRAKES. We can't do dat, man, you hear what Harper say.

ALLEN. Ter hell wit Harper an what he say. Harper is a mad man an you know dat all we have ter do is let dem sit dey an do notting.

DRAKES. No, man, de people order drinks an dey have ter have it. Dat's what dis place . . .

ALLEN. You is a real focking slave you is. You have a real slave mentality. Just because dey want someting dey must have it. Yer see how yer born a slave, yer die a focking slave.

DRAKES. No, man, take yer luck you say it was a gamble an yer lose.

DRAKES *pours out two rum punches, rings up the price, puts the ticket on the tray.*

ALLEN *looks at them, puts them on the tray.*

DRAKES. You want me take dem?

ALLEN. No, I go do it. (*He takes the tray over.*)

MAN. That's it, the course, the fine course.

WOMAN. What dear?

MAN. That's what's wrong, the course is missing. I told you something was missing.

WOMAN. Yes dear.

MAN. Well that's it, the golf course is not there. Don't you remember it?

WOMAN. I'm not sure.

MAN (*points*). Over there, that's where it was, all along there.

ALLEN *puts down the drinks.*

WOMAN. Thanks, those look very nice.

MAN (*to* ALLEN). What became of your course?

ALLEN. What sir?

MAN. The golf course. There used to be a golf course over there along that side there.

ALLEN. I'm sorry sir, it's a Community Housing Block dere sir. I can't see no golf course.

MAN. I see, it's behind the blocks.

ALLEN. No sir, it's all roads dere.

WOMAN. It's no longer there dear.

MAN. Shame, thank you.

ALLEN *leaves*.

MAN. Such a fine course too.

WOMAN. I think I remember it dear.

MAN. I said it was there.

ALLEN *sits on a stool*.

ALLEN. Dey got me calling dem sir now.

DRAKES. Do' worry bout dat man, dey mad.

ALLEN. You know anyting bout any golf course?

DRAKES. Yes, where de housing is.

ALLEN. Dat what a tell dem.

DRAKES. Dey must a been here a long time ago.

ALLEN. Like you.

DRAKES. Dat course went in, let me see, in forty-five, no some a de soldiers was still here playing, no not forty-five, forty-six. No it was forty-seven, dat's wen it went. Nineteen Forty-Seven.

ALLEN. I wasn't even born den what dey asking me . . .

DRAKES. Yes, forty-seven it was, I was here, dey use some a de big bulldozers de American had, I remember all de noise an dust. Man, dem bulldozers cut through dat hill like butter.

ALLEN. Yes.

DRAKES. Yer see after de war dat's wen tings started getting different. Everybody started pulling out so dey didn't need de golf course any more.

ALLEN. No dey needed house.

DRAKES. Yes, dey had nobody ter use de course so what is de use a it standing dere.

ALLEN. Yes.

DRAKES. Yes, man, de old golf course, fancy dem remembering dat.

MAN. What was that chap's name?

WOMAN. What chap dear, you know I'm not very good at names.

MAN. Colonel in the Engineers he was, at least I think it was the Engineers. Got a hole in one, saw the same thing myself. I was sitting right here, at least I think it was here. No, he was a major, we made him a colonel after he got the hole in one, Scotsman he was, well so he should, they invented the damn game you know.

WOMAN. Yes dear, I do know that, but I don't remember his name.

MAN. Mac something or the other, Donald, Dougall, one or the other. Pretty as pie it was, one minute it was on the ground, the next it was flying through the air, the next it was in the hole. Simple as that. Never saw anything like it. Yes, Donald it was, definitely Donald. We made him colonel in the bar. You know he had to stand everyone a round don't you?

WOMAN. No dear.

MAN. Yes dear. It's a rule. It all got pretty outrageous after a while, we were ordering the most exotic and bizarre concoctions and we made him a colonel right there in the bar. (*The* WOMAN *looks.*) No dear not there, over there, that's where the bar was. The commanding officer was also there and everyone began chanting colonel, colonel. You know how things like that happen, slowly at first and then everyone was shouting, and the commanding officer simply smiled and said, Yes, why not. Nothing else he could say.

WOMAN. Yes dear, and did he mean it?

MAN. Of course he meant it. Those days you said something . . . you meant it. You didn't say it otherwise.

WOMAN. Yes dear.

ALLEN. How long yer tink dey go stay here?

DRAKES. I do' know, leave de people dere man, you en' see dey enjoying deyselves.

ALLEN. You enjoying yerself too eh?

DRAKES. Yes, dat's what dis place for, dat's what it built for.

ALLEN. For dem.

DRAKES. Yes, fer dem. Is dem build it but just not fer dem fer people ter enjoy deyself, no hurry, no rush, take yer time, sip yer drink, watch de sun go down, dat's what it for.

WOMAN. It was very nice of them to ask us dear.

MAN. Nothing else they could do. It is a public place, I must say . . .

WOMAN. No dear, to attend their Independence celebrations. It was very nice of them to invite us, after all they didn't have to.

MAN. No my dear, you're quite right. Damn good manners, if we taught them nothing else, at least we taught them that, and some of the young chaps are not half as bad as I expected.

WOMAN. No dear.

MAN. What's his name, the one who collected us at the airport?

WOMAN. I think it was Harper dear and he addressed you as governor dear. Wasn't that nice of him?

MAN. Yes, he did.

WOMAN. Do you think they'll mind us slipping away from the party?

MAN. No, my dear, they'll understand.

WOMAN. I had to see it again.

MAN. I understand my dear, don't fret.

WOMAN. It hasn't happened has it?

MAN. What's that my dear?

WOMAN. Changed, it hasn't changed?

MAN. No my dear the old place looks as good as the day we walked in.

WOMAN. I mean me, it hasn't changed me has it?

MAN. You didn't expect it would did you?

WOMAN. I thought, no hoped, that coming here, seeing it, being here, it would happen, but it hasn't?

MAN. It . . .

WOMAN. But I feel the same, the same dark . . .

MAN. Don't my dear, it's over.

WOMAN. It isn't for me, I carry it wherever I go. It's like a cloud hanging, it never used to be there, I can vaguely remember a time when it wasn't there, it didn't exist. It's foggy and hazy but I see it . . . then it flies away. I want it to return, those days Gerald, I want them to come back, we were happy those days. It's not too much to ask is it?

MAN. No dear.

WOMAN. But why don't they?

MAN. Give it time it will.

WOMAN. I've given it everything, Gerald, I've spent the best years of my life, seeing it come and go again. Our best years, when I could have been so happy and be more of the wife you wanted. Why, Gerald, why?

MAN. I don't know my dear. We, all of us carry things, it's how we do it that matters.

WOMAN. I don't Gerald, don't you see, you can. Coming here I hoped . . .

MAN. Maybe it wasn't such a good idea after all. It was selfish. If I knew it would upset you I would never have agreed to it. What's past is past. We should never have come.

WOMAN. No, Gerald, we were right to come. Whatever happens, I know that now. Something told me those years being looked after, something told me I must return here, that much was clear to me, the doctors agreed.

MAN. There's no need . . .

WOMAN. I want to, don't you see, I need to, don't you see, it happened too quickly, everything happened too quickly. I didn't have the opportunity to . . . We should have stayed here Gerald, and seen it through. I should have, but I was rushed away to England before I knew . . .

MAN. It was for the best, dear, at the time it was decided . . .

WOMAN. Whose best, Gerald?

MAN. For all concerned, it was decided that you should not attend the hearings, the ordeal . . . of going into the witness . . . to . . .

WOMAN. For whose best?

MAN. For all concerned. For you, the chap concerned.

WOMAN. Yes.

MAN. For the administration, it was decided the best course of action in the circumstances was that you should return to England as soon as possible.

WOMAN. I was not consulted.

MAN. You were not in a proper state to make such a decision . . .

WOMAN. That man. That poor man.

MAN. Margaret . . .

WOMAN. He spoke the truth, Gerald. He came to my room because . . .

MAN. Margaret.

WOMAN. I did ask him to, I did, Gerald. The look on his face, I'll never forget.

MAN. Your appearance at the hearings would have served no useful purpose, Margaret. It was a very serious period, the Nationalistic parties were emerging, I tell you it was a very sensitive time. As it was he got a very mild sentence. It was decided . . .

WOMAN. He hanged himself. Because we believed . . .

MAN. That was not your fault, that had absolutely nothing whatsoever to do with you, Margaret.

WOMAN. Don't you see it has, Gerald. He did it because he was innocent.

MAN. No my dear.

WOMAN. It has everything to do with me, Gerald, and you and your administration and the island, it's all here. We came here and caused things, we took things and left some, we made scars, deep scars, we can't pretend we didn't . . .

MAN. Don't torture yourself so much.

WOMAN. I am tortured, Gerald. Everywhere I go it goes with me. I have no excuses you see, for you it's easy, you can blame the times, the delicate political situation. I have nothing, I was not drunk, I knew what I was doing. I wanted him, I invited him. I needed . . .

MAN. Margaret, don't go on.

WOMAN. You must let me Gerald, you must understand. Yes I asked him, yes the governor's wife wanted a waiter. No one even considered it did they?

MAN. No, my dear.

WOMAN. No, they didn't, they couldn't could they if even they . . . No, madness, the sun's got to her, those blacks, what was it someone said, some fool. Oh yes, he heard the drums and his eyes turned in, and he went wild, it gets them, he said, something to do with the moon I think it was, the fool. (*A beat.*) It could have been his, any of the wives on the island.

MAN. Are we ready to leave my dear?

WOMAN. Not just yet Gerald, there's one thing, one thing more I'd like to say and that is what happened, what I wanted to happen, in no way reflected on what I felt for you.

MAN. I understand my dear.

*A beat.*

WOMAN. Thank you, now I think we're ready to leave. (*They get up.*) You walk on, I'll pay the bill.

MAN. Are you sure?

WOMAN. Yes, have a wander round, I'll find you.

MAN. I would like to.

WOMAN. Well then.

MAN. I'll start at the reception area then.

WOMAN. I'll find you.

DRAKES. Look, dey ready ter leave, go an get yer money or yer want me go?

ALLEN. It's all right a going (*He walks over.*) Did you enjoy your drinks?

WOMAN. Yes thank you. Here. This is for you. (*She takes a bundle of dollar bills, puts it on tray.*)

ALLEN. But dis is more dan, is too much.

WOMAN. It's for you. Take it. (*She begins to walk off.*)

ALLEN. But lady, it only five dollars. Yer do' understand, we . . .

WOMAN. Take it, take all of it it's yours now. (*She leaves.*)

ALLEN. But yer.

*He stands looking at the tray. He puts the tray on the table, sits, stares at the money.*

*DRAKES goes over.*

DRAKES. What happen dey en' pay? (*He arrives.*) What is dat?

ALLEN. She leave it on de tray.

DRAKES. No man, dat can't be.

ALLEN. She put it on de tray, walk off an say, take it, take all of it, it's fer me.

DRAKES. Yer lie.

ALLEN. No man, she . . .

DRAKES. But dere is more dan five hundred dollars dey.

ALLEN. Is more dan dat. What ter do Drakes?

DRAKES. How yer mean what ter do? Go an fine she an give it back ter she before she call de police.

ALLEN. But she say, take it, man. Is mine, she . . .

DRAKES. Do' mind what dem kinda people say, man, go an find she, she could say she forget it, she could always change she mind an say she forget. Go an fine she before de police come, because once dey . . .

ALLEN. No Drakes, I en' going, is mine, dis is it. I need it a tell yer, a woulda get, now a get it I en' going ter find nobody. Dis is mine.

DRAKES. A warning yer, I en' have notting ter do wit it. I not responsible for what happen if I get involved I go kill yer.

ALLEN. Drakes, listen.

DRAKES. I en' listening ter notting. Yer not involving me in notting yer hear. I din't see it, I didn't see no money. I didn't walk over here, so I do' know. I honest, yer hear.

ALLEN. Drakes she say it's mine, take it, dat's what a doing man. You see me try an call she back, you see she walk away.

DRAKES. I en' see notting.

ALLEN. Oh shit, man.

DRAKES. If you do' report it I go have to.

ALLEN. Drakes, she give it ter me. I know wen somebody mean

someting der say. I know de difference. She give it ter me.
Look a tellyer what, a give yer me word on dis, if any police
or trouble happen if anyting bad turn out I go take full blame
fer it.

DRAKES. Yer was never so right in yer life, yer hear.

ALLEN. Okay, le' we cool down den, is my neck go get cut.

DRAKES. Yer right again.

ALLEN. So what we go do?

DRAKES. We, is not we is you.

ALLEN. All right a mean me den, right. (*He takes the money
up, folds it, puts it in his pocket.*) I go keep it, I keeping it, it's
for me, it's mine whatever happens is mine.

DRAKES *puts empty glasses on the tray.*

DRAKES. Right. (*He goes to walk off.*)

ALLEN. Hey, Drakesey, yer do' see what happen, yer do' see.

DRAKES. I en' see notten, man.

ALLEN. Is what a was waiting on, man. Drakes we could tell
dis place ter go, we could tell Harper ter go, we could tell
everybody ter fock off man. We independent now, no more
Yes, Sir, Yes, Marm, How are you, Sir, ter nobody. We got
we land now, man, an dat mean we feed we self an de rest we
sell. Yer know what dat mean, man, we free, an I know how
ter do it, man, I know it here in my head, nobody could have
dat, it dere. Come wid me Drakesey, join me as a equal share.
I go do all de work, man, all you have ter do is come an
water. Come an see me do it, just sit down an take it easy, no
rush, no hurry, an see a dream come true dat's all. Come wit
me.

DRAKES. I still have work ter do yer hear. Dis place still open an (*Walking off with the tray.*) de sun en' set as yet an Harper coming, so you better get up.

ALLEN *gets up. He takes off his jacket, throws it on the ground. He takes off his bow-tie, his shirt, throws them on the ground.*

ALLEN. Fock dis place, man, fock de sunset, fock Harper, man. We free a all dat shit, man. You is a born slave yer go never see, look (*He brings up his arms in a body builder's pose.*) free.

DRAKES. Put on yer uniform, Allen.

ALLEN. No, no more.

DRAKES. Allen – Allen man, put back on yer uniform, man.

ALLEN. No, I en' putting on nobody uniform no more. Nobody en' go hide me no more. I do' care I resign.

DRAKES. Allen man, listen ter me, pick it up man before Harper get here please.

ALLEN. Come wit me man, join me man.

DRAKES. Allen – you car' resign.

ALLEN. Sack me den, you could sack me, you is my superior. You could sack me.

DRAKES. No, I en' doing it.

ALLEN. Right, I is my own superior, I sack myself.

DRAKES. Look, man . . .

ALLEN. Join me, Drakes, if yer say yer join me a pick it up. A do everyting yer want, go through de channels, everyting in writing eh, join me.

DRAKES. I can't leave dis place man, I . . .

ALLEN. No, come an see . . .

DRAKES. I . . . spend my life . . .

ALLEN. Yer still alive.

DRAKES. I old . . .

ALLEN. Yer is a slave.

DRAKES. No.

ALLEN. Yes, an yer go die one.

HARPER *comes on.*

HARPER. Brother Drakes what is going on here?

DRAKES. Notting Mister Harper.

HARPER. What is all de shouting about an why is Allen half-naked, Brother Drakes?

ALLEN. I resign Harper, no Mister neither, you is Harper.

HARPER. What he doing, Brother Drakes?

DRAKES. He . . .

ALLEN. Yer didn't hear me a say a resign.

HARPER. Resign, did you give dat boy permission to take off his uniform, Brother Drakes?

DRAKES. Yes . . .

ALLEN. No, I take it off, he lie, yer do' know de truth wen yer hear it or what yer so blind yer so stupid.

HARPER. What's . . .?

ALLEN. I sack meself, I resign, I give up dis job, dis place, dis establishment, yer understand.

HARPER. Allen you are committing a serious crime. No Government employee can absent himself from his post unless ordered to do so by his superior.

ALLEN. What is dat, who is dat, you, you en' my superior.

HARPER. I am your senior officer appointed by the minister in charge of this Department. Do you know what you have done?

DRAKES. Brother Harper.

HARPER. No, Brother Drakes, stay out of dis I know you want to help, I realise he took advantage.

ALLEN. Harper, yer deaf or what, you en' have no more authority over me.

HARPER. Yes, I do, you disobeyed a strict order. I specifically said until sunset. No one is to consider this establishment closed and you anticipated no one coming, you thought you were clever, cleverer dan (ALLEN *begins to laugh*.) everybody, but I caught you and Brother Drakes here is my witness.

ALLEN. I do' care.

HARPER. Right, Brother Drakes, you are my witness, I am now officially dismissing Allen from his post.

ALLEN. I do' care.

HARPER. For the reasons I have already stated.

ALLEN. I do' care.

HARPER. He is as from dis moment no longer an employed person, right.

DRAKES. Brother Harper.

HARPER. Brother Allen you are no longer an employed person, you are a burden to the Repubic you are an idler and a anti-social element. (ALLEN *laughs*.) You have no means of supporting you' self, and the Republic cannot allow you to live off the sweat of other hard-working citizens' labour, is de camp fer you, yer criminal.

ALLEN. Harper, I am capable of supporting myself as you will certainly discover, wen your spies from de Social Security Department come to snoop, dey will see a farmer at work, a man, a free man at work doing de most natural ting in de world, de ting dat God make man ter do, work an be free. (*He goes off.*)

DRAKES. Brother Harper he young . . .

HARPER. No, Brother Drakes, you don't have to explain, I hold you in no way responsible, he was always a troublemaker, a dangerous anti-social criminal. He's not de first I come across, dey have a lot like him but we get dem in de end. Dis is a progressive country, in de days of de British dey could get away wit dat kinda attitude, because de English expected dem ter be lazy, but not any more, everybody have ter work. No excuses, he go end up in a camp a promise you. Dat go make a man out of him, or it go teach him ter see no one can put dey feelings before de needs of de people, dey go break him. I'll put in a special report on him, do' worry he en' go get away.

DRAKES. Brother Harper you do' understand.

HARPER. I understand.

DRAKES. No, you don't.

HARPER. What a don't understand?

DRAKES. I told him to do it.

HARPER. What?

DRAKES. I told him ter take de uniform off.

HARPER. No, Brother Drakes.

DRAKES. Yes, I told him ter get someting out a de pool so he was undressing wen you come.

HARPER. No Brother Drakes, dat en' go work.

DRAKES. Is what happen.

HARPER. It do' matter anyway, yer see I never like him, I wanted ter get him. He make it easy fer me now.

DRAKES. But . . .

HARPER. What, Brother Drakes?

DRAKES. Notting, Brother Harper.

HARPER. The sun is beginning to set so if you'll be so kind as to let me have today's receipts, that will be included in my report that there were two customers here today, distinguished customers in fact. A ex-governor and his wife. So if you will let me have the receipts I will go and find them and take them back to the reception.

DRAKES *takes the roll out of the cash register, gives it to* HARPER.

HARPER. Thank you, Brother Drakes, now did you see which direction the governor and his good lady went.

DRAKES. Yes, Brother Harper, dey went towards reception, dey was having a look around.

HARPER. Thank you. Happy Independence Day.

HARPER *is about to leave.*

DRAKES. Harper.

HARPER. Brother Harper Brother Drakes if yer don't mind.

DRAKES. No you is definitely Harper.

HARPER. What is it, I'm very busy an' a en' have much time, a have ter run . . .

DRAKES. What I have ter say en' go take long an it en' go slow yer down but — yer know me I work fer you fer a long time, we work together fer a long time.

HARPER. Get ter de point Brother Drakes.

DRAKES. De point is I never give yer no trouble, me an you had a understanding, you used ter ask me advice about people working here an I used ter tell yer.

HARPER. You have supplied me with certain assessments on brothers working here, yes.

DRAKES. I didn't spy fer you, I was senior here coming down from you, I see it as part of my job.

HARPER. Yer losing me Brother Drakes, yer still . . .

DRAKES. Leave Allen alone.

HARPER. What Brother Drakes did I hear you . . .?

DRAKES. I say leave de boy alone.

HARPER. Brother Drakes I'm afraid you have no say in de matter, dis has notting ter do wit de running of de bar so it does not come under . . .

DRAKES. A say —

HARPER. I heard you Brother Drakes I admit we had a certain understanding but dat was because you wanted ter keep in wit me an keep yer job. I wanted ter replace you, wit a younger more progressive brother long ago. To me and I'm sure to many people coming here, you represented the past of this place and all that went wid it. I don't know how much you are responsible for its decline, so you see your influence with me is nil.

DRAKES. I do' care what yer say bout me, I know who I is, all a say is leave de boy alone. People like you just take over wey de English leave off, dat's what dey leave you but not him wen I hear dis country was getting Independence an we was going ter run we own affairs, I tought good it might be too late fer me but at least de young people go benefit, but you an people like you spoil it, all, yer jump in de water like fish an carry on de same ting, power, power in yer mind.

HARPER. Careful Brother Drakes, old age or no old age dere's a limit.

DRAKES. All yer corrupt. What could a be a good ting, all yer spoil. He is de only chance we have.

HARPER. I'm warning you.

DRAKES. But all yer en' learn notting. But Allen he's de future he have hope an good intentions, he en' want ter drive no big car an wear no big suit he want ter do someting good, what Independence was for, so keep off him a beg yer don't harm de boy.

HARPER. Brother Drakes I have listened to your points, and have given careful consideration to what yer say, so listen ter dis an listen good, Allen do' work here no more, so he is my business, as fer yer own business, I go deal wit you too, you are a disgrace ter de Republic wit yer sentimental negative attitudes you represent everyting dat is bad wit de past and wat de Republic is trying to eradicate, but dat's what yer get fer mixing wid colonisers, yer car' change and changes is in de air, if yer car' change yer go get run over, dat is a promise.

DRAKES. I do' care.

HARPER *goes*.

DRAKES *takes two full bottles of rum punch from under the counter, empties the contents, puts the bottles on the counter, goes to the phone, dials.*

DRAKES. Hello, pool bar here, yer know who have de key ter de store room . . . all right. (*He walks off.*)

*Complete and instant blackout, sounds to be heard instantly.*

WOMAN (*calling out*). Gerald, where are you, Gerald? (*She knocks on a door.*) Are you there?

MAN. Yes, my dear in here.

*The sound of a door opening.*

WOMAN. What are you doing in here? It's so dark, why don't you put on the lights . . .?

MAN. I tried my dear, they don't seem to be working.

WOMAN. I was so worried I thought you'd got lost you know . . .

MAN. Mind your step, dear.

WOMAN. Where are you, Gerald?

*Lights on.*

DRAKES *is pouring petrol from a small drum into the bottles.*

*Blackout.*

MAN. I'm here on the bed, reach out your hand my dear.

WOMAN. What are you doing? Don't you feel well. Why don't you open the shutters? There you are . . .

MAN. Be careful.

*Lights on.*

DRAKES, *jacket off, shirt off, is tearing shirt.*

*Blackout.*

WOMAN. It feels very rough.

MAN. There are no sheets, just a mattress. Do you remember this suite my dear, how many times we stayed here on this very bed and watched the sun go down? Those marvelllous sunsets when the whole sky seemed to be on fire. And time seemed to linger forever . . .?

WOMAN. Yes, my dear, that's something I never forgot.

MAN. That's what I thought we'd do my dear, open the shutters and watch the sun go down, would you like that?

WOMAN. Yes, is it time?

MAN. Almost.

*Lights on.*

DRAKES *lights a match. He throws or runs into the hotel carrying a lighted bottle.*

*Blackout.*

WOMAN. Are you getting up?

MAN. Just to open them, my dear. I can see it's beginning to set now.

*A dark, rich, orange glow to appear and arch the stage.*

## ACT THREE

*One year later. The pool bar. Night. The bar is wrecked. The table, chairs, umbrella are overturned.*

YVONNE. We go miss we truck, yer know.

ALLEN. Nar dey go wait fer we.

YVONNE. Yer mad.

ALLEN. Yes.

ALLEN *and a* GIRL *appear in high area. She is his age, pretty.*

YVONNE. Is just a old mess man it breakdown. What yer bring me here fer?

ALLEN. A wanted ter see it an you say yer wanted ter see it too.

YVONNE. Yes in de daytime you make it sound so nice but look at it it en' notting is a burn down place, it en' notting.

ALLEN. A know yer car' see notting but is being here, dis place used ter be smart, yer know.

YVONNE. I getting scared.

ALLEN. Why, dey en' have notting here ter harm yer, I do' fraid dis place it harmless now, it dead.

YVONNE. I do' understand you, you tell me how bad dis place was, how dis place used ter remind you a all dat was bad about de colonial days an now yer bring me here. Yer want ter come here, yer crazy, man.

ALLEN. It used ter be bad it was everything a told yer about it wid black people spending dey whole life running about ter serve white people, till dey dead but look at it now, look at it, it dead now it harmless, I wouldn't a bring you wen it was

still standing because in dem days just ter come near it, yer
had ter change, yer had ter, yer manner had ter be different,
ter come in, dat's de kinda effect it had on people an dat went
on fer whole generations a people dis place affect, come let us
sit down. (*Picking up chairs.*)

YVONNE. All right. (*She sits.*)

ALLEN *picks up the table and umbrella. He sits.*

ALLEN. Dis place, colonise we, it showed we someting we
never had an someting we could never get.

YVONNE. An what we doing here?

ALLEN. Notting a just wanted ter come an have a look dat's
all, is once a year a come into de town so what is de
difference, an a wanted you ter see it.

YVONNE. Why?

ALLEN. Because is here it started, fer me.

YVONNE. Yer mean de money?

ALLEN. Yes, yer still do' believe dat eh?

YVONNE. No.

ALLEN. But is true, right here right over dere.

YVONNE. Allen, I do' car, I do' care how you get de money,
why yer do' understand dat, yer tief it, yer rob it, I do' care.

ALLEN. But I en' tief it, she give it ter me, a tell yer, she put it
in me hand. No a lie.

YVONNE. Yer see.

ALLEN. No she put it on me tray, right dere I en' lying, right
over dere.

YVONNE. Yes, I know, yer shame, dey en' have notting ter be

shame about, I do' care. Money en' have no guilt on it, is money yer could do anyting wid it.

ALLEN. An I do it.

YVONNE. Yes.

ALLEN. An I buy a piece a land wid it.

YVONNE. Yes.

ALLEN. You tink if I had tief it or rob it I coulda get through wid it someting bad woulda go round.

YVONNE. Why?

ALLEN. Because dat's de way ting work out.

YVONNE. You believe dat?

ALLEN. Yes.

YVONNE. Well I don't, money is money, it en' have no . . .

ALLEN. Yer do' understand.

YVONNE. Yes I understand. I understand although you hate dis place you make me climb over a wire fence, walk through all kinda rubble, in de middle a de night ter come here an sid down, an tell me bout some old beat up English woman who yer serve here, two coke or someting an she give you a tousand dollars fer dat, dat is de truth eh?

ALLEN. Yes, yes, dat's it, dat's what happen, dat's how.

YVONNE. All right, you tink I foolish, you tink I is one a dem girls yer could give a story – stupid Yvonne, look I read colonial history at college, not de white man one but black history, an it was a series a rule an oppression, cultural, as well as economic oppression, governed by greed, de English people drain dis colony dry an all de resources dey had so do' tell me one a dem give you anyting, because a know yer lie, if you tell me you kill one a dem fer dat money, a would admire

yer an say yer is a hero, because yer take back what was
yours an yer fathers' an yer used ter improve yer own life,
so . . .

ALLEN. Yes.

YVONNE. So do' tell me . . .

ALLEN. Yes what yer say is true everyting yer say is true but I
do' know why she do it, I still do' know why, I en'
romantising dis place, a tell yer what it was like wit me, an I
was here at de end but I hear stories wen I was here about
how worse it was.

YVONNE. Right so . . .

ALLEN. But it happen . . .

YVONNE. Look, we could a been in town celebrating dis is
Independence Day, we is a Republic we could a been in de
grandstand dancing or drinking or celebrating we deserve ter,
we work hard all year ter bring in we crops we should be in
de streets dancing instead we sitting here in dis wreck so you
could, what, relive de good old days wen de white man was
boss.

ALLEN. No.

YVONNE. Well dat is what we doing (*She gets up.*) I going, if
yer want ter see me I go be at de terminus, waiting by de
truck dat is if I en' meet a real brother, who know how ter
enjoy he independence from de white man witout guilt or any
kinda sadness.

ALLEN. Yes, all right.

YVONNE. All right, what yer coming?

ALLEN. No, a go meet yer by de terminus, I just want ter . . .

YVONNE. Dat is if a en' meet nobody.

ALLEN. Do' forget we have work ter do in de morning.

YVONNE. You do' forget it neither.

ALLEN. Right.

YVONNE. Well, enjoy . . . (*She turns to go.*)

ALLEN (*gets up*). Yvonne yer do' understand, I do' love dis place, but dis is where I saw – we here – we come from, dis place, yes, I needed dis place ter show we where we come from an where we going yes, we need places like dis dat is one a de jokes about it, we need de horror ter show we or else we could never know, my eyes open in dis place, ter what we was, what we used ter be an I value if fer dat ter push off, push off from it, yes I need it, I need dis place, an anodder one a de jokes about it is dat de more dis place treat yer like a boy is de more I felt like a man, de more I wanted ter be a man, I felt alive here, I saw tings clear here fer de first time in my life how de system operated how it killed people, dere used ter be a fellar here working wid me call Drakes. I en' know what happen ter him, but he was one, he was somebody who dis place enslave, because he couldn't see how it worked, but he help me, he is a man. I would never forget him an fer men like him it was too late fer dem, dey was born into it, but we lucky we had a chance ter look at tings an see dem clear fer de first time, but fer dem who gives us dat chance, all de Drakes a dis world.

YVONNE. Yer going ter show me how ter get outa dis place or yer expect me ter trip over an fall down.

ALLEN. You could find your way out just go back de way we come in, I go be . . .

YVONNE. Right brother . . .

YVONNE *goes.*

ALLEN *watches her go.*

DRAKES (*his voice*). She was right yer know.

ALLEN *turns.*

ALLEN. Who's dat, yer sound . . .?

DRAKES *comes to the edge of light area, feet in light, face, shoulders in darkness.*

Is you Drakesey?

DRAKES. She was right.

ALLEN. Is me Allen, a car' believe is you.

DRAKES. What yer doing here, dis place en' have notten fer you, she was right, yer girl was right.

ALLEN. A just come man, a just wanted ter see . . . what yer doing here man, dis place?

DRAKES. I is de watchman here, you shouldn't come ter dis place dis place dead, dis is de past, what you doing here?

ALLEN. How yer is man?

DRAKES. I all right, I keep watch here, I is de watchman here nobody do' come here, nobody suppose ter come here yer do' read de sign say dis place is condemned Trespasser will be Prosecuted.

ALLEN. Is good ter see yer man, I get me farm now yer know.

DRAKES. Yes.

ALLEN. An a doing well, everyting a say woulda happen happen.

DRAKES. Yes.

ALLEN. We was just in town fer Independence Day parade, we co-operative win best village dis year, an I was driving de lead tractor.

DRAKES. Yes.

ALLEN. An de Prime Minister take de salute.

DRAKES. Yes.

ALLEN. Why yer do' come an see me man, yer could . . .

DRAKES. No, tanks.

ALLEN. We have a nice piece a land on Maracas Hills, we could see all de ships coming in man bringing fertiliser, fertiliser fer my crops, we feed we self yer know if yer see de yams we grow man, big, big yam, an dasheen, like dis (*Shows*.) an rice, enough ter trade wid man why yer do' come an see we man?

DRAKES. No, I have ter stay here I have ter watch dis place. My job is ter watch over dis place, ter see dat notting ever move in dis place, ter see dat notting ever change in dis place, ter see it never rise up again, in no shape or form, no bulldozers or crane must come near dis place. Nobody must touch it, I is de only one, because I build it, what man build man could pull down, an I en' only I could pull it down, an I do dat every day, I crumble a wall, an I stamp a board an dey giving, a feel it, I hear it, only I an I en' want no help, de only ones who come here in de night is de dogs dey have work ter do like me dey have bones ter pick, hundred a years a bones ter pick an dust ter turn ter dust, we have a big job but we have time ter do it all we life, in a hundred years time people go come here an say what was dis place what did it stand fer what did it do, who did it benefit, what BC was dat or what AD was dat. Yes an interesting period dat was yer see dust . . . On a graph or a chart . . . a date, a date on a map . . . But we go be still here, so go, do' look back, do' come back, it en' go be here, you have notting ter look back here for dat's what I'm here for I is de watchman.

ALLEN. Yes, yes.

DRAKES. Yer better go now, de dogs go start coming an I have ter go an greet dem, bring dem in, dey belong here, not you, go go an enjoy yer Independence.

ALLEN *walks off, a slight smile.*

DRAKES *stays a beat. Sound of dogs barking. Then he returns to darkness.*

*Welcome Home Jacko* was first staged on 12 June 1979 at The Factory, Paddington, London, and subsequently at the Riverside Studios, Hammersmith, with the following cast:

| | |
|---|---|
| JACKO | Gordon Case |
| MARCUS | Victor Evans |
| ZIPPY | Trevor Laird |
| FRET | Alrick Riley |
| SANDY | Maggie Shevlin |
| GAIL | Dorrett Thompson |
| DOLE | Chris Tummings |

*Directed by* Charlie Hanson

## ACT ONE

*Scene: a Youth Club.*
*Time: afternoon.*

*A bar counter on the side with stools, also tables and chairs against the wall. Posters of Africa, Ethiopia, Haile Selassie, Youth Employment, a Police PR poster. Across the ceiling a larger banner saying: WELCOME HOME JACKO. The rear stairs leading to an office upstairs. In the corner a Juke Box-Football machine.*

*Four black boys (seventeen to twenty-one), ZIPPY, MARCUS, DOLE and FRET are playing a football machine.*

ZIPPY. Ras Clart me a beat yer.

MARCUS. Bet what you a miss ter Ras Clart, you a hit one ball you a call dat beat.

ZIPPY. Aright, make we play one more game, Dole yer ready?

DOLE. Me no want te play no mor Man, him a make ter much Ras Clart noise make we play some Dominoes.

ZIPPY. Cha Man, I we play.

MARCUS. Me an Fret go clart yer ras, eh Fret?

FRET. Yea, yea, make we play, en last round, first five win.

MARCUS. Wha yer say?

ZIPPY. Me ready Dole.

DOLE. Aright, make we play, him a make ter much noise make we shut him Ras Clart mouth.

MARCUS. Wait, wait, wha we a play for?

ZIPPY. Wha him mean?

MARCUS. Coke, make we play fer Coke, who a lose him have ter buy, wha yer a say?

ZIPPY. Cha why not you no win.

DOLE. Yea.

MARCUS. Make we see.

ZIPPY. Aright.

*They play. ZIPPY and DOLE, MARCUS and FRET.*

ZIPPY. Move dey, yer Ras shift, eh.

DOLE. Block him Ras.

MARCUS. Go way Block yer Bomba, dat . . . go in, go in.

ZIPPY. Block him Cha.

MARCUS. Move Fret, block im Fret.

ZIPPY. Goal.

MARCUS. Cha Fret you a let de Ras Clart Man score him a get easy goal, me no why him a score me no had me sounds wit me punch me a dub, Fret.

FRET. Him a lucky, him a lucky.

*Goes, punches Juke Box (Reggae). Throughout the later games music is played.*

ZIPPY. Lucky me Ras Clart dat a skill, skill from above, skill from Jah.

MARCUS. Jah, me Ras, wha you no bout Jah, dat a luck.

ZIPPY. Me no Jah, me talk ter Jah, him talk ter me, me an him communicate him a tell me hit de Ras Clart ball square, me hit it square it a go in square.

MARCUS. Cha.

ZIPPY. Me an Dole, we hand guided wha yer say Dole?

DOLE. Cha, him a seek him revenge.

MARCUS. Him a right me a hit yer Ras wid de Rod a
Correction come Fret, block him Ras.

*They play.*

DOLE. Go way, go way yer Ras.

ZIPPY. Block him, block him Ras Clart.

MARCUS. Go in, go in, go, go.

ZIPPY. Block in, cha him gone.

MARCUS. Block him break Fret, Fret, block him, cross.

FRET. We have him de Fret ter Ras.

MARCUS. Good him Ras worry now, go in, go in.

ZIPPY. Dole.

MARCUS. Goal, goal ter Ras.

ZIPPY. Dole you let de Ras Clart Man jinx yer.

MARCUS. Whey yer communicate wid Jah gone me just cut yer
wires. Jah do' want ter know you, him a have better Ras
Clart ting ter do.

ZIPPY. Aright one all.

MARCUS. Dat goal was scored by de Lion of Judea, de warrior
of Redemption ter Ras Clart, me no me should have me dub.

ZIPPY. Make we play. Make we play.

MARCUS. Fret like him in a hurry ter buy Coke, him feeling
rich come, Resurrection is at hand all Hypocrites I will shed
blood come to Canaan.

*They play.*

ZIPPY. Block him Ras.

DOLE. Me block im.

ZIPPY. Up, up.

MARCUS. Me have it, me have it.

ZIPPY. Have me Ras, dey.

MARCUS. Me have it.

ZIPPY. Take him Dole.

DOLE. Me have im, him gone.

MARCUS. Fret him coming.

FRET. Me have im.

ZIPPY. Have dat yer Ras.

MARCUS. Fret.

ZIPPY. Goal, goal, fer Ras.

MARCUS. Cha Fret you let de Man walk round yer.

FRET. Me stop him.

MARCUS. Him score Man.

ZIPPY. Two one, yer see Jah will guide him servant to Paradise him will guide him Warrior ter wreck vengeance on dose who face Judgement, de Sword of Jah is sharp and swift, wit love on one side an blood on de odder.

MARCUS. Judgement me Ras we have two more ter come we a go see who have Judgement.

ZIPPY. Righteousness is mine to give said Jah, you a get him punishment him wrath.

MARCUS. Shut yer Bomba.

DOLE. Make we play him, don't believe him have ter see yer

him ter believe, him a unbeliever, him one a dem who have ter feel him pain.

*They play.*

MARCUS. Watch im Fret.

FRET. Me see im.

ZIPPY. See, im, yer could see Lightning yer could see de Desert Wind, see dat.

MARCUS. Good Fret.

FRET. Me see him Ras me read him like Genesis, Chapter One.

ZIPPY. Block him Dole.

MARCUS. Judgement come to him deserving.

DOLE. Me have him.

MARCUS. Have Ras.

ZIPPY. Watch im Dole, him wait.

DOLE. Me have im Ras covered.

MARCUS. Cover dat yer Heathen.

DOLE. Me have im.

MARCUS. Cover dat yer Hypocrite.

DOLE. Me cover im.

MARCUS. Cover dat yer Pagan.

DOLE. Me . . .

MARCUS. Goal, goal.

ZIPPY. Dole, him . . .

MARCUS. Him what him cover dats what him do, him conquer all Jericho is dats what him do, eh Fret?

FRET. Cha.

MARCUS. Make we show one unbelievers who take de road ter greed an vanity dat rudenss do' pay, Cha me could taste de Ras Clart Coke already.

ZIPPY. Last game, two all.

DOLE. Him a make himself, Ras lose make him see.

MARCUS. Me a want one large glass ter Ras Clart, wid big ice an a straw, eh Fret?

FRET. Cha, dem a miss, dem goal.

ZIPPY. Aright make we see.

*They play.*

ZIPPY. Watch im Dole.

DOLE. Me have him.

MARCUS. Have . . . Fret him come.

FRET. Me have him.

ZIPPY. Have Bomba, him come Dole.

MARCUS. Dole a sleep ter Ras, me a shepherd.

MARCUS. Me a once walk round him.

DOLE. Me have him.

ZIPPY. Him a want ter sneak in, like Judas.

MARCUS. Judas me Ras, me a son of Jah, yer Hypocrite, take im Fret.

FRET. Me have im Ras.

ZIPPY. Have dat yer Ras.

FRET. Me tell yer me have him him path block im power miss.

MARCUS. Give him Judgement ter Ras.

ZIPPY. Dole im . . .

MARCUS. Judgement come.

ZIPPY. Him try Dole, block him.

MARCUS. Goal, goal, in yer Ras Clart, yer Bomba Clart, yer tink yer could escape de Sword of Correction you Hypocrite, Jah a say all will succumb, an him word is law.

ZIPPY. Dole you let dis Ras Clart beat we, Cha.

DOLE. Him lucky, Man.

MARCUS. Me no beat yer me righteousness beat yer, Cha Fret, dem a Ras Clart, en know de Warriors of Haile Selassie de Lion of Judah, de Lord of Lords de King of Kings, wen dem see him.

*He beats his chest.*

FRET. Whey de Coke dem, me a tirsty, all yer a deal Coke.

MARCUS. Cha yea, me a hot too, me a want me nice cool down make me gather me wisdom, ter confront dem Hypocrites, get dem Cokes.

ZIPPY. Make we wait till Sandy a come.

MARCUS. De Coke behind de Bar Man.

ZIPPY. Sandy have de keys Man.

MARCUS. Cha go behind de Bar and break him Ras, Man, me want me Coke.

ZIPPY. Nar Man.

MARCUS. Whey Sandy?

ZIPPY. She upstairs in de office.

MARCUS. Well call she down ter Ras, like yer want me break de Ras Clart lock or yer do' want ter pay fer yer sins.

ZIPPY. Me a pay, me a pay, Dole give Sandy a call.

DOLE. Cha make dem call, she na drink dem, Jah say, 'Make men toil fer him rewards', me do' like asking she Ras fer notting.

ZIPPY. Call de Ras Clart woman nar.

MARCUS. Cha me go call she nar fraid no Hypocrite me power stronger dan dem. (*He goes to the bottom of the stairs, shouts.*) Hey Sandy.

SANDY (*from upstairs*). What?

MARCUS. Come an open de Bar. Zippy want some Coke.

SANDY. I'm on the phone, hang on a minute.

MARCUS (*to the boys*). She a on de phone. Phone me Ras, dis place suppose ter be fer we, ter keep we outa danger, an you suppose ter be running dis place ter look after we, so come an do yer Ras Clart job. Wha de Ras Clart yer doing on de phone, making date for.

SANDY. I'm not making dates, give me a minute.

MARCUS. Me give you more den a Ras Clart minute, me box yer Ras Clart head. Cha if yer do' want ter interrupt yer romantic conversation trow down dem keys den, we go open up take four cokes an send back dem keys.

DOLE. Yea.

*The others laugh.*

SANDY. No.

MARCUS. Well come down or else me break him Ras Clart.

SANDY. Coming.

MARCUS. She a come, a know what a bring she, Ras-

> *They laugh.* SANDY *comes downstairs. She is white, thirty to thirty-five, plump. She wears glasses, a long Indian skirt and a T-shirt and keys and a crucifix on a chain round her neck.*

SANDY. What's all the fuss about? I told you I was on the phone. It wouldn't of killed you to wait a minute, just for a few cokes, which are only going to rot your guts anyway. I told you.

MARCUS. We like Coke.

SANDY. You boys have no consideration. I was on the phone trying to find out what time Jacko's train gets in.

DOLE. Yer coulda fling down dem keys.

SANDY. You know that's not allowed, I'm responsible for them.

DOLE. Cha.

SANDY. You can Cha all you like, but what's the point in locking something if you don't keep the keys for it.

ZIPPY. Locks could get break.

SANDY. Yes, I know locks could be broken, so could doors and chairs and tables, and windows and I can go on for a month, but you know, don't you, so I won't but the whole purpose of having a lock is to make sure some one is responsible for the key, and that is why I have it. If the lock is broken that is not my responsibility.

MARCUS. So we could break the lock.

SANDY. I did not say that, you know, you all know that. That is the last lock I am replacing. I've told you if that lock gets broken, you will have to go to the corner for your cokes. I mean it. I'm not going to keep up this farce.

DOLE. But dis a Youth Club, suppose ter have coke, I know some Youth Club have not only coke but orange, and food.

ZIPPY. Yes.

MARCUS. Me know an dat have Billiards an even machine fer French Letter.

SANDY. Yes, I'm sure you do, I know of some that even have sensible boys who take part in activities and protect their centre and do repairs and paint also.

*They laugh.*

Yes, crazy as it may sound, they even feel proud of the centre so don't you start telling me about orange and Johnny machines. We've had all that and what happened? Someone was always putting money in and the machine was always jamming and someone always had to have a refund.

ZIPPY. De machine did jam.

SANDY. And who had to hand out the refund? Me.

MARCUS. Well you responsible.

SANDY. And when the engineers came, could we find the jammed coins, no they disappeared.

ZIPPY. It jammed.

SANDY. And what happened when someone broke open the machine? Did you all go and put those packets to some use to the good use they were designed specifically for? No. I wish to god you had.

ZIPPY. You leave Jah out of dis kind a talk.

SANDY. Oh I see I'm not allowed to have my god am I? Why? OK, don't tell me I know. I am white, and we white people don't have a god, we don't believe in a god, we are devils. Is that right?

MARCUS. Cha, yer right, all a believe in money an greed an oppression, all yer oppress people.

SANDY. I see, and we are not oppressed as well. Look at me. I am as oppressed as you, more I think. I've got to worry about this place, to make sure it's run and keep it open, and clean and keep writing letters begging for money so that you harmless creatures have a quiet life, so that you good little boys keep out of trouble and so that I don't have to spend all my life in court saying 'Your Lordship he's never been in trouble before. I have found him responsible and sensible, and no I cannot put up the bail for him but I'm sure if you give him a suspended sentence he will have learned his lesson.' That is my oppression and I feel it so don't you tell me about oppression. Back to the Johnnies, those Johnnies you wanted. What did you do with them? You blew them up and strung them up on the ceiling didn't . . .

ZIPPY. We . . .

SANDY. Yes, you did, and you thought it was a big joke, when the girls came in didn't you?

MARCUS. Dem know what Johnny look like.

*The boys laugh.*

SANDY. Yes, yes very funny they were upset and insulted I know that. You know what it told them, it told them you did not respect them, that they, black women, had not earned the respect of you their men. They didn't say it, but I saw their faces, and I also was insulted, me a white woman, I was also insulted. Are you surprised they don't want to come back? How many discos have we had?

DOLE. Two.

SANDY. And how many girls came?

DOLE. Not much.

SANDY. You see.

DOLE. But dem do' like heavy music, dem want soul, and all that funky business, dem en want Rasta music.

SANDY. The music has nothing to do with it, it's this place. We have got the worst name as far as centres go and that's saying something.

MARCUS. Dat en true you is a hypocrite me know places wid worse name den here, where wen one crowd inside de rest have ter pay dem money fer dem ter get inside.

SANDY. Yes all right we are perfect, one bright peaceful, little family.

ZIPPY. Hey Sandy, yer like dem Johnnys.

*The boys laugh.*

SANDY. No love they're for little boys like you to try an inflate.

MARCUS. Cha she call him little boy.

*The boys laugh. Not ZIPPY.*

DOLE. Sandy, what inflate mean?

SANDY. It means to try to make yourself larger than you are.

DOLE. I taught dat was erection.

*The boys laugh.*

SANDY. No love, that is trying to make yourself smaller than you are. All right now how many cokes and who's paying?

ZIPPY. Marcus.

MARCUS. Nar Zippy.

ZIPPY. Nar Marcus.

MARCUS. Zippy Ras him lost me but, him carry him lost so him pay, ask Fret.

FRET. Him right.

SANDY. Now look, I don't care who's paying but I'm not unlocking that door until I see some money. I haven't got all day to waste here whilst you decide . . .

ZIPPY. All right here.

*He gives her a pound.*

Wha happen yer no joke?

SANDY. I'm sorry Zippy. Yes I joke. How many?

ZIPPY. Four. Make it five if ye want one.

SANDY. Thanks.

MARCUS. Watch im Sandy, he a try ter catch yer.

ZIPPY. Do' mind him. Catch what? Me like Sandy, she know dat.

MARCUS. Yer see.

SANDY. I see, I'll watch him. I think he's a nice boy. He's the only one of you who's offered to buy me a coke, that's for sure.

MARCUS. Is him lose, him have ter pay.

SANDY (*taking the cokes to the table*). Nevertheless thanks all the same for the drink Zippy. I'm sure you would have bought even if you had won. Who beat who then?

MARCUS. Me an Fret lick dem Ras.

SANDY. Ah I didn't know you played Fret.

MARCUS. Me teach him, once an we lick dem me could teach anybody ter lick dem, dem no good.

SANDY. I see, so you're our champion.

ZIPPY. Champion what, him is champion.

MARCUS. Me lick dem me an Fret.

DOLE. Do' mind he Sandy, he a make one set a noise him put me off.

ZIPPY. Yes, him just lucky.

MARCUS. Luck, me Ras, me give dem all me powers of righteousness, Rasta Man en depend on luck, all him a have is him righteousness. Right Sandy?

SANDY. Right, you'll have to play against Jacko when he comes to see who is the real champ.

MARCUS. Him good?

SANDY. He was our champion.

ZIPPY. Whey him is?

SANDY. He was inside and he's coming out today.

*She looks at her watch.*

He's out. He's on the way home and I've got to meet him at the station at half-three.

MARCUS. What him went in fer?

SANDY. He's a nice guy you guys will like him and yes, that's something I wanted to say. When he comes he's going to be feeling a bit strange so no aggro.

MARCUS. We do' give aggro.

SANDY. You know what I mean.

MARCUS. No.

SANDY. Come on.

MARCUS. Cha all right. What him like, him a Rasta?

SANDY. No, I don't think so. I don't know. He's been inside for . . .

DOLE. How long him get.

SANDY. Five years.

DOLE. Dat long?

SANDY. Yes.

DOLE. Dem barstard. Wen dem lock up blackman dem make sure him lock up long.

ZIPPY. What him get lock fer?

SANDY. Rape; he and three boys.

ZIPPY. An him get catch, him en rape good.

*The boys laugh.*

SANDY. Very funny.

ZIPPY. Me never rape, but if me rape me go rape so good no girl en go get Police, she a go want more an more.

*The boys laugh.*

SANDY. Now stop that. That is not funny. That's what you and a lot of men think. That's why so many women are raped and so many men and boys — boys like you and Jacko — are sent to prison. No, it is not funny, I'm sorry, no man has any right to rape a woman, no matter what his reasons are or what he thinks she wants, you hear, and it's not funny. Jacko took part or the girl said he took part.

MARCUS. Dem girl tell lie, dem is hypocrite.

SANDY. All right and she recognised him, she knew him.

ZIPPY. An she inform on him?

SANDY. Yes.

ZIPPY. Him no rape good me say.

*The boys laugh.*

SANDY. I said it wasn't funny.

ZIPPY. Me bet yer it was one white girl, dem Ras Clart, always want ter pretend dem good.

SANDY. How much?

ZIPPY. What?

SANDY. How much you'd like to bet?

ZIPPY. Why?

SANDY. How much you want to bet it was a white girl, because I'd bet you.

MARCUS. It was a black girl.

SANDY. That's right. Why do you think it was a white girl?

MARCUS. I didn't say it was a white girl, it's him.

SANDY. It's him I'm talking to. Eh Zippy why, you don't think black girls are sexy too?

ZIPPY. No, black girls sexy, me like black girls.

SANDY. So you think white girls should get raped.

ZIPPY. No, me never say dat, but dem like boys ter gang dem an wen dem finish an dem realise what happen, dem start ter feel ashamed and say it happen widout dem consent, me see dem in de back a disco, plenty, if me wanted to me coulda just walk up an . . .

SANDY. All right Zippy and you know why? It's because young girls go there, and they have something to drink.

Something like whisky which they can't or shouldn't drink and that's what happens.

ZIPPY. Dem like it.

SANDY. Would you like –

ZIPPY. No, me tell yer, me never do it.

SANDY. No, I mean would you like five men to . . .

ZIPPY. Me like five women.

*The boys laugh.*

SANDY. All right, very funny.

MARCUS. Do' mind dat Zippy, Sandy. Tell me beat dis champion, me want ter know all bout him, him strategy, how me go lick him, him does flick or him does stroke.

SANDY. Both, sorry Marcus I don't know much about it, but he was always winning.

MARCUS. All him games?

SANDY. Yes, he used to teach . . .

MARCUS. Cha, him a cheat.

SANDY. No, Marcus.

MARCUS. No man car win all him games, you a miss . . . so him a warrior me go have ter watch him.

SANDY. Yes, Marcus.

DOLE. Him lost one game an him get five.

MARCUS. If him so cool Sandy how come him get catch ter Ras.

SANDY. He didn't get caught, I told you the girl remembered him and told the Police, and he refused to give the other boy's name so . . .

MARCUS. Cha.

DOLE. Yes.

MARCUS. Cha him a genuine warrior ter Ras.

SANDY. Call him what you like, just try and be nice to him. When he comes he's bound to feel a bit . . . just try.

MARCUS. All right Cha.

SANDY *looks at her watch.*

SANDY. I better leave now or else I'll miss him.

MARCUS. Sandy what about dem robes yer was making fer me.

SANDY. You want them now?

MARCUS. Yes, we must look like proper Rasta, to greet de warrior.

SANDY. All right, they're in my office on the floor behind the cabinet. Now look, I'm leaving you in charge Marcus.

MARCUS. Wid de keys.

SANDY. Oh – no, you don't need them.

MARCUS. We might need some cokes.

SANDY. I won't be that long. Christ I almost forgot.

MARCUS. Leave Jah out of dis.

SANDY. Listen, there's a girl coming here, she was meant to be here by two but she's late so tell her I won't be long, will you.

MARCUS. Who's she?

SANDY. My new helper or warden, whichever you like, and don't give her a hard time, practise being nice on her so that when Jacko comes you'll be perfect, we don't want her to get the right impression on her first day do we?

MARCUS. What?

SANDY. Never mind just be nice to her for my sake. Right, keys yes, gloves in the car, yes, right, I'm off. Be good.

*She smiles and goes.*

MARCUS. Cha, me in charge a what dis Ras Clart place, en worth notting she no give me no keys so how me a in charge, she a hypocrite man genuine hypocrite dat.

ZIPPY. Marcus make me get dem robes nar.

MARCUS. Cha why yer ask me?

ZIPPY. You are General.

MARCUS. Cha me no General if yer want robes go find dem yerself, come Fret make me get some practice, before me face dis Goliath.

FRET *and* MARCUS *go to the football machine. They play.*

ZIPPY. Dole make we go upstairs get we robes.

DOLE. Cha me do' want no robes man, me a stay here, fight ya.

ZIPPY. Cha.

*He goes upstairs.*

DOLE. Hey Marcus, you a practise yer Ras you still en go beat nobody.

MARCUS. Shut yer Ras, me beat you, me beat you an Zippy, yer no hear what Sandy a say? She say me champion.

DOLE. Champion what? Champion caretaker? She a left you in charge a de broom ter Ras.

MARCUS. Shut yer mouth, Bomba hypocrite, you a interfere wid de working a Jah.

DOLE. Jah me Ras, you a scheming to beat one guy, de guy out a practice, him been put away for five year, you a want to outnumber de poor guy you en no genuine warrior you a Herod ter Ras.

MARCUS. Shut yer mouth before me box yer Ras.

*ZIPPY comes down in an African robe.*

ZIPPY. Cha, me a genuine Ethiopian now me a warrior of de Lion, ter Ras Clart, all yer a see Rasta ter Ras Heavy Cloth.

MARCUS. Cha you look good boy.

ZIPPY. Me look genuine no hypocrite ting dis a genuine robe.

MARCUS. Whey we own?

ZIPPY. Dem a upstairs.

MARCUS. Cha.

*He runs upstairs followed by DOLE. FRET walks. Sounds from upstairs.*

Cha, give me dat.

ZIPPY (*jumping, sings*). By de waters of Babylon . . . Cha

*A girl, GAIL, enters. She is black, attractive (twenty to twenty-five) and is wearing a jacket, skirt and jumper.*

GAIL. Hello.

ZIPPY. Yes?

GAIL. I came to see Sandy.

ZIPPY. Yes, she a gone out but she left a message she say she en go be long ter wait fer she.

GAIL. Yes, I'm a bit late, I couldn't find the place.

ZIPPY. Yes, Cha take a seat, she a come soon.

GAIL (*sits*). Thank you, it looks nice.

ZIPPY. It aright, it have office upstairs you ar want to see it?

GAIL. No, I better wait till Sandy comes.

ZIPPY. Yea, you a come ter work?

GAIL. I hope so, it's up to Sandy if she likes me.

ZIPPY. Cha, Sandy cool she a like you she a like everybody, you en help she out.

GAIL. Yes.

ZIPPY. What you a do?

GAIL. I . . . Lots of things, try to keep you busy most of all. Are you the only one here?

ZIPPY. No de rest a guys upstairs dey look fer dem robes, you like it? (*Stands.*) It a genuine Ethiopian robe.

GAIL. Yes, it's very nice.

ZIPPY. Sandy a make dem fer we. She a cool, you a ask she, she make you one.

GAIL. Yes, I'll ask her, so what other rooms do you have?

ZIPPY. Cha, not much, we a have office an phone upstairs, toilet over dey.

GAIL. One?

ZIPPY. Nar two, one for de girls.

GAIL. Yes.

ZIPPY. An in de back dey it a have a room for discos.

GAIL. Ah, I like dancing, how often do you . . . ?

ZIPPY. Cha, not too often, it a some time one week, some time two weeks, not steady. Whey you from?

GAIL. London.

ZIPPY. But yer people black.

GAIL. Yes.

ZIPPY. Cha, me know dat me take one look at yer me know yer people a dem black. You is a Rastafarian?

GAIL. No, I don't think so, not that I have anything against it, I just don't know anything about it.

ZIPPY. Me tell yer, me explain everything not Marcus him a hypocrite.

GAIL. Who's Marcus?

ZIPPY. Him a upstairs. Yer see Rastafarian is a man who believe in de Bible, all peace an love an him a believe in Emperor Haile Selassie to be de Lion a Judah, de King of Kings and Lord of Lords.

GAIL. Yes?

ZIPPY. Dat is something eh, dat is Rasta man, him belief. Yes, an all white people all a dem, dem a genuine hypocrite dem.

GAIL. Yes I see.

ZIPPY. See dat what Rasta man believe.

GAIL. And you're a Rasta man?

ZIPPY. Cha all a we a Rasta an all Rasta man believe in him dread locks.

GAIL. Yes, the hair.

ZIPPY. Dat not him hair, dat him dread locks.

GAIL. I see, so tell me what sort of things you do here?

ZIPPY. Cha me nar do much, we a play some dominoes, some football, some sounds.

GAIL. You have a team?

ZIPPY. Nar, over dey.

GAIL. Yes. What else?

ZIPPY. Fool around, talk.

GAIL. Ah, what do you talk about?

ZIPPY. All kinda ting, Rastafarian tings, an Ethiopia.

GAIL. Would you all like to go to Africa?

ZIPPY. Sure all a we want go dey some day.

GAIL. Good, well maybe we could go on a trip to see some exhibits from Africa.

ZIPPY. Where?

GAIL. In London, there's always something going on concerning Africa, you'd be surprised.

ZIPPY. But dat not Africa, dat a white man ting, dem a hypocrite, dem not genuine Africa, is Africa we want ter see, we want ter see real lion not dem circus ting.

GAIL. I see, but it would give you some idea, of what life is really like in Africa.

ZIPPY. Cha, but not Africa, we want ter know we in Africa dats what we want ter know, you a see.

GAIL. Yes, where are you from?

ZIPPY. Me from Jamaica.

GAIL. You were born in Jamaica?

ZIPPY. No, we born in London, but me people from Jamaica.

GAIL. But you speak with a Jamaican . . .

ZIPPY. Cha, me could talk London if me wanted to but me is a Rastafarian so me talk Ja.

GAIL. I see.

ZIPPY. Yer all genuine Rasta man him a talk Jamaican or else him not genuine.

GAIL. Yes, and all the other boys they were born in London?

ZIPPY. Some a dem born in Jamaica some born in London me do' know.

GAIL. Are they allowed to be upstairs so long?

ZIPPY. Cha Sandy she a cool, she left Marcus in charge. Him upstairs. You a want to see him we call im fer you.

GAIL. No. (*She gets up.*) I'll just look around. (*She looks at a poster.*)

ZIPPY. Dat is de Emperor Haile Selassie.

GAIL. Yes.

ZIPPY. You know him face?

GAIL. Yes.

ZIPPY. Cha, you is Rastafarian.

GAIL. Are women allowed to be Rastafarian?

ZIPPY. Cha yes man all black people is Rastafarian. Is what dem believe.

GAIL. I see you have a bar.

ZIPPY. Yes.

GAIL. Do you run it yourselves?

ZIPPY. Nar Sandy, it a only keep coke.

GAIL. Would you like to run it yourselves?

ZIPPY. Cha what for, it en make no profit, it fer someting ter drink, it do' need no running.

MARCUS, DOLE *and* FRET *come down in robes.*

MARCUS. Cha Zippy, a pick up chick.

ZIPPY. Me no pick up no chick Ras dis Gail come to help out Sandy.

GAIL. Hello, I'm Gail.

MARCUS. Yes me know, Gail Roberts.

GAIL. How did you know, have we met?

MARCUS. No me know yer name, Sandy a tell me yer come an ter take care a you, she left me in charge, me name is Marcus, me was named after de great black warrior Marcus Garvey.

GAIL. Yes, . . .

MARCUS. Dis is Dole, cause since him born him a draw dole an dis is Fret, him is my warrior an him do Fret.

GAIL. I see. Hello. Your friend was telling me all the good things you do here.

MARCUS. Who Zippy? Him do' know notting, me is in charge, me running ting, Sandy say fer me ter look after you not Zippy.

GAIL. Well he was the one I met first and –

MARCUS. Cha, yer shoulda wait fer me, me in charge.

ZIPPY. Do' take no notice a he, yer know him just want ter prove him point, him didn't want to be in no command.

MARCUS. Cha shut yer Ras mouth.

GAIL. It's OK, I'm fine. How long is Sandy going to be?

MARCUS. She a back soon, she gone to get a guy, him Jacko.

GAIL. Oh yes, who's Jacko? I see you're having a party for him.

MARCUS. It no party, him a coming out today dat all, him a Sandy friend.

GAIL. I see.

MARCUS. You a work here?

GAIL. I hope so. I was saying to Zippy, I hope I can organise some outings and get you guys to come along.

MARCUS. What kind a outing? Ter museum an ting?

GAIL. No, I thought maybe we could visit a Safari Park, and see the animals they have. Lions and tigers.

MARCUS. Me do' want ter see no Sarfari Park, Sarfari is a white man ting dat a fer white people, in dem car to visit.

GAIL. I just thought maybe you might like to see some lions.

MARCUS. Cha me know what lions look like.

GAIL. Or maybe a factory or something.

MARCUS. Factory what, what kinda factory?

GAIL. Any kind of factory where they make things. We could see how its done.

MARCUS. What?

GAIL. Anything. I have a friend who works for a record studio. We could maybe go and see how they make records, see how it's done. You like music?

MARCUS. Me like Reggae. Heavy Dub. Who him a cut?

GAIL. They cut all kind of records there. Maybe we could go when they are doing some Reggae.

MARCUS (calls out). Hey all yer hear dat, dis girl know people who make reggae record.

GAIL. A friend.

DOLE. Cha, dat good.

MARCUS. She a take we ter see.

GAIL. I could try and arrange it.

MARCUS. Cha you cool, me dig dat.

GAIL. What other sort of things do you like? Sports?

MARCUS. Yer mean running in dem shorts.

GAIL. Yes.

MARCUS. Nar, cha, dem a school boy ting. Me like chick and
me disco.

GAIL. I see.

MARCUS. Me like Rasta man ting.

GAIL. Yes Zippy was explaining to me.

MARCUS. Him no explain notting. Him no genuine Rasta man.
Him is real hypocrite. Is me de Rasta man here. Anyting you
want to know bout Rasta man you ask me. Me know all bout
Ethiopia.

GAIL. And Haile Selassie.

MARCUS. Him to him is de King of Kings, Lord of –

GAIL. Lords.

MARCUS. You know him?

GAIL. Yes.

MARCUS. Dis friend wit him record studio, him yer boyfriend?

GAIL. How did you know it was a him?

MARCUS. Me know, me know dem tings, me is a righteous

man, an me righteousness tell me dem ting, it tell me all kinda ting, me know yer name was Roberts before anybody.

GAIL. He's a friend, yes.

MARCUS. Boyfriend.

GAIL. Friend.

MARCUS. What kinda friend?

GAIL. A sort of friend.

MARCUS. A sort of boyfriend?

GAIL. A sort of friend.

MARCUS. What sort?

GAIL. A sort, any sort really. You have friends.

MARCUS. You mean like me an Fret?

GAIL. Is Fret your boyfriend?

MARCUS. Cha shut yer Ras clart mouth.

GAIL. I'm sorry.

MARCUS. Me is genuine Rasta man, Rasta man do have no boyfriend dat is white man ting.

GAIL. I said I was sorry, it was a joke.

MARCUS. Cha, me nearly box yer face if Sandy did ask me look after you, me box. Rasta man don't do dem kinda tings, da is hypocrite ting.

GAIL. I'm sorry (*She takes out a cigarette.*) Would you like a cigarette?

MARCUS. Me no smoke tobacco, me smoke ganja, Rasta man he smoke no tobacco.

GAIL. Look I'm really sorry, it was a joke right? OK, a bad one, OK . . . ?

MARCUS. Cha.

*He walks off and joins the others. He says something. They laugh.* ZIPPY *comes over to* GAIL.

GAIL. Hi.

ZIPPY. Hi.

GAIL. I think I upset your friend.

ZIPPY. Who, Marcus? Do' mind him him a have a big mouth dats all him have.

GAIL. Yes, but all the same I think maybe I shouldn't have.

ZIPPY. Do' mind him, him just want to prove him is big man dats him problem.

GAIL. Yes a lot of men have that problem. I think I'll go upstairs and wait in the office.

ZIPPY. Yer want me show yer?

GAIL. No thanks.

ZIPPY. It right at de top a de stairs, make yerself at home.

GAIL. Thanks.

*She goes.* MARCUS *comes to* ZIPPY. *Music.*

MARCUS. Cha, punch me a dub dey . . . Cha whey she a gone?

ZIPPY. She gone upstairs ter wait for Sandy.

MARCUS. Me do' know if she fer wait in office.

ZIPPY. Cha shut yer mouth, Sandy say look after she, you a give she one get a heavy sound. Wha rang wit yer? Yer brainy, or what? De chick is a nice chick, man.

MARCUS. She a hypocrite, me nearly box she face.

ZIPPY. Box me Ras, you not boxing nobody face.

MARCUS. Who go stop me?

ZIPPY. Me, me and de lion of Ethiopia to stop yer cha, you like
   ter go en wit dis Ras clart ting too long, me vex now, me vex,
   me spirit go an get vex now Ras clart, me no heavy guy yer
   know but wen me get vex, me vex, Cha, go way duck me ter
   Ras —

   ZIPPY *walks off, goes in the corner and sits.*

MARCUS. All right, brother man me duck yer.

   MARCUS *goes to the boys.*
   SANDY *enters with* JACKO.
   JACKO *is tall (twenty to twenty-five).*
   *He is wearing a suit and tie.*

SANDY. Hi everybody, this is Jacko, come and say hello.

   ZIPPY *goes and shakes his hand.*

ZIPPY. Hi man.

DOLE (*slaps his hand*). Hi.

MARCUS. Hey brother how yer is?

   FRET *comes.*

FRET. Hi.

SANDY. His train was late and I got held up, so how's things?
   What's been happening? I see everything's still in one piece.

MARCUS. We had some cokes.

   SANDY *goes to the bar.*

SANDY. Oh no, I warned you, I warned . . . (*Looks.*) Shit
   Marcus I must be stupid, you get me every time, don't you? I

never learn, it's my trusting nature. OK, you guys relax. Take a seat Jacko, you're no stranger.

JACKO. Tanks.

SANDY. And the place hasn't changed that much, some paint here and there that's all, so make yourself at home.

JACKO. It feels good.

SANDY. That's because it's home.

ZIPPY. Sandy that girl come.

SANDY. Christ and what happened?

ZIPPY. She upstairs, waiting.

SANDY. Christ, OK, I'll go and see her. You, look (*Gives the keys to* ZIPPY.) open the box, let's all have some cokes, I'll get her.

*She goes upstairs.*

ZIPPY *goes behind the bar and brings out some cokes.*

MARCUS. Hey look Zippy, nar him is now barman in hotel.

ZIPPY *opens coke and gives one to* JACKO.

ZIPPY. Here brother man try dis.

JACKO. Tanks.

ZIPPY. All yer help all yer Ras.

SANDY *and* GAIL *come down.*

SANDY. Have you met everybody?

GAIL. Yes.

SANDY. But you haven't met Jacko. This is Jacko.

GAIL. Hello Jacko.

JACKO. Hello.

SANDY. Oh I'm sorry Gail, it is Gail isn't it?

GAIL. Yes.

SANDY. Let's have a coke then, I'm paying for the damn things.

*She takes one for* GAIL, *gives it to her. She looks at* JACKO.

Oh you've got one. All right everybody, to Jacko, welcome home Jacko.

*They all repeat this. They drink.* SANDY *sits.*

Right let's relax now, I needed this. (*The coke.*) I've been rushing all day. First it was you and I had to get Jacko, and I haven't stopped. So come on then tell me what you think of us.

GAIL. I think you're all nice, great.

SANDY. Well I wouldn't go that far, but we're all right. Let's say we're not as bad as we appear.

GAIL. OK.

SANDY. So what do you think? You think you'd like to work with us?

GAIL. Yes, I think so.

SANDY. Great, hey everybody, Gail is going to work with us.

*ZIPPY goes and shakes* GAIL's *hand.*

ZIPPY. Yea, welcome sister.

SANDY. That's the spirit. Anybody else?

MARCUS. Cha.

*The others wave.*

SANDY. Take no notice, they're all rushing to welcome you. Let's drink to Gail.

*They drink to* GAIL.

GAIL. Thank you. What do I have to do?

SANDY. We'll talk about it, it's not much. Things like answer the phone, take messages, be in charge here when I go out, which is going to be more often I hope. Those sort of things, oh yes, and any bright ideas you have for keeping these guys occupied, except dominoes, the Juke Box or football; we've got those.

GAIL. I noticed.

SANDY. Yes. Now, we're not much of a candidate for Youth Club of the year.

GAIL. We'll make it better. When can I start?

SANDY. Right now. Come upstairs, I'll show you what's what and what goes where.

GAIL. Great.

SANDY. OK, you guys look after Jacko, and don't let them cheek you Jacko.

JACKO. I'm all right.

SANDY. Come on then.

SANDY *is on the stairs.*

ZIPPY. Hey Sandy, how yer like dem robes?

SANDY. Great, they look genuine.

SANDY *and* GAIL *go up.*

ZIPPY. Cha, hey brother how yer like dem robes?

JACKO. Dey look nice.

ZIPPY. If yer ask Sandy she a make yer one too.

JACKO. What dey for? All yer doing a show or what?

ZIPPY. Show, no man, Ras dis is genuine Ethiopian robes, we is Rasta man, genuine Rasta man yer do know bout Rastafarian?

JACKO. No, not much.

ZIPPY. Cha me forget you been lock up for long time, well Rastafarian is black man ting now we discover we identity is Rastafarian dats it.

JACKO. I hear bout it in Jamaica long time.

ZIPPY. Well it a come ter Britain now, we call it Babylon da is Britain so tell me brother man what it like inside de man place, fer how long?

JACKO. Five years.

ZIPPY. What is a like?

JACKO. It's not bad, as long as you follow de rules.

ZIPPY. Follow dem rules, me no follow nobody rules.

JACKO. Well when yer inside dere yer have ter or else . . .

ZIPPY. Or else what?

JACKO. Or else, dey make yer pay.

ZIPPY. Cha nobody car make me a do what me do' want ter do.

JACKO. Well inside dey do, a only hope you don't have ter go in.

ZIPPY. Cha me nar go inside dem never catch me, me smarter dem all dem ras.

JACKO. OK.

ZIPPY. But you is a warrior ter ras.

JACKO. How yer mean?

ZIPPY. Sandy she tell we. Sandy tell we how yer en give dem Babylon yer friend en dem names how yer no tell dem notting.

JACKO. Yes.

ZIPPY. Dats heroic ting man, dats what genuine Rasta man go do man.

JACKO. Yes.

ZIPPY. Genuine hero man even Sandy a call yer hero.

JACKO. Tanks, so what you guys do all dey just come here?

ZIPPY. Cha yes is a good place man. Dis is de only place in dis town whey we could come an relax an en get no harrassment. We could do we own ting here, an dey en have nobody ter tell we what ter do or asking we what we doing. If we go by de corner, is Panda Car come up, ter ask we question, Ras clart, dem do' like ter see we doing notting. Everybody must be doing someting, working or going somewhere or coming from somewhere. If dem see people relaxing dem tink dem up ter someting. Dem people do' relax so dem do' like ter see people relax. Dem like ter have heart attack an give people dem heart attack.

JACKO. Yes.

ZIPPY. Cha brother, me like you me could make you genuine Rasta man.

JACKO. I do' know, I do' know.

ZIPPY. Cha it no sweat you a catch yer spirit.

MARCUS comes over.

MARCUS. Hey brother man yer know how ter play dat game?

JACKO. Yes, ah used ter . . .

MARCUS. Come den nar, me give yer a game, make we play.

JACKO. All right.

*He goes.*

MARCUS. Hey Zippy you a come watch.

ZIPPY. Nar, Cha, go long.

JACKO *and* MARCUS *go to the football game.*

MARCUS. Make we toss fer kick off.

JACKO. All right.

*Puts his hand in his pocket.*

MARCUS. Me have coin, me have coin. (*Tosses.*) Head nor tail?

JACKO. Head.

MARCUS. Head a win, make we punch me tune . . .

*Music.*

JACKO *kicks off. They play.* DOLE *and* FRET *go to watch.*

MARCUS. Cha go in.

DOLE. Him block yer Marcus.

MARCUS. Shut yer Ras. Cha go in dat Ras.

DOLE. Him cover yer Ras Marcus.

JACKO. All yer take dis game serious.

MARCUS. Serious Ras it a warfare ter Ras go in.

DOLE. You know about him Ras Marcus him block all yer Ras clart move. Look how him cool, him a real warrior, him worry yer Ras.

MARCUS. Worry who Ras, me a righteous man. Righteous man no lose no contest.

DOLE. Win it den nar.

MARCUS. Cha go in, go in.

JACKO. Yer good man.

MARCUS. Cha course me a good, goodness breed goodness, go in.

DOLE. Him a block yer Ras.

MARCUS. Block . . . goal, cha me win, me win.

JACKO. Good goal.

MARCUS. Goal ter Ras me is now champion warrior, me win, all yer a see how righteousness does triumph over evil.

JACKO. Good game, da was a good goal. Yer want ter play another game?

MARCUS. Nar, nar me no play no more me win.

DOLE. But Marcus yer only win one game ter Ras clart de rules . . .

MARCUS. De rules what rules? Who makes rules? Me Ras clart me win da is all. We no play.

DOLE. Dat en justice man, de man rusty ter Ras, him a just come out, him not proficient, him just a warm up.

JACKO. I do' mind.

ZIPPY. No him right.

MARCUS. Cha me do' defend no title, right away me get me crown first.

ZIPPY. Cha. (*Goes and sits. To* DOLE.) Leave him Ras.

MARCUS. Me champ ter Ras.

JACKO. All right, but a hope yer go give me another game.

MARCUS. Cha sure, sure me give yer plenty game ter Ras, all a dem go be like dat ter Ras.

DOLE. Marcus you is not a righteous man, me say dat now, an me never change it, you is not righteous.

MARCUS. Cha, ne warrior you a Ras clart hypocrite, what you know, me have de blood of Haile Selassie an all dem great warrior a pumping in a veins, blood a true warrior cha. (*Sits with* FRET.)

DOLE *goes and sits with* ZIPPY.

DOLE. Dat man is a . . .

ZIPPY. Cha, left him Ras.

DOLE. Brother man de mind dat Ras, him profess ter be genuine, but him crooked, him a take de wrong path, but him go learn some heavy wisdom wen him come ter me him maker. Do' let him attitude distort yer destiny, ter Ras.

JACKO. Nar is all right. I know guys like him, dey have guys like him inside, dey have ter be big, bigger dan everybody or have more dan everybody else.

DOLE. Him a Lazarus man, is him sores him want ter spread.

JACKO. If he went inside, he see how big he really was, one night a would give him.

DOLE. What it like inside brother man, it tough?

JACKO. Yes it tough, if you tink tings tough outside a prison, it ten time more tough inside, de white screws . . .

DOLE. De is de guards?

JACKO. Yes dem do' like yer at all an if yer black den is worse. Dey do' give yer a chance. Yer have ter ask dem fer everyting, everyting. An de white cons dem come next, dem higher dan yer, dem have tings under control an yer have ter ask dem fer favours too. An every favour yer get yer have ter pay back wid interest, an yer car miss no excuse or yer pay more an more an den everyting yer do have a rule an regulations ter cover it. So all yer guys tink outside hard eh all yer do' know how easy it is . . . take my word fer it, I en going back inside. I make dat pledge de first night I spend, notting go get me inside again. I en care if a man killing me modder I go let him . . .

DOLE. Yer hear dat Zippy.

ZIPPY. Me hear.

DOLE. Like what kinda tings dem do . . . ?

ZIPPY. Cha rest de man nar, yer en see de man en want ter talk . . .

JACKO. Nar is all right, I do' mind, I en mind talking bout it, is . . .

DOLE. Me hear dat is man does fock man.

JACKO. Yes.

DOLE. Me would never let no man get me.

ZIPPY. Cha.

DOLE. Me would kill him first.

JACKO. How much people yer could kill, ten, five, three?

DOLE. All a dem.

ZIPPY. Cha rest yer Ras nar.

DOLE. Me kill all a dem, Ras, me poison dem, me choke dem, me.

ZIPPY. Cha man go way wid dat Ras nar.

JACKO. Yes.

DOLE. Aright, me stop.

SANDY *and* GAIL *come downstairs.*

SANDY. All right who missed me?

MARCUS. Me win Sandy, me win, me is now de reigning champion me beat yer Jacko licks.

SANDY. I see.

MARCUS. Me beat him.

SANDY. Is that true?

JACKO. Yes.

MARCUS. Me say it true yer no have ter ask, you now have ter put up one sign saying Marcus is reigning champion pon wall.

SANDY. All right Marcus, but I still don't believe it. Why don't you write the sign yourself? You'll find some card and the felt-tips upstairs.

MARCUS. Cha champion shouldn't have ter write his own sign.

SANDY. Yes Marcus, but you know exactly what you want to say and how it should look. Make it pretty, use lots of colours.

MARCUS. Cha yes, me use de colours of Ethiopia, de red, de gold an de green ter Ras.

SANDY. Yes.

MARCUS. All right, Cha all yer hypocrite do' know how ter say glorious ting.

SANDY. Why not do it now.

MARCUS. Cha.

SANDY. Dole run upstairs and get the card and pens for me.

DOLE. Me en going Cha, make him go an get him.

SANDY. For me.

DOLE. Cha.

GAIL. I'll go. (*She moves.*)

SANDY. Thanks Gail.

SANDY *calls out to* GAIL.

SANDY. You'll find some in the cupboard.

MARCUS. Cha, dat is power of righteousness.

SANDY. That is downright laziness. I don't know why I put up with it. I must be stupid.

MARCUS. Cha, you is a maiden at de Palace of Kings Marcus ter Ras.

SANDY *goes to* JACKO *and* ZIPPY.

SANDY (*to* JACKO). How are we then, you OK?

JACKO. I'm cool.

SANDY. Zippy's looking after you then.

ZIPPY. Cha, me do' have ter look after nobody him a big man, him look after himself.

GAIL (*at the top of the stairs*). Sandy should I bring all the pens?

SANDY. Christ. (*Calls out.*) Yes bring them.

GAIL *comes down. She gives pens and card to* MARCUS.

GAIL. Here you are.

MARCUS. Tanks sister me go make you second hand maiden to me court.

GAIL. Do you want me to give you some ideas?

MARCUS. No tanks sister, me is one heavy designer wen we start ter use me righteous hand me goodness does come out, me do' need no hypocrite to guide me hand.

GAIL. I only . . .

MARCUS. Cha, me know yer went ter Art School an ting but me is a natural.

GAIL. How do you know, I did . . .

MARCUS. Me know everyting bout you sister, me know yer background yer foreground yer cricket ground and yer football ground, me know all bout you, me know yer people an dey respectable, an yer come from posh school.

GAIL. Not really.

MARCUS. Chas, yes really you a one English black woman, you a not one a we, you look genuine but me know bout you, every ting . . .

GAIL. Really?

MARCUS *starts to draw.*

MARCUS. Yes, me ask me guardian spirit bout you an him tell me everyting cha.

GAIL. Okay, but it's better if you do an outline sketch first.

*She goes to* ZIPPY, SANDY *and* JACKO. *She sits.*

GAIL. That guy is crazy.

SANDY. Who Marcus? No he's not, he's sweet and tender and kind and understanding and totally unselfish, but he's a lazy infuriating bastard. He'll tease the life out of you if you let him.

GAIL. He's doing it all ready. He knows so many things about me, I can't understand how he . . .

SANDY. He's got you worried has he?

GAIL. Yes, he . . . he makes me feel as though we've met before, but I know we haven't.

SANDY. That's Marcus, he's a cunning bastard. That's his best trick. He tries to undermine you and . . .

GAIL. Yes, that's what he does and he's so good at it.

SANDY. You'll get used to it.

GAIL. I hope I don't, it's so scary.

SANDY. He's harmless, a bastard, but harmless.

ZIPPY. Cha him a want somebody put a stop ter his life, dat what.

JACKO. No man, do' say dem ting, dat is trouble, guys like he always run away but dey leave you to answer for dem actions.

SANDY. Marcus is one of life's crosses that's all. We all have to bear him that's all. So (*To* GAIL.) you think you're ready to take over for a little while?

GAIL. Yes, sure.

SANDY. I've got to run Jacko over to his place.

GAIL. I'll be fine.

SANDY. Good. I won't be long but you never know. Come on Jacko let's go. (*Rises.*) Now listen everybody, I'm going to take Jacko to his place and see him settled in, so I'm leaving Gail in charge. I won't be long, so if you need anything see Gail, OK? Be good.

MARCUS. Cha, yer leaving she dem keys me bet.

SANDY. Thank you Marcus, I almost forgot. (*She takes the*

*keys off her neck and gives them to* GAIL.) Don't let him eat you.

GAIL (*laughs*). Go on I'll be fine.

SANDY (*to all*). OK, enjoy yourselves. Come on Jacko.

JACKO (*to all*). See you guys.

ZIPPY. Right, take care.

DOLE. Cool.

MARCUS. Cha.

JACKO *and* SANDY *leave.*

GAIL. OK. I'll be upstairs if you need me.

*She goes upstairs.*

MARCUS. Cha me do' need she Ras. Hey Dole how dis a sound in nineteen-seventy-nine in dis place me de warrior of de Lion of Judea, Emperor Haile Selassie, Lord of Lords, King of Kings, defeated no conquered a fellow call Jacko who was de champion at football. Cha how yer like it?

DOLE. Like me Ras, it a bomba.

MARCUS. Me know yer would like it ter Ras, signed, who a go sign it, Dole?

DOLE. Sign it yer Ras self.

MARCUS. Nar, me have ter have impartial Judge come beat witness, come nar Dole.

DOLE. Go way yer Ras, ask Zippy.

ZIPPY. Cha.

MARCUS. Nar, Fret, nar nar Fret, Sandy me go get Sandy, me do' want no Corporal me go get General, me go get Sandy she a respectable, yes or me could get what she name upstairs, Madame Roberts ter sign, wha yer a say ter dat eh Zippy?

ZIPPY. Cha why you do a rest de girl, de girl come here ter do she ting, yer keep up one set a Ras, what wrong wit yer man, yer keep up. Keep up dis Ras so long.

MARCUS. Dis is part a she job, dis is what she a here for yer tink is like me like she Cha. Man is you a like she, you afraid me power a righteousness capture she eh?

ZIPPY. Yes, me like she know what.

MARCUS. Me do' care, man. Me know dat dat is clear vision me get. Cha, pon she say if we a need she ter come, fer she me need she now, eh me a need yer baby.

ZIPPY. Cha, you a Ras clart satan, you a want tempt somebody into some wilderness but you en go tempt me, you go tempt you Ras self go dey, yer dey already cha.

DOLE. Whatap, good, blow Zippy, him never go recover dat spirit blow, him get him Rod of Correction. Cross him back ter Ras.

MARCUS. Cha all yer a miss all all yer a blow miss because me is a genuine Rasta, no stone car touch me, me have de protection of Daniel, cha, all yer not even Lion. Fret go ask she fer me.

FRET. What?

MARCUS. Go ask she ter sign me record.

FRET. Nar me no go up dem stairs.

DOLE. Cha, even his own man a left him.

ZIPPY. Cha, him get wise.

MARCUS. Hey Mister Zippy you fer want ter go me know yer need one excuse ter need she.

ZIPPY. Excuse me Ras, you a look in mirror ter Ras.

MARCUS. All right me going, me en want see she Ras but she
come fer dis.

MARCUS *goes upstairs*.

DOLE. Cha.

ZIPPY. Dat Ras cha make me a take a walk round de corner.

DOLE. Yer do' want for stay.

ZIPPY. Cha what for him (*Going to the door*.) a go just come
down wit him Ras, talk.

DOLE. Yer a come Fret.

FRET. Yea.

They all leave.

## ACT TWO

*The centre*

MARCUS's *board in a prominent position. A large football on top.* MARCUS *is at the Juke Box dancing.*

ZIPPY, DOLE *and* FRET *run in.*

MARCUS. Cha, whey all yer a go. Me tought all a get lock up.

DOLE. We was up de road.

FRET *pulls out a pair of jeans from under his robe.*

MARCUS. Cha. Jeans a hippy ting. Wha happening up dey?

DOLE. Notting much. Some chick a walk about.

MARCUS. Any a know?

DOLE. Julie en she friend.

MARCUS. Cha, dem a make some style.

DOLE. Dem say dem was coming down, but wen dem hear you was here dem change dem mind.

MARCUS. Cha yer Ras clart mouth lie.

DOLE. It a true dem say you a too weird, dem say you a favour Frankenstein monster, ter Ras clart.

MARCUS. Tell dem me a favour Casanova ter Ras, me d' want dem, me have me own chick.

DOLE. Yer a pull a new chick?

MARCUS. Yes nar.

DOLE. Who?

MARCUS. De new chick, what she name, Gail.

DOLE. You pull she?

MARCUS. Cha, wha so had in dat? It was a easy, me do' let dem night class chick frighten me. Dem brains do' distract me, me cope wid all a dem have ter trew at me.

DOLE. Yer hear dat Zippy?

ZIPPY. Me hear, what dat have ter do wit me? Dat him Ras clart business what him do.

DOLE. Whey she is?

MARCUS. You want it, it a upstairs resting.

DOLE. It good?

MARCUS. Cha it en bad, me make it good.

DOLE. Cha man yer a quick ter Ras.

MARCUS. Cha me give she me power, me make she tink me is wise man, an she car keep no secret from me. Me make she believe me know everyting bout she dat me know all she dark secret, an make she a beg me tell she how me know. But what she en a know is me a read she application letter to Sandy an me know all about she, she believe me have power man, wisdom ter Ras clart me is she savior ter Ras.

DOLE. Cha, you is champion now.

MARCUS. Cha, who want one game? Me feeling strong.

MARCUS *punches the juke box.*

DOLE. Me play yer ter Ras.

DOLE *goes to the game. They play.* SANDY *and* JACKO *enter.*

SANDY. Well I see everything's still normal, football and noise. How's everything?

DOLE. All right. Cha.

SANDY. Zippy?

ZIPPY. All right.

SANDY. Fret?

FRET. Easy.

SANDY. Good then. How's Gail?

MARCUS. She a OK, take me word for it.

*He laughs.*

SANDY. Yes?

DOLE. Him know.

SANDY. I see. Well Marcus, Jacko wants a return match.

MARCUS. Cha me beat him Ras already. Look pon wall we put up me award. Me is champion.

SANDY. Go on, give him a game.

MARCUS. Cha all right make me finish beat Dole first.

SANDY. All right I'll just go and see how Gail is coping.

MARCUS. Cha she coping fine.

SANDY. That's what I'm worried about.

SANDY *goes.* JACKO *sits next to* ZIPPY.

ZIPPY. So how yer fine tings, it change?

JACKO. A bit, a just have ter get use ter some new . . .

SANDY *brings* GAIL *downstairs.* GAIL's *face is bloodied.*

SANDY. For Christ sake Marcus what did you do this for?

MARCUS. Me no do notting.

JACKO. What happen?

SANDY. Marcus you did this. Why for Christ sake did you hit the girl? You had no right to.

MARCUS. Me no hit she.

SANDY. She said you did, look at her, why should she lie?

GAIL. He hit me, he came.

MARCUS. Me no hit you, you fall down, me no hit she, she a fall down, me try an pick she up.

SANDY. Shut up for Christ sake, shut up. What happened Gail?

GAIL. He came upstairs, and started to play his game and tried to get me going putting me in a corner, and wanting to touch me and putting his hands . . .

SANDY. Did he . . . No OK, all right OK, all right, all right, don't cry, don't . . .

MARCUS. Me never touch she.

SANDY. You're a wicked, dirty, vicious bastard that's what you are, I always knew one day . . .

MARCUS. What?

*A beat.*

Go en take she word for it, just because she's a woman, an better educated you tink dem people do' lie.

SANDY. What's that got to do with it? Look at her. (*A beat.*)
Zippy go upstairs and get the First Aid Box, you know where it is.

ZIPPY. Yea. (*He runs upstairs.*)

DOLE. So Marcus you a pull she eh, you a one focking mad Ras clart.

MARCUS. Me no try a touch she, me box she Ras clart. She a tink cause she a educated she a better dan me, but me have 'O' levels just like she, me do' show off da is all an try an talk like de Englishman, and beg him for job in him office. She a black just like me how come she get a job in dis place? She no better, me proud just like she, cha she a Ras clart hypocrite black woman.

*ZIPPY returns with the box.*

SANDY (*takes the box*). Thanks.

*She takes out cotton wool and a small bottle.*

This won't sting. I'll just clean off the blood. There, there, how does that feel, is that better?

GAIL. Yes – Sandy he –

SANDY. Don't worry, it's all right.

GAIL. He's a liar.

SANDY. Yes, yes I know.

MARCUS. Dats right believe she, me know you like woman, you always take woman side in tings.

SANDY. What do you mean by that?

MARCUS. Me know you do' like man, all dem young girls who come here you always nice ter dem always want ter touch dem an get dem ter like you, but dem do' come no more, dem know yer, dem know yer secret, yer do see dem no come.

SANDY. Marcus, you're nasty and dirty and vicious, they don't come because you frighten them away, they know you better than I did. I – I – now go away and take your dirty mind with you.

*MARCUS moves. He sits. The boys go to the football game and play.*

(*to GAIL.*) What do you want to do now? Do you want to go home?

GAIL. No, I want to go to the Police Station.

SANDY. What?

GAIL. I want to report it.

SANDY. Gail, you don't . . .

GAIL. I want to report that nasty vicious thing. I want to report what he did to me.

SANDY. You don't know what will happen.

GAIL. It will show him. He's got to realise he cannot hit a woman, an get away with it.

*She gets up.*

SANDY. Gail, please – (*She sits her down.*) If you go to the Police you know what they'll do? They will come here and take him away, he's already on suspended sentences. He'll go in for sure and what will that prove?

GAIL. It will show him he can't treat people like this and get away with it.

SANDY. He's an animal that's what he is that's how he's been made, that's how he's been treated.

GAIL. Sandy, you . . .

SANDY. I know he's a liar, and vicious. What did you think you were doing when you came here? Did you think you were coming to a kindergarten? These boys are all vicious, not as bad as Marcus but, that's why they're here, that's why society pays us, to keep them away from good clean society, out of trouble, out of prison. That's why this place is open. You know how I had to fight to get you here? If you go to the Police, they'll close us down. We're meant to be qualified to do it, to do their dirty work for them.

GAIL. Sandy.

SANDY. Jacko, you tell her, tell her what it's like . . . tell her what will happen if he goes in.

JACKO. I en involved in dis, I en know what happening.

SANDY. Can't you see what's happened?

JACKO. I en know, I en know.

SANDY. You want him to go inside, you want him to go through what you went through?

JACKO. Why yer asking me? I do' know, me en no judge or jury, do' ask me.

SANDY. Well I'm asking you Gail, I'm begging you. I'll ban him from here. I'll do anything, but don't report him. Believe me that's the worst.

GAIL. I'm going.

*She goes to leave.*

SANDY. Gail, I know Marcus lied, you think I don't? I know what he's like, you think I haven't been jammed in a corner before and had hands all over me? But when I looked in their eyes they were as puzzled as I was and as frightened. They do it, they don't even know why they . . .

GAIL. He hit me, Sandy, he . . .

SANDY. I was just like you when I started here, full of bright ideas. I was going to make it happen. I knew exactly what was needed, but there is a world outside that I can't change. They haven't got a chance, the moment they walk on the street they're guilty, that's why we're here to occupy them, to contain them because society doesn't want to know, not even their parents . . .

JACKO. Dat en true.

SANDY. You went inside right?

JACKO. Yes.

SANDY. Did your Mother visit you?

JACKO. No.

SANDY. Did any of your family visit?

JACKO. No.

SANDY. You told me how nice it would be if your Father came. I have the letters to prove . ...

JACKO. Dat was foolishness. I was too soft. I believe in your fairy story.

SANDY (*to* GAIL). Yes, I let them dress up and fool around and dream about Africa. What else is there? That's all they've got.

JACKO. All dat is foolishness too. Ethiopia is a Marxist country an Haile Selassie is dead an he exploit he own people more dan anybody. Dat en true blackness, blackness is seeing tings de way it is nothing more. Inside, inside prison. I was in prison, but me en know whey all yer was. I read all de time I in dey, everyting, I read about how de National Front an dem terrorising black people an nobody en doing notting, an how dis Rastaman ting saying peace and love an smoking dope an dreaming bout Africa an de Bible, an de National Front attacking people. I car understand all yer. Wha happen, all yer car see, all yer blind? I say wen I come out I go meet de youth fighting back, because de paper en go print dem ting, an I go join dem. But de paper right. Wen I went in people eye was opening, now I come out it close. Wha happen, wha happen ter all yer? We fight de racist in prison. All yer outside, wha all yer do?

MARCUS. What all yer listen ter he for? He en no genuine black man.

JACKO *approaches* MARCUS.

JACKO. So you're going to Ethiopia den?

MARCUS. Sure.

JACKO. What you going ter to do wen you get dere?

MARCUS. Me go do my ting. (*He backs off.*)

JACKO. So you believe in peace an love, eh?

MARCUS. Yes, dat's what de Bible good book say.

JACKO. You love me? (*He pushes* MARCUS.)

MARCUS. Me do' want know . . .

JACKO. Give me some peace and love.

MARCUS. Me do' want no fight man, Sandy, tell him.

SANDY. Jacko . . .

MARCUS. Sandy, tell him. (*He pulls out a blade.*)

SANDY. Marcus, don't.

JACKO. Where your peace an love? Give me a kiss you black
    bastard.

MARCUS. Me warn you.

*He lunges at* JACKO. JACKO *overpowers* MARCUS, *grabs
the knife and holds it against his throat. Then he lets*
MARCUS *go.*

SANDY. Oh my god.

*MARCUS runs out. Music.* ZIPPY *walks out. They all follow*
ZIPPY, *one by one leaving* SANDY *alone on stage.*

*Meetings* was first performed in Britain at the Hampstead Theatre, London, on 25 March 1982, with the following cast:

| | |
|---|---|
| HUGH | Rudolph Walker |
| JEAN | Corinne Skinner-Carter |
| ELSA | Angela Winter |

*Directed by* Mustapha Matura
*Assistant Director* Alby James
*Designed by* Peter Hartwell

*Meetings* had previously been staged at the Phoenix Theatre, New York, in 1981.

**Scene: a kitchen**

*A very large modern table – chairs, smart wall units, labour-saving devices.*

**Morning**

*Man (40–45), HUGH, well-dressed, business suit, tie, reading paper, drinking coffee.*

RADIO. Here is the news, read to you by Gail Ramsingh. The Government has announced a major programme of building that will modernise the country's transport facilities. This will include the national airline, the dock area and a major road building scheme as well as improving existing facilities. The programme is meant to tackle the present large unemployment problem. The entire programme will cost an estimated 15 million dollars and will, for the first time, be co-ordinated by a new computer.

*Wife, JEAN, enters also smartly dressed, (business suit) smoking. Also drinking coffee.*

HUGH. Five per cent, five per cent, he's a joker; if my company aimed for a five per cent increase we'd be bankrupt, what a fool dat man is. He only get de job because he sister is de Prime Minister Personal Assistant.

JEAN. What you talking bout?

HUGH. Davis. De Minister of Finance. So called, de one who car' even count to ten.

JEAN. Oh him.

HUGH. I remember him wen he just leave school, he was

looking fer a job like everybody, now he is in charge a
Finance.

JEAN. Did you interview him?

HUGH. I sat in on it, I voted against him.

JEAN. Why?

HUGH. He wasn't any good, he couldn't en talk properly.

JEAN. I remember now, you say he wear a grey suit wit brown
shoes.

HUGH. Yes. Dat was him.

JEAN. His Mother phoned up Mummy, and asked her ter have
a word wit me, ter have a word wit you, about de job.

HUGH. I do' remember dat.

JEAN. I didn't bodder.

HUGH. Is a good ting, a woulda have ter vote against you too.

JEAN. I agree wit you.

HUGH. Now he is de one us companies have ter depend on, dis
country really in a mess.

JEAN. Yer always say dat.

HUGH. Is true, if it wasn't for de private companies like ours I
do' know what would happen, dey en' have no brains in
Government, all de bright boys in business.

JEAN. An girls.

HUGH. Yes, girls too. I sick a dis Government getting into
trouble an coming an ask us ter get dem outa it, like de water
– de latest joke is dey buy about two hundred big water
pumps, and forget ter buy de pipes ter channel de water, now
dey run ter us can we tell dem where ter get pipes.

JEAN. I heard about dat.

HUGH. How you hear?

JEAN. I was having lunch yesterday wit Jim Allen.

HUGH. What he want?

JEAN. He wants us ter handle his company.

HUGH. Yer going ter?

JEAN. It's worth fifty thousand a year.

HUGH. Dat's good.

JEAN. He told me about it.

HUGH. De joke is, it just so happen we ordered too many pipes for Logan, an so we had dem lying about, so I said to de Permanent Secretary: How urgent? He say, yesterday. Yer see, I know him, we went ter school together, he come de ole boy wit me: Look Hugh yer have ter help me out, pardner. Is he forget ter order de pipes, an before de Minister find out he have ter find dem.

   JEAN *laughs*.

So a say ninety thousand.

JEAN. What he say?

HUGH. He say, tanks boy, a know a could count on yer.

   *They laugh*.

JEAN. Where dey for?

HUGH. It's dat new reservoir in Talparo.

JEAN. Yer mean de one dat go put a end ter all we water problems?

HUGH. Yes.

JEAN. Yer know some girls in de office en' have a shower in years.

HUGH. I believe you.

JEAN. Oh well a must tell dem.

HUGH. Tell dey boyfriend too, is I helping dem ter keep clean.

JEAN. What you have on terday?

HUGH. Meetings, is meetings all morning, dis afternoon a going ter visit a site, an later we háve some more meetings. What about you?

JEAN. Is de same, I have some meetings in de morning, den a work lunch.

HUGH. Wit Jim?

JEAN. Yes, den some more meetings, all afternoon.

HUGH. What about dinner?

JEAN. Car' make it, I'm meeting an American to sound out, representing dem down here, de cigarette company a told yer about.

HUGH. So what I go eat?

JEAN. I do' know, find someting yer could eat at de Country Club, or someting.

HUGH. I getting tired a dat yer know.

JEAN. A what?

HUGH. Eating out, somebody else cooking, in a club or somewhere, I would like to eat in my own house fer a change.

JEAN. Well I do' have de time ter cook dat's all, yer know dat.

HUGH. I know, but look at dis kitchen, it have everyting in it except food, and dat is what a kitchen is for, my modder used ter spend all day in she kitchen.

JEAN. I en' yer modder.

HUGH. I know dat.

JEAN. Yer modder never wen ter college.

HUGH. No.

JEAN. Yer modder never had a job, a job dat was demanding.

HUGH. No.

JEAN. She only had you, and yer father, and de resta allyer to cook an clean for, so she could afford ter spend all day in a kitchen.

HUGH. Look, I en' criticising, or complaining yer know, I understand.

JEAN. What yer doing den?

HUGH. I'm just saying how nice it would be ter eat some real old Trinidad food instead a chicken and chips, or burgers an macaroni.

JEAN. Look, wen we get married I told yer, I was going ter work an earn my own money, I do' want no man keeping me, yer hear.

HUGH. Right.

JEAN. Look at Shirley Loo Kong, wen Henry walk out an leave she didn't even have a penny to she name, not even a car, she had to go back home to she modder with four children. She modder didn't even know what ter do wit she, de old woman tought she marry off all she children and she go take life easy, an suddenly Shirley turn up on she doorstep wid four children, dat en' go happen ter me yer know.

HUGH. Yer tink I go leave yer?

JEAN. I do' know, but I en' taking no chances, I too big to go an live wit my mother.

*A beat.*

HUGH. I do' know bout you. But I remember eating good food, tings I never taste nowadays, tings I grow up on, like cocoo an saltfish, an ochro, an yam an dasheen.

JEAN. I grow up on dat, we had a servant call Flora, dats all she used ter cook, but times different. Flora dead an gone.

HUGH. I was in a meeting yesterday, an it was a boring one, an I started tinking about all de old tings we used ter eat, an yer know what?

JEAN. No.

HUGH. I got up, an said excuse me, I have ter call New York.

JEAN. Yes, so . . .

HUGH. An I went out to de corner, an dey had dis old woman wid a basket selling mangoes an pomcété, an I buy ten dollar mangoes zabico.

JEAN. Mango.

HUGH. Yes, an I eat evry single one, even de soft ones, I never taste mango so sweet in me life.

JEAN. I do' believe yer.

HUGH. It's true.

JEAN. You leave a meeting to go an eat mango?

HUGH. Yes.

JEAN. I must tell Jim bout dat.

HUGH. I do' care, I never feel so happy for a long time. It was just like going to school again.

JEAN. Yer should a wear short pants.

HUGH. I didn't care one shit, an yer know what?

JEAN. Yer was sick afterwards.

HUGH. No. She – de old woman.

JEAN. What.

HUGH. Every day she go bring mango, an pomarac an downes, an governor plum an chenette fer me.

JEAN. I do' believe dis.

HUGH. Is true, a have a standing order she promise, I going ter be her best customer.

JEAN. But nobody do' eat dem tings anymore.

HUGH. I do. I go start a new ting.

JEAN. Yer crazy.

HUGH. No, forget yer apples an grapes, dem fruit is what we grow up on, dey is what give we de brains ter become what we become, so why stop eating dem because we grow up, dey grow here like us. Apples and grapes do' grow here.

JEAN. Well if it do' make yer sick I do' see why not, all I remembered is mango used ter bring me out in spots.

HUGH. Dat was adolescence.

JEAN. Well, I do' know.

HUGH. An I en' finishing wit fruits, I want ter eat all de old foods I grow up on.

JEAN. Where yer go find dem? I en' cooking.

HUGH. A servant, we find a servant who could cook dem.

JEAN. You know how hard it is ter find a servant nowadays.

HUGH. Yes.

JEAN. Well you find one, yer lucky if yer find any girl nowadays who want ter work servant, an dat's if yer could afford dem.

HUGH. I know.

JEAN. An dat's if dey could do de job, as well, I hear so much stories.

HUGH. I know.

JEAN. I wish yer luck den, yer have ter find some girl from one a de small islands who want a work permit ter stay here.

HUGH. I know.

JEAN. An after she get she residence, she going ter work in a factory.

HUGH. Yes.

JEAN. Long ago yer could get a young girl from de country but not any more.

HUGH. I know, I go find one though, one who could cook all de old foods, I do' care if she do' clean, I do' care how much she cost, what is de point a making money if yer car' get a benefit from it.

JEAN. Yer call eating old food, benefit.

HUGH. Yes, it benefit me, I felt so good eating long ago an I want dat feeling again, if she could cook dat's what matters.

JEAN. Well boy you is someting.

HUGH. It's what I want, you wanted yer own Mercedes, yer get you own Mercedes, you wanted a swimming pool . . .

JEAN. You use it too.

HUGH. Yes, I like it, but is what you wanted, everyting in dis house is what you wanted, yer even get a fur coat. A fur coat is de West Indies.

JEAN. Dat's fer wen I go to New York.

HUGH. I do' mind, I en' complaining but dis is what I want, an you tink is such a big ting.

JEAN. I en' tink is such a big ting, a just surprise dat is all, I tought maybe yer like a new set a golf clubs or . . .

HUGH. No.

JEAN. Yer birthday coming up an I was tinking . . .

HUGH. Nope I know what I want.

JEAN. Or a weekend in Miami.

HUGH. Nope.

JEAN. My treat yer know.

HUGH. No, I know what I want.

JEAN. Well, I could ask de girls in de office if dey know bout anybody.

HUGH. Yes, you look, an I go look, we must find one, dis country still must have people who know how ter eat an cook good food.

JEAN. Well a go try.

HUGH. Dat's de birthday present I want, I want somebody who could cook red fish in butter with yellow gravy in onion, an mash de yam in butter wit a fork, an I could see de rows where de fork went, an a want ter eat de fish eye last, dat's brains. Dat gives yer de brains an some green fig as well, dat give yer iron, dat's what my mother used to say.

JEAN. All right, all right den.

HUGH. Yer see what a talking bout?

JEAN. A see.

HUGH. Right, a have ter go, or else de old woman go tink I let she down. Where is my briefcase?

JEAN. By yer foot.

HUGH. Tanks, right, have a good day an I'll see yer. If I awake yer could tell me how yer get on.

JEAN. Wid what.

HUGH. De girl.

JEAN. Yes, yes.

HUGH *kisses* JEAN's *hand.*

HUGH. Bye, bye den.

JEAN. Yes, bye.

HUGH *leaves.*

JEAN *goes to the phone in the kitchen, dials.*

Hello Gloria, is Jean, I all right. Is Mum dere? Yes, call her 'fer me. What you doing home? . . . Hello Mum, yes I all right. No everyting okay. What Gloria doing home? Dat's what she say. De last time, she car' keep blaming de teachers, tell she I say dem private school fees have ter come from somewhere, an I en' paying no fees if she en' goin ter school. Teacher my ass, all teacher like dat you tell she I say ter go, yes, all right, all right. Look a want yer to do someting fer me. No, it en' go kill yer is just – you listening? – good. Hugh want me ter find a servant girl, no ter cook, somebody does clean already, yes. I do' have ter tell yer everyting, yer know how busy I am, yes de job. Look, Hugh say he want ter eat old food, an I tought you might know somebody, yer understand. No a do' want a cook book, no, I do' want ter know how to do it, look a have ter go now, yer remember what a ask yer, just somebody ter cook, no, no cleaning involved, an tell Gloria get she ass ter school. Yes, only if yer hear anyting, yes, a see yer.

*She puts down the phone – dials again.*

Hey Beverly child, I all right, like a tiger, yes, I saw him. He look a bit soft, not my type, no yer joking, no I tought is only French men like dat, true, all night, yer need a holiday now, yes.

Look Beverly, I looking fer a servant girl. No not for me I do' swing dat way, no child, not in a million years. Hugh, de man, suddenly decide he want somebody ter cook, yes cook fer him.

You keep you' tail quiet, I could look after myself darling, I en' get a complaint once. What happen, yer French man soft? Yer too greedy dat's what. A have a Yankee fer yer, if yer behave yerself, fortyish, Robert Redfordish, blue eyes, blonde streaks, de works. If yer in Blue Room ter night yer go' see him, but do' try notting wen I ready ter let yer have im, a let yer know. (*She laughs.*)

Seriously if yer know bout anybody let me know. No child, I have ter take it where I get it, yes, okay.

*She puts down the phone, picks up her bag, cigarettes – leaves.*

**The next morning**

HUGH *is sitting reading a newspaper.* JEAN *enters.*

JEAN. Morning. (*She kisses his head.*)

HUGH. Bonjour.

JEAN. Any coffee?

HUGH. In de pot, Marie say we should drink cocoa.

JEAN. What, who is Marie?

HUGH. De old woman, de old woman a was telling yer bout.

JEAN. Oh, she, yes, a forget, yes.

HUGH. Ah asked her.

JEAN. Yes. What, sorry?

HUGH. A asked her what she had in de morning fer breakfast.

JEAN. Yes.

HUGH. She say she do' have no breakfast, all she have in de mornings is a cup of cocoa wit coconut, an salt sprinkled on it an a hops bread wit piece a salt fish.

JEAN. Yes – yer want any toast? (*Putting bread in the toaster.*)

HUGH. No – yer wasn't listening ter me or what?

JEAN. I listening, but we do' have any a dat.

HUGH. So a don't want any toast.

JEAN. Okay a heard yer de first time.

HUGH. How did yer meetings go?

JEAN. Good, good, very well, Rick . . .

HUGH. Who's Rick?

JEAN. The American feller.

HUGH. Yes.

JEAN. We definitely going to handle all de promotion side of de launch.

HUGH. Yes.

JEAN. He bringing out a new tobacco.

HUGH. What is it?

JEAN. It's purely scientifically grown, but wid dis special chemical added; fer de tropics, it's a secret, de chemical, de scientist been working on it fer years. Rick say he do' even know what it is.

HUGH. Yes.

JEAN. Low tar, low risk, everyting, specially designed to meet all health requirements, yer want ter try one, he give me a carton to try.

HUGH. Marie says cigarettes is all paper, she say is paper yer smoking.

JEAN. Well, even de paper is specially grown to . . .

HUGH. She say she does just get a tobacco leaf, an dry it an just roll it an smoke it, she say dat is de ting ter smoke.

JEAN. Yer want one?

HUGH. No tanks.

JEAN. I'm very excited about dis account. Yer realise dis is de first one I going ter see all de way through, from concept to creation?

HUGH. Yes.

JEAN. From de initial stage to de launch.

HUGH. Yes.

JEAN. I've got so many ideas, I'm bursting, wen we finish, if dis country do' know what Luna is, a go shoot meself.

HUGH. What is Luna?

JEAN. De cigarette.

HUGH. Oh.

JEAN. Why is so important, is we is de first.

HUGH. What?

JEAN. We, is de real market dey launching, it en' even available in America yet, dey went in fer a huge population research programme, an after dey feed de information into de computer, guess where come up first? Trinidad, we, yer could beat dat, little old Trini . . . who would believe dat anybody know about we, much less a big computer. Rick showed me a picture of it, it take up a whole room.

HUGH. But we are in all the financial reviews as a growth economy, per capita income so . . .

JEAN. Yes, but dey choose us, ter launch it on, so if we suceeed de whole world go come after, we go set de pattern fer everywhere.

HUGH. Yes.

JEAN. Yes, yer see how important it is that people like it.

HUGH. Yes.

JEAN. Rick say is a big day fer Trinidad an I agree wit him.

HUGH. What time yer came in? It must a been late.

JEAN. Yes, a didn't wake yer, a didn't even know what time it was, it was so late, we spend de whole evening outlaying plans, a just lose all idea a time. He was hitting me with a idea, an I was hitting him back with one, it was a real ping pong match, if yer had seen yer girl, yer woulda been so proud a she, a more dan hold me own.

HUGH. Yes.

JEAN. At first a register he had some doubts about me, down here. Yer know, small island mentality, yer know how some a dem is, dey come down here an tink we soft, but wen a start ter hit him yer coulda see him change, an start ter fight back,

ter capture ground, de man shut up an just start ter listen. It
turn out I know more bout de cigarette dan him, an wen a
tell him, Luna means moon an how it go appeal ter de
woman buyers, he almost choke on de rum punch.

HUGH. So yer went for a drink?

JEAN. Of course, dat is de best way ter do busines. Yes, a had
him eating out me hands, yer know how we finish up?

HUGH. No.

JEAN. Drinking champagne.

HUGH. Why?

JEAN. Ter clinch de deal, an guess who order it, me. He say he
woulda order it but he didn't know we had it down here so a
show him, we have everyting in Trini – an we know how ter
do it in style, a really show him.

HUGH. Yes, good, good.

JEAN. What about you, how your meetings go?

HUGH. Good, good, a saw Marie.

JEAN. What a mean –

HUGH. A know, Marie was dere.

JEAN. What you mean in de meeting?

HUGH. Yes.

JEAN. What.

HUGH. I took her.

JEAN. De old woman who sell de tings?

HUGH. Yes, why not.

JEAN. No reason it just . . .

HUGH. It was my idea, she know a lot dat woman, she pass
   through a lot.

JEAN. But how you could carry a woman like dat in a meet – a
   business . . .

HUGH. She came ter de office, I bring her up, if I could see
   where she work, why she can see where I work, eh, what is
   de difference?

JEAN. De difference is work, one is work de odder is . . .

HUGH. What?

JEAN. Look, me en' have notting against de woman yer know, I
   like talking ter dem old people, but dey en' know notting
   about . . . look . . . what de people at de meeting say?

HUGH. Notting.

JEAN. Yer mean dey didn't ask who she is?

HUGH. No.

JEAN. Dey didn't ask what she doin dere?

HUGH. No.

JEAN. Well.

HUGH. She sit down next ter me with she basket.

JEAN. An what?

HUGH. She en' say notting, wen de meeting finish we discuss
   tings.

JEAN. Like what?

HUGH. Like, if she tink Ronnie was a good engineer.

JEAN. Who, Ronnie Look Hong?

HUGH. Yes.

JEAN. But he is de best engineer in Trinidad, in de whole Caribbean. Everybody know dat, I do' understand what going on, you take a woman off de street an bring she in a business meeting.

HUGH. She en' a woman, she is Marie.

JEAN. I en' care what she name is, an asking she if de most brilliant engineer is good.

HUGH. What wrong in dat?

JEAN. I . . . you want . . .

HUGH. De trouble wit Trinidadians is we accept everyting people tell we. Who say Ronnie Look Hong is de best engineer we ever had, eh? All somebody have ter do is come down here wit one set a certificate, an we believe dem. Who say dey en' forged eh? We do' know, so de ting ter do is ter get an objective view. A outsider who knows.

JEAN. Dat old woman know bout engineering?

HUGH. No, but she know bout people, she know if somebody lying or not, dat's it, dat's what she know.

JEAN. What she say, what she . . . ?

HUGH. She say, he was a good engineer.

JEAN. So what, anybody . . . ?

HUGH. Yea but she didn't say he was de best, or greater dan anybody else.

JEAN. All right . . .

HUGH. Yer see what a getting at?

JEAN. Yes.

HUGH. Dat woman know so much ting, an she en' read it in no book, is ting she learn herself an tings dat was handed down ter her. A was coughing an she tell me what bush ter boil, an prepare an how ter drink it ter get rid a de cough. Wen she see I en' know bout bush, a tell she, she say she go bring some tomorrow, she go pick it she self, she have it growing in she back yard . . .

JEAN. What about yer visit ter de site?

HUGH. She liked dat.

JEAN. Yer took her?

HUGH. Yes, a tell yer we spend de whole day.

JEAN. Yer didn't tell me dat, why?

HUGH. Well we did, she like de drive yer know, she never drive in a private car before.

JEAN. No.

HUGH. All de years dat woman live she never travel in a private car. Wen de meeting finish it was too late fer her ter go an start selling, anyhow she didn't have notting ter sell. I eat all she had.

JEAN. In de meeting.

HUGH. Yes, so we went ter de site, she really enjoyed de drive. All along de way she was telling me tings bout who had houses dere in de old days, what life was like on de old plantations, amazing tings bout de trees. Yer know pesie vine is not just ter make whip, if yer boil an mash de leaves it good fer fever.

JEAN. No.

HUGH. Or yer put alloes on a boil it would go away.

JEAN. No, Hugh how was tings at de site?

HUGH. We pass through Valsyn.

JEAN. Yes, yer drop in on Peter?

HUGH. No, no, notting like dat, Marie showed me de exact spot where de first rebellion of de slaves took place in Trinidad, de exact spot, her grandmother showed it ter her. De slaves attacked a British post an soldiers, horses, everyting was chopped up, an de slaves went into de hills. She pointed ter de bush tracks where dey went, if yer do' know where ter look yer car' see it, but it dere between all de big houses. She told me how de slaves prepared fer weeks de attack, an how one Saturday dey deliberately work late so dat wen dey had ter hand in dey cutlass nobody was dere ter take dem, an early de Sunday morning dey creep up, an wit one chop all de sentries was down an de commander in de bed didn't know what hit him, he en' even wake up. Dey sharpen dem cutlass all night, she say she grandmother tell she de noise was de most frightening ting she ever hear. An yer know someting?

JEAN. No.

HUGH. De same spot de reservoir going ter be, is where de British poisoned de water.

JEAN. What?

HUGH. Yes, dey couldn't catch de rebels, dey couldn't go up in de hills, but dey know dey had to come down fer water, an dey poison de pool, yer didn't know dat, eh?

JEAN. No.

HUGH. De man and woman died, with blood coming out dey mouths, but dey drink first, an dey never let de children drink, wen dey know, dey make sure all a dem make sure de children didn't drink, dey sent dem higher up de stream ter drink. Wen de children come back everybody was dead, she grandmother was dere. Wen Marie get out de car she went into de pool wit some bush an was just beating de water wit it, like a child, beating it an scolding it!

JEAN. Was Francis dere?

HUGH. Oh yes, he was dere.

JEAN. Did he like de pipes?

HUGH. De pipes?

JEAN. De pipes he wanted, was he pleased ter have dem?

HUGH. Yes, he was pleased. Yer shoulda see him, he almost dive in an went fer a swim wen a tell him he could have dem fer eighty thousand.

JEAN. Eighty? But yesterday you say yer was giving it ter him fer ninety. What happen yer let him beat yer down?

HUGH. No, it do' matter, it do' matter.

JEAN. What happen?

HUGH. It was Marie idea.

JEAN. De old woman, what she have ter do wit it? You mean you let dat old woman decide what price you ask dat idiot fer, you let she negotiate . . . ?

HUGH. Ah say she was dere, I didn't let she negotiate, she listen, she was dere.

JEAN. A hear you, yer take she.

HUGH. Yes, an she say how de water go help de people in de area. An how it go help dem grow better vegetables and rice an fruit an . . .

JEAN. So you drop de price.

HUGH. A didn't drop it.

JEAN. But yer said ninety, if it so important yer shoulda say a hundred.

HUGH. No.

JEAN. Yer lose ten thousand.

HUGH. No, we make seventy, dey cost us ten.

JEAN. Yer coulda make ninety clear, I do' understand yer, you
fall on yer head, yer let Francis off ten thousand, because
some old woman show you what people could do wit water.
Yer know de size of Francis budget?

HUGH. Yes.

JEAN. You know Francis allocation fer dis year was increased
ter eighty-seven million?

HUGH. Yes.

JEAN. An dat's just fer special projects.

HUGH. Yes. Marie said de water is more important dan
anyting, it must flow wit pipes or no pipes, it must run, an if
not it go waste, an dry up. We have ter move it, so fresh
water could come in all de time, we making seventy
thousand.

JEAN. Yes.

HUGH. Clear.

JEAN. Yes.

HUGH. Dat woman is someting.

JEAN. Yes, yer should put her on de board.

HUGH. I asked her.

JEAN. What!

HUGH. I did, she refused.

JEAN. Yes – Hugh?

HUGH. What?

JEAN. You know what yer doing?

HUGH. Yes, an I want ter do more. What is de point a making money by itself? It . . .

JEAN (*up*). Look, I go be late, I have a lot a meetings terday, contracts ter see about. What about you?

HUGH. I have a lot as well too.

JEAN. What about dinner? I could arrange fer us ter meet tonight.

HUGH. Oh by de way, do' worry bout looking fer a girl.

JEAN. Why.

HUGH. Marie get one fer me.

JEAN. Who, she . . . ?

HUGH. Her grandaughter.

JEAN. Yes.

HUGH. Yes. A told her a was looking fer somebody an she have a grandaughter who looking fer a job, an she could cook, Marie teach her.

JEAN. A glad ter hear dat.

HUGH. She coming terday, so do' worry bout dinner, come home early an eat some real food.

JEAN. Yes, a go do dat, bout seven.

HUGH. Yer go see what a was talking about, yer go see.

JEAN. Yes, you mustn't be late either.

HUGH (*looks at his watch*). Oh, Christ, no . . .

JEAN. A see yer den. (*She goes.*)

  HUGH *goes to the telephone, dials.*

HUGH. Let me talk to Jam Singh right, Jam Singh. Who? Let

him wait. No, I'll see him after lunch. Look a old woman coming ter see me, she should have a young girl wit her. She dere? Ah, well, look show dem in me ofice, an tell dem I on de way, an ter wait fer me, a coming now. Yes. Make sure dey stay, yer hear me, dis is important, okay, good, a leaving now. (*He puts down the telephone. He goes.*)

**Evening, the same day**

*With HUGH, in the kitchen, is a young woman, ELSA, 18–20, dressed in a floral print dress. Her head is tied.*

HUGH. An dis cupboard is where we keep de Hoover an cleaning tings.

ELSA. Yer do' have brooms?

HUGH. Just fer de outside yard.

ELSA. A cookea.

HUGH. No, no, is a long time I en' hear somebody talk about cookea.

ELSA. Dat is all right.

HUGH. Yes, but yer do' have ter worry bout cleaning or anyting, a just showing yer.

ELSA. Is okay.

HUGH. An dis one is more important.

ELSA. Yes.

HUGH. All de cooking pots we keep in here.

ELSA. Dey look new.

HUGH. Yes. (*He takes one out.*) Brand new, we never used dem.

ELSA. Yer have any iron pots?

HUGH. Yes, a tink we have one my mother gave us, wait, is somewhere in de back here, yes a have it, here . . .

ELSA. Dat's new too.

HUGH. Yes, a forget we had it.

ELSA. You never cook?

HUGH. No.

ELSA. Yer modder never teach yer?

HUGH. No.

ELSA. Yer wife never cook?

HUGH. No, she know how ter dough, but no she never.

ELSA. So how allyer eat?

HUGH. Outside, we get food outside, dat's why we need you, we busy you see.

ELSA. Dat is all right.

HUGH. Cookea broom, I forget all bout cookea, dat is de long middle of de leaf, an yer get it wen yer peel off de dry coconut leaf.

ELSA. Yes, is a good broom.

HUGH. An yer tie a lot together.

ELSA. Yes.

HUGH. I remember as a boy, I used ter tief my modder cookea ter make kites, yer know we used ter bend de cookea ter made de frames.

ELSA. Me little brodders does still do it.

HUGH. An we used ter break razor blade, an put it in de kite tail ter cut odder fellas thread.

ELSA. Yer never used ter make manja.

HUGH. Manja, manja, oh yes, manja, a forget all bout manja, an zwill.

ELSA. Yer grind up de glass bottle, an mix it in a paste an put it on yer thread, an wen yer rub it on odder people thread, it cut it.

HUGH. Yes, manja, how I could forget bout manja, yes, an zwill.

ELSA. You used ter fly a lot a kite den.

HUGH. Yes, a lot, every Sunday during kite season we go in de Savannah an spend all day flying kite, an de big men an dem used ter bring dey mad bull, an fly dem too.

ELSA. My uncle does fly mad bull.

HUGH. I remember I used ter be fraid a dem, because dey was so big, an used ter make so much noise, an people used ter say if a little boy hold on ter a mad bull string it would pull yer up in de sky wit it, yer see.

ELSA. Yes a hear dat too.

HUGH. Yes.

ELSA. Yer big enough ter fly one now.

HUGH. Yes – right, in dose two drawers is de knife an forks an spoons, an tings, an in dat cupboard we keep cups an ting.

ELSA. Okay.

HUGH. An dat is de fridge dere, fer keeping tings fresh.

ELSA. Okay.

HUGH. Now we come ter de special tings.

ELSA. Yes.

HUGH. Dat is a mixer, yer see yer switch it on, an it start mixing.

ELSA. Yer do' have a clay bowl?

HUGH. Eh.

ELSA. Dat is what I use ter mix anyting, wit just a woodspoon, a just take it, an mix.

HUGH. All right, if dat is what yer want a give yer some money ter get one.

ELSA. Yer do' have ter give me money fer dat, we have plenty home, next time I go home I go bring mine wit me.

HUGH. All right, den, dis is de coffee grinder, yer switch dat on too an yer put de coffee in here.

ELSA. Dat's all right, but I have a mortar an pestle in me bag, dat I go use.

HUGH. Yes, all right, well look a was going ter show yer how ter operate de dishwasher but you use anyting you want to, whatever suit you and you happy wit.

ELSA. I happy wit everyting.

HUGH. Good, good.

ELSA. What's dat?

HUGH. Dat's a washing-machine.

ELSA. Fer clothes?

HUGH. Yes, but you en' go be doing any a dat.

ELSA. Okay.

HUGH. I just want you to concentrate in de cooking an do'

mind bout anyting, whatever you want ter cook or yer feel like eating, you do it, I go give you money everyday ter get it.

ELSA. Every day?

HUGH. Yes.

ELSA. All right den.

HUGH. An dis is de microwave oven.

ELSA. Yes.

HUGH. A suppose you used ter a coal pot?

ELSA. Yes.

HUGH. Well dis is de stove, is gas, like a kinda coal pot, is de same fire, hold dis here an yer just turn de knob an de flame come up an yer could adjust it, so, like dat.

ELSA. Yes.

HUGH. Wen me wife come home, her name is Jean by de way, she go show you yer room, an explain everyting ter you.

ELSA. Dat is all right.

HUGH. Is a nice room, is right next ter de kitchen.

ELSA. Yes, is one ting I do' understand.

HUGH. Yes, what? Anyting you ask me an I go explain it ter yer.

ELSA. What kinda food you go want ter eat?

HUGH. What you eat, Creole food, real Creole food, Marie yer grandmodder didn't explain ter you?

ELSA. No.

HUGH. Yes, I tell her I want ter eat all de old food.

ELSA. All she said, was dis man wanted somebody ter look

after him, an he would make sure I have somewhere ter live, an food ter eat.

HUGH. Yes, dat is it.

ELSA. Oh . . .

HUGH. An yer could cook.

ELSA. Yes.

HUGH. Well dat is de way I want looking after, yer see I want ter eat de old food . . .

ELSA. Like saltfish bull-gou?

HUGH. Yes, dat is it.

ELSA. An souse an cucumber?

HUGH. Yes, Sunday mornings.

ELSA. An pelau?

HUGH. Yes, on Mondays, wit beef left over from Sunday.

ELSA. An chipp-chipp soup?

HUGH. But you can get chipp-chipp in town?

ELSA. Yes, I know a place in George Street.

HUGH. Yes den, chipp-chipp soup.

ELSA. Dey does come in evry morning, fresh from Manzanilla.

HUGH. Good, good.

ELSA. By truck.

HUGH. Good, yes. What bout co-coo? Yer could make dat.

ELSA. Wit ochro an ting.

HUGH. Yes.

ELSA. Yes.

HUGH. An green fig.

ELSA. Yes, how yer like it dry or slippery?

HUGH. Slippery.

ELSA. Dat is de best way.

HUGH. What bout dumplins, yer could make dumplins?

ELSA. In soup.

HUGH. Yes, in soup.

ELSA. What kinda soup?

HUGH. Beef soup, fish soup.

ELSA. What bout cow heel soup an turtle soup, yer like dem too?

HUGH. Yes, yes, a could . . .

ELSA. What about cornbeef dumplins?

HUGH. A do' know dat.

ELSA. Yer cook de cornbeef in onions an stuff it inside de dumplins an boil de dumplins, dat's nice too.

HUGH. Yes, yes, all dem kinda tings.

ELSA. Yes, what bout black pudding, yer like dat too?

HUGH. Yes. Yes, on a Saturday afternoon, good, good.

ELSA. An breadfruit how yer like dat?

HUGH. Plenty, plenty.

ELSA. Roast or boil?

HUGH. Both, both.

ELSA. Well so is all right den, so dat is all?

HUGH. Yes, dat is it.

ELSA. Well I could do dat den, Mister Hugh you remind me a uncle I used ter have, I never see a man who like he food so.

HUGH. Yes, good. Good, is dem kinda tings I want.

ELSA. An he was bad, he was always causing trouble, an mischief.

HUGH. Is dem kinda people we do' have in de Island anymore.

ELSA. Yes he dead, a truck knock him over, but he was weak before dat. He went for a sea bath an he stay too long an come out wit a chill, an all de bush we give him ter drink en' help, an den de truck come round de corner an hit im.

HUGH. Yes.

ELSA. A miss him, he was nice, he used to whistle all de time, whatever he was doing he'd be whistling.

HUGH. Yes.

ELSA. If he was walking yer would hear im coming up de road whistling, or sitting in de back yard, de birds used ter whistle an he used ter answer dem back, just like a bird, he was a bird.

HUGH. Yes, I remember fellers used ter whistle a lot, I remember de first guy who teach me ter whistle, how ter keep in de wind an ter let it out, I en' whistle in years.

ELSA. Yer should, is good fer yer, his favourite was a slow Italian tune -- Come back ter someting . . .

HUGH. Sorrento.

ELSA. Someting like dat, a tink dat is it.

HUGH. Is dis. (*He whistles.*)

ELSA. Yes, yes, a always used ter ask fer dat, an he used ter hold de notes long, long, den let it go, an a used ter sway just a Gru-Gru-Bef, Palm.

HUGH. Yes, I remember Gru-Gru-Bef too, I used to suck a Gru-Gru-Bef all day.

ELSA. Yes, dey last long.

HUGH. Yes, one more ting.

ELSA. Yes?

HUGH. Marie say anyting about money – yer salary?

ELSA. No, all my granmodder tell me is . . .

HUGH. Yes, well yer go get a hundred an fifty dollars a month.

ELSA. Fer cooking?

HUGH. Is not enough? All right a go make it two hundred, how is dat?

ELSA. No, a didn't mean it wasn't enough, a mean, a didn't want no money as well as somewhere ter live an food ter eat.

HUGH. Or, but it do' matter I want ter pay yer as well, I want ter.

ELSA. All right den.

HUGH. Dat's all right wit you?

ELSA. Yes.

HUGH. Yer happy wit dat?

ELSA. Yes, I always happy.

HUGH. Yes, if anyting boddering you, you come an tell me yer hear.

ELSA. Notting do' bodder me Mister Hugh.

HUGH. All right den. An feel at home, if yer want ter use de pool or anyting, feel welcome, Elsa.

*The sound of coughing.* JEAN *enters.*

JEAN. Hello (*She kisses* HUGH's *head*.) everybody.

HUGH. Jean, dis is Elsa.

JEAN. Hello Elsa.

ELSA. Hello Miss Jean.

JEAN. Yer know me name already.

ELSA. Mister Hugh tell me.

JEAN. So you is de one who go do all dis fantastic cooking eh?

ELSA. Yes.

JEAN. A hope yer come good.

ELSA. Yes Miss Jean.

JEAN. Well we do' care how good yer is as long as yer could cook. Yer could cook?

ELSA. Yes.

JEAN. Good, because yer was so hard to fine, yer know how much people I ask, nobody could suggest anyting (*She coughs*.) an suddenly my husband fine you, you is a miracle. Yer hear dat girl?

ELSA. Yes.

JEAN. Dat is a nice name Elsa.

ELSA. Yes.

JEAN. Well girl, if you know how my husband build you up, yer have a lot ter carry. Yes, so he show yer around an ting?

HUGH. Yes I explain everyting.

JEAN. A see, as yer could see girl, we en' no stylish couple yer know, we does live we life as we know it. So we en' want no formal ting, we en' have no time fer dat.

ELSA. Yes.

JEAN. We go curse an carry on as dough yer en' here. Yer se what ah mean?

ELSA. Yes Miss Jean.

JEAN. Because we en' have no time ter worry bout notting. (*She coughs.*)

HUGH. You getting a cold.

JEAN. No, a tink someting stick in me troat. (*She clears it.*)

HUGH. Maybe, Elsa could give yer someting fer it.

ELSA. I could . . .

JEAN. Nar, nar, is just a tickle, yer could make me a drink, yer know how to do dat.

HUGH. What yer want, scotch or rum?

JEAN. A martini.

HUGH *makes drinks.*

Nar is all right, do' worry child – now yer do' have ter worry bout me. Sometimes I go eat, sometimes I en' go eat, but is he yer have ter keep happy, he is de one who worried bout he food.

ELSA. Yes Miss Jean.

JEAN. A must say yer wasn't what a had in mind, yer look so young.

HUGH. De only ting a didn't do is ter show her her room.

JEAN. What, yer getting slow. Is he old age catching up on him, do' mind me girl I like ter tease people, I go show yer, yer bring yer tings wit yer?

ELSA. Yes.

JEAN *and* ELSA *go off.*
JEAN *returns –*

JEAN. Lord a needed dat. (*She coughs.*)

HUGH. What yer tink.

JEAN. Bout she, she's a nice girl, I tink yer dam lucky ter fine she, an if she could cook yer all right.

HUGH. Yes.

JEAN. A must say dat is a load off my mind. Yer know how much people I phone up, all a dem laugh at me. You wait till I tell dem you fine one.

HUGH. Yes.

JEAN. Dey go say: How child? Where child? Yer go se dem.

HUGH. Yer tink she go like it here?

JEAN. She go be all right, man, what wrong wit yer, she get a nice house ter stay in. An all she have ter do is cook, she bound ter like it. Dem country girls en' stupid yer know. An yer paying she too.

HUGH. Yes.

JEAN. How much yer tell she?

HUGH. Two hundred a month.

JEAN. Well den you en' have notting ter worry about. (*She coughs.*)

HUGH. Dat cough sound bad.

JEAN. Nar is all right a just tired.

HUGH. What kinda day yer had?

JEAN. It wasn't long enough, it coulda go on an on if a didn't have to get back here but a well glad fer de break, we spend all day terday working out which groups an which part a de country we go give de cigarettes ter try from nine dis morning, till just now. An discussing how we go get people ter try dem, an fill in de reaction forms. I tell dem de cigarettes en' go be no problem, people go smoke dem. Dey en' have nobody who like freeness more dan Trinidadian, soon as dey know somebody giving away someting, dey dere.

HUGH. I remember wen dey just bring Vicks Tubes ter Trinidad, a man in a truck was just trowing dem ter children.

JEAN. What I tell dem is ter get people ter remember ter write down dey opinion go be another story. Yer go have ter beg dem fer dat, anyhow tomorrow we going an give dem out, so if a come home as dough a was in a cattle stampede do' be surprised.

ELSA *enters in a thin cotton white nightdress.*

ELSA. Good night Mister Hugh. Good night Miss Jean.

HUGH. Oh good night Elsa, everyting all right?

ELSA. Yes Mister Hugh, tanks.

JEAN. Goonight girl. Yer en' have a dressing-gown?

ELSA. No Miss Jean.

JEAN. I have a old one, a go leave it out fer yer in de morning.

ELSA. Tanks Miss Jean. (*Going.*)

JEAN. Sleep well girl, I tink I go follow she too. Yer coming. I have a heavy day tomorrow.

HUGH. Yes, a go just put out de lights.

JEAN. Right. (*She goes.*)

**Morning**

ELSA *at the stove – dressed.*
HUGH *enters dressed for work.*

HUGH. Morning.

ELSA. Morning Mister Hugh.

HUGH. Yer up early.

ELSA. Yes.

HUGH. Yer sleep all right?

ELSA. Yes, I does always sleep all right.

HUGH. What is dat yer preparing?

ELSA. Is just some saltfish a frying. An a get two Zaboca ter go
with it, a tought you and Miss Jean might like it.

HUGH. Yes, yes, I go like, Miss Jean gone already.

ELSA. A see, you want me leave some fer she.

HUGH. No, no, no bodder, I go eat it.

ELSA. Here den. (*She puts the plate on the table.*)

HUGH. Tanks. Ah ha, dis is it.

ELSA. It nice?

HUGH. Umm, dis really good.

ELSA. Yer like it?

HUGH. Umm, yer really good, Elsa.

ELSA. Tanks Mister Hugh.

HUGH. Umm, good, I feel like a lion, dis is de way – umm, ter,
start a morning. Where yer get dis?

ELSA. I get up early an went down de market.

HUGH. Good, good, really good, a ready to fight anybody after dis.

ELSA. You funny Mister Hugh.

HUGH. Yer tink so?

ELSA. Yes.

HUGH. Dis good, why because I like me food?

ELSA. Is de noise yer making.

HUGH. Dat's good, dat's how a enjoying it.

ELSA. Yes, a like dat.

HUGH *finishes eating, sits back.*

HUGH. Dat was good.

ELSA. Yer enjoy it?

HUGH. Yes.

ELSA. Yer want some more?

HUGH. No, a full up, if a eat anymore a go fall asleep.

ELSA. Dat is all right.

HUGH. No, an a didn't sleep too well last night. Miss Jean was coughing a lot, you should give she someting, Elsa.

ELSA. I could fine she someting.

HUGH. Good. I go make sure she take it.

ELSA. Dat is all right.

HUGH. I go be in early for dinner tonight bout seven.

ELSA. Dat is all right. What bout Miss Jean?

HUGH. Do' worry bout Miss Jean a tink she go eat out.

ELSA. All right.

HUGH. So what yer hitting me wit ternight?

ELSA. A tought some fry fish would be nice.

HUGH. Yes.

ELSA. A see de man in de market had some nice grouper.

HUGH. Yes.

ELSA. An some rice. Yer does eat rice?

HUGH. Yes.

ELSA. An a gravy wit some onion?

HUGH. Yes, yes.

ELSA. An some cassava bread ter soak it up?

HUGH. You could make cassava bread?

ELSA. Yes, all de time.

HUGH. Good, good, good, da sound good, a go look forward ter dat.

ELSA. Yer make me laugh Mister Hugh.

HUGH. Well I go make yer laugh all de time, if you cook me good food. How is dat?

ELSA. Dat is all right.

HUGH. Good, I go leave yer money, you get anyting yer like, yer hear.

ELSA. Yes Mister Hugh.

HUGH. Right a see yer later den.

ELSA. Yes Mister Hugh.

HUGH *goes.*

**Later the same night**

HUGH *is at the table eating.* ELSA *is standing.*

HUGH. Dat was good. Dis is what a come home for. Yes, good, all day dis is all a tinking bout. Yes, good, if yer ask me. I en' know what happen terday. Umm, good.

ELSA. Mister Hugh, yer going on as dough yer never eat food in yer life.

HUGH. Dat is true girl, dat is true, yes is such a long time since a taste someting so nice.

ELSA. Yes, so what yer been eating all de time?

HUGH. Chips-chicken-chips.

ELSA. Yes, well dat en' good fer yer.

HUGH. Yer right.

ELSA. Is dat what Miss Jean does eat?

HUGH. Yes, a was telling Marie terday, is de best day a my life wen a meet she.

ELSA. You see my granmodder ter day?

HUGH. Yes, I does see she every day now.

ELSA. How she look?

HUGH. Great, she all right. She wanted ter know if a was pleased wit yer. I tell she yes, more dan pleased, yer hear dat.

ELSA. Yes.

HUGH. An after ternight a wasn't lying.

ELSA. Yer finish, Mister Hugh?

HUGH. Yes, Elsa.

ELSA *takes the plate.*

ELSA. Yer want anyting else?

HUGH. No tanks.

JEAN *enters*.

JEAN. Yo ho, anybody home?

HUGH. Hi.

ELSA. Evening Miss Jean.

JEAN. What happening girl?

ELSA. Yer want anyting, Miss Jean?

JEAN. What yer have?

ELSA. A make some sour sop juice.

HUGH. Sour sop juice, good.

JEAN. Who yer make it fer?

ELSA. Fer you and Mister Hugh.

JEAN. A go try some.

HUGH. Me too.

ELSA *pours*.

Good, good, yer see.

JEAN. Yes, it's nice. (*She drinks a little.*)

HUGH. A tell yer she was good.

JEAN. A believe yer.

HUGH. Good.

JEAN. Elsa a hope he en' giving yer too much work, yer know.

ELSA. No Miss Jean.

JEAN. Do' let him drive yer crazy wit all he foolishness.

ELSA. No, Miss Jean. (*Washing up.*)

JEAN. Dat is all right den.

HUGH. Yer eat?

JEAN. Yes, we stop on de way down, at dis new Italian place dey open on de highway.

HUGH. Where?

JEAN. Near Barackpore.

HUGH. Yes.

JEAN. Boy a so tired, is all dat fresh air. It go kill me, we hand out so much cigarettes is a joke, if yer see people hand grabbing all over de place.

HUGH. Yes, so it was good?

JEAN. More dan good, but dey do' want ter take de forms at all, we had to hold back de cigarettes till dey take dem.

HUGH. Dat is a good idea.

JEAN. Well we made it out alive, we cover ten villages, dat was a day's work.

HUGH. Yes.

JEAN. Everyting going according ter plan.

HUGH. Yer have ter collect de forms or dey posting dem?

JEAN. We tell dem post dem, but we know dat en' go happen, but we en' really care, de important ting is dat dey smoke Luna, like it, an go in de shops an ask fer it, de forms is ter make dem feel good.

HUGH. A see.

JEAN. From start ter finish my idea.

HUGH. Yes, yes.

JEAN. So what bout you? How your day went.

HUGH. Quiet, quiet, just some routine meetings, I skip a few.

JEAN. Why?

HUGH. I wanted ter get back here ter eat some good food, ter taste Elsa hand. I was just sitting down dere tinking, what I doing listening ter dis boring old talk for, wen I could be eating some nice food.

JEAN. Yer hear dat Elsa?

ELSA. Yes Miss Jean.

JEAN. Yer is really someting girl, yer is a success.

ELSA. A hope so Miss Jean.

JEAN. Yes.

HUGH. Well, I going an see what on de television. (*He goes, whistling 'Sorrento'.*)

JEAN. A didn't have a chance ter talk ter yer dis morning. How de room, everyting all right?

ELSA. Yes Miss Jean.

JEAN. Yer get de dressing-gown?

ELSA. Yes Miss Jean, tanks.

JEAN. Dat is all right, girl, so what part a de country yer from?

ELSA. Yer wouldn't know it Miss Jean.

JEAN. Look child after terday, I know every village on this island.

ELSA. Is a place outside Santa Cruz.

JEAN. We stop dere, near ter Las Cuevas.

ELSA. Yes.

JEAN. We was dere today, I didn't know dat or else I woulda tell yer people.

ELSA. Is all right.

JEAN. We give out a lot dere ter day.

ELSA. Yer – yer cough get better?

JEAN. Dat is gone, is de fresh air.

ELSA. Yes, we live in one a de houses on de hill.

JEAN. Yes, we pass a lot a dem. So dat is where you grow up?

ELSA. Yes.

JEAN. Yer went ter school up dere too?

ELSA. Yes Miss Jean.

JEAN. What age yer leave school?

ELSA. Ten.

JEAN. Why what happen?

ELSA. Notting. I learn ter read and write and count, an I didn't go back after.

JEAN. Yer family didn't make yer go?

ELSA. No, none a my brodders an sisters went back.

JEAN. A see.

ELSA. I turning in now.

JEAN. Yes, good night child.

ELSA. Say good night ter Mister Hugh fer me.

JEAN. Yes. (*She switches on the radio.*)

RADIO.
Luna will drive your troubles away,

Luna will help you work and play
Luna will make you happy and gay,
    So smoke Luna,
    So smoke Luna.
At the office or on the beach, whatever
yer doing – be positive – smoke Luna.
Now available in hard or soft pack,
    king size or normal,
    plain or menthol.
Ask for Luna.

JEAN *leaves*.


**Next morning**


HUGH (*eating*). Dis is good. Yes, yer should try some.

JEAN. No, tanks (*Smoking*.) de coffee go do me fine.

HUGH. You mean dat plastic coffee.

JEAN. Yes.

HUGH. Dis is real bread. An real sausage.

JEAN. A believe yer.

HUGH. Yer really forget what it like ter enjoy nice tings yer know.

JEAN. What you call nice, hops bread an sausage? What de man say? Wen a was a child, a behaved like a child, now I'm a man a behave like one. Yer get it?

HUGH. No.

JEAN. Well do' bodder, you eat yer hops bread an leave me

alone. I do' know what happen ter you, yer must be catch someting.

HUGH. What?

JEAN. I do' know, yer going on as dough you is de only person in de world who know how ter enjoy tings, odder people want ter enjoy life too yer know, not only you.

HUGH. What yer mean? Yer not happy?

JEAN. Forget it.

HUGH. No what yer mean? I tought yer was happy.

JEAN. Well I en' *happy*.

HUGH. But yer have yer job, yer like dat.

JEAN. Course a like it.

HUGH. What den?

JEAN. I en' know man, a fed up.

HUGH. Wit what?

JEAN. I en' know a tell yer, if a had know a would do someting.

HUGH. Yer tired.

JEAN. Yes, but dat en' it.

HUGH. What den?

JEAN. I en' know a tell yer, shit.

HUGH. Well look, maybe yer should take a day off.

JEAN. A car' do dat, a have de whole ting ter look after.

HUGH. I know what le' we take a day off an go by de sea, le' we go ter Maracas.

JEAN. What for?

HUGH. How yer mean what for? Because it would be nice, we could take some rum and some food and spend de day . . .

JEAN. Doing what?

HUGH. Anyting. Anyting yer want ter . . .

JEAN. I do' know.

HUGH. What yer do' know?

JEAN. I do' know bout you. I really do' know what going on in your head. Maracas full a one set a married man an woman who go dey wit dey boyfriend or girlfriend ter hide an have a good time, yer could see me doing dat.

HUGH. We used ter go dere.

JEAN. But we wasn't married.

HUGH. But . . .

JEAN. Is childishness man, fer young people who en' have notting better ter do, a waste a time, yer could see we walking bout on a beach, playing beachcomber, is not fer me, is not what I want ter do. I want ter be wit people wit ideas ter give me ideas. I do' want ter go ter de toilet behind some coconut tree.

HUGH. A tought we could drink some fresh coconut water, an help de fishermen pull in de nets. An after, dey might give we a fish, an we could cook it on de beach.

JEAN. Wen last you help a fisherman pull in a net?

HUGH. I do' know, long time.

JEAN. Wen yer was a little boy.

HUGH. Yes.

JEAN. Yer know dey have outboard motors now.

HUGH. What? I tought it might be nice if we get away for
a . . .

JEAN. From what? . . . Look if you want ter go an play tourist,
you go ahead, I have appointments, an meetings ter keep. I
like dat, dat is what make me feel alive, dat I'm somebody
involved in tings.

HUGH. I have a business ter run too, but dat do' mean we car'
do other tings.

JEAN. Look a going. (*She gets up.*)

HUGH. Yer go be in fer dinner?

JEAN. A do' know. (*She goes.*)

*A beat.*

ELSA *enters.*

ELSA. Yes Mister Hugh, yer want me for anyting?

HUGH. No tanks, Elsa.

ELSA. Yer enjoy de bread and sausage?

HUGH. Yer know I did.

ELSA. A could hear yer, yer do' have ter worry, yer know I
know what yer like now.

HUGH. I know dat, I en' worried.

ELSA. Well, a tought as we had some beef, an it have some big
bone on it, a make a soup, I'd boil up de bones so all de
marrow go come out. An I'd trow some split peas in it, not
much, bout two han full. (*A beat.*) All right den.

HUGH. A go look forward ter dat.

ELSA. I know dat.

HUGH. A goin now, a seeing Marie terday, yer want me ter tell she anyting?

ELSA. No, just tell she a well.

HUGH. All right den. (*He goes whistling.*)


**The same night**

JEAN *enters, switches on the radio.* ELSA *enters a beat later.*

RADIO. The minister also added, the new system will allow the large airliners to land in any weather, and so the extra cost will be offset by an increase in passengers.

JEAN. Elsa.

ELSA. Yes, Miss Jean.

JEAN. Mister Hugh didn't say what time he was coming?

ELSA. No Miss Jean, but a know he was coming ter eat, dat is all.

JEAN. So what happen ter him?

ELSA. A tell him what he was having ternight an he say he looking forward to it.

JEAN. Is nine o'clock now, well is he look out, me en' worrying bout him.

ELSA. Yer want ter eat, Miss Jean?

JEAN. No child, I eat already. (*She coughs.*)

ELSA. Miss Jean.

JEAN. What girl?

ELSA. If yer could tell me de kinda food you like, a could cook fer you too, yer know.

JEAN. No child, yer have enough to do wit he funny dishes.

ELSA. I do' mind. I would try dem, because sometime a get tired cooking de same tings.

JEAN. Is de time girl, I really en' have de time, I en' know if a go be in ter eat anyting like dat. It go just waste, dat damn man. A bet you he gone playing cards an giving way all he money.

ELSA. Men like ter play cards.

JEAN. Yes.

ELSA. Dey like ter make noise, an beat one another, every Friday night my uncle an he friends used ter get together an play cards and smoke and drink, wen a tell yer dey could drink, a never see men drink so much, dey would set up a table an chair under de tree in de back yard an put a flambeau in de middle, an all night dey would play an send me brodder an me ter get rum an cigarettes, backwards an forwards we would go, ter de Chinese shop. Ten, twelve bottles dey would drink, especially on a holiday or a feast day.

JEAN. Yes. Well dis is damn foolishness, I could be out having a damn good time an . . . he . . . (*She coughs.*) Yer car' depend on dem either, de one blasted night a want him here ter talk bout de Luna, he en' here, he late, he decide ter be late.

ELSA. If you want, I go wait up fer him, yer know.

JEAN. No child, is all right, I go stay up, if you want ter turn in you go ahead, do' mine me.

ELSA. I en' sleepy.

*A beat.*

JEAN. Yer have a boyfriend?

ELSA. No.

JEAN. Yer mean yer en' have one, yet.

ELSA. No Miss Jean.

JEAN. Well it en' go be long a nice girl like you, a sure some feller must be have he eye on you already. Men smart yer know, yer have ter watch dem, dey does take dey time, but man wen dey ready ter pounce watch out, you mark my words.

ELSA. I do' take dem on.

JEAN. Yer right child, is ter let dem take you on, eh, you let dem get excited, an den yer have dem.

ELSA. Yes.

JEAN. I have dem work out. All a dem, a have dem eating out of me hand, a bet yer had one in yer village.

ELSA. Yes.

JEAN. What was he name?

ELSA. Errol, he had a bike.

JEAN. Yes.

ELSA. A nice bike, wit pretty colour tings on it.

JEAN. Yes.

ELSA. He used ter ride round an see me.

JEAN. Yer must be miss him.

ELSA. Miss, no. We just used ter talk, he used ter talk an ride round and round me, a used ter get giddy, we used ter just talk.

JEAN. Why?

ELSA. What Miss Jean?

JEAN. Yer mean all yer never.

ELSA. Yer mean – no Miss Jean. If my modder catch me she would beat me.

JEAN. But yer coulda – nobody had ter catch yer.

ELSA. Yer mean hide an ting?

JEAN. Yes.

ELSA. We used ter do dat.

JEAN. Yes.

ELSA. But we never do notting.

JEAN. You have a lot to learn child. Wen I was half your age, I new what men was after, an if yer let dem tink dey could get, yer'd be surprised what dey would do fer yer.

ELSA. He used to say a lot a ting like he love me, an he want ter marry me, but I never take him serious, he was only sweet-talking me.

JEAN. Yer didn't believe him?

ELSA. No, he was only joking.

JEAN. Yes . . .

ELSA. Men does say dem tings because dey tink yer like ter hear it, dat is all.

JEAN. You do' like ter hear it?

ELSA. It do' bodder me, I tink it funny.

JEAN. Yer car' tell me yer en' like it wen a man give yer a sweet eye and get close ter yer an tell yer some nice tings, eh, if even

yer en' want ter believe it. Or yer know it en' true, yer car'
tell me dat.

ELSA. No, but I do' take it serious.

JEAN. But yer like it.

ELSA. It do' bodder me.

JEAN. Well girl you is one in a million yer hear.

ELSA. Yes.

JEAN. You is de only woman I know who say she do' like dat.

ELSA. A didn't say a do' like it, a say a do' take it serious, a
know what dey like.

JEAN. Yer right, girl, a only teasing yer.

ELSA. Yer like ter tease people Miss Jean.

JEAN. Yes girl, a know, dat is me, a tease everybody, a was
always so, since a small.

ELSA. Yer modder never stop yer?

JEAN. Nar. She couldn't stop me, nobody could stop me, a
used ter tease people till dey cry.

ELSA. Yes, yer like it wen people tease you?

JEAN. No, wait, it depend on who it is, if a like dem yes, a like
it when a feller a like tease me, yes a like it, dat is how yer
know people like yer, people notice yer.

ELSA. Yes.

JEAN. Eh?

ELSA. Yes.

JEAN. Everybody know me. Now dey know I like ter tease, so
dey get used ter it, but dey have a lot of people yer know,
who only want ter hold yer back an stop yer from enjoying

yerself, dey do' like me cause dey car' stop me. I tell dem kiss my backside, yer know what I mean. I en' fraid a soul.

ELSA. Yes.

JEAN. You tell dem de same ting. If yer want ter do someting you go ahead an do it, you hear, you tell dem to come see me if dey do' like it.

ELSA. Yes, Miss Jean.

JEAN. An dat ass could fine he own way home. I going ter bed, you too. (*Going.*)

ELSA. Goodnight, Miss Jean, an tanks.

JEAN. All right girl.


**Morning**

ELSA, HUGH, JEAN.

HUGH. How yer mean what time I come home? I en' know what time I come home, de house was dark, dat was all.

JEAN. De house was dark, because yer come home late. Dat is all.

HUGH. Look, I tired yer know, I just get up, I really en' want ter have a row first ting in de morning.

JEAN. I do' want ter have a row either, I have a hard day ahead a me, but if you come home late you car' complain about de lights bein' off. What yer want we to leave de lights burning for you? An another ting, yer get poor Elsa ter cook food fer you an yer en' come home ter eat it.

HUGH. A go eat it ternight it go taste even better, it en' go waste I go eat it. Anyhow what you worrying bout food for? It en' costing yer notting.

JEAN. I know it en' costing me notting is your money, but yer make such a big fuss a dis food ting, an wen de girl cook it, yer en' here.

HUGH. A go eat it a tell yer.

JEAN. Yer know how late I wait up for you? Ask Elsa.

HUGH. I do' have ter ask Elsa, a believe yer. A know a was late but yer didn't say anyting bout us meeting.

JEAN. I had someting a wanted ter ask yer I didn't know yer wasn't coming in, yer come home early every night.

HUGH. Only lately.

JEAN. You told Elsa yer was coming early, I believe yer. Elsa believe yer, look she dere ask she.

HUGH. A do' have ter ask she a know what a say. A went out dat is all, someting come up. What yer wanted to ask me?

JEAN. Where yer went?

HUGH. A went out a say. Dat is what yer stay up for?

JEAN. No.

HUGH. I do' ask you where you go, wen you come in late.

JEAN. I does tell yer.

HUGH. I know, but I do' ask yer.

JEAN. So is a secret.

HUGH. No it en' no secret, but I en' go tell you shouting like dis, yer must be waking up de whole neighbourhood.

JEAN. I en' give a shit bout dem, dey could kiss my ass. Both cheeks, dey need waking up, all a dem dead already. All dey

could do is wash dey little Japanese car an cut dey Japanese
grass, as if anybody care how long dey grass is, so do' tell me
bout dem yer hear or a go shout even more.

HUGH. All right.

JEAN. All right.

HUGH. What it is yer wanted ter ask me den?

JEAN. A car' ask yer now, I have ter go. Yer go be in tonight?

HUGH. Yes a . . .

JEAN. Yer sure?

HUGH. Yes, a say so.

JEAN. All right a go know more about it terday, too.

HUGH. Someting happen?

JEAN. I en' know a tell yer, a go know more about it, a tell yer.

HUGH. All right, I go be in.

JEAN. All right den. (*She goes.*) A gone.

ELSA. What yer want ter eat Mister Hugh?

HUGH. What?

ELSA. Ternight, what yer feel like?

HUGH. Yes, yes, I en' know.

ELSA. Yer'd like me ter fix yer some meat, a could go down de
market and get yer a manicu, it only mean a have ter season
it all day, yer know how dem manicu strong. What wrong
Mister Hugh?

HUGH. I eat manicu last night.

ELSA. You eat manicu last night, where you eat manicu last
night, Mister Hugh?

HUGH. A went up de hills wit Marie.

ELSA. My granmother give you manicu last night? What was last night? Yes, a see, a ferget, yes.

HUGH. She took me to a Shango meeting.

ELSA. Last night was Shango?

HUGH. Yes, you ever went?

ELSA. Yes, all de time but I forget bout last night.

HUGH. Yes.

ELSA. Yer like it?

HUGH. The manicu?

ELSA. No, de Shango.

HUGH. I en' sure. It was strange.

ELSA. It en' strange, dey does have it all de time. Yer get frighten?

HUGH. A bit.

ELSA. It does frighten yer de first time, but after yer get used ter it . . .

HUGH. But I never know it went on.

ELSA. Yes, all de time.

HUGH. All dose people.

ELSA. Yes, sometimes it does get really pack.

HUGH. An de drums, I never heard a sound like dat in my life.

ELSA. Yes, dey good eh.

HUGH. An all dem woman in white dresses an headties, singing an dancing in a circle an carrying de torches, an de shadows . . .

ELSA. I like de flambeau light.

HUGH. Yes, dere was men beating drums.

ELSA. Any spirit catch?

HUGH. Right in de middle a Port of Spain. What? What yer say?

ELSA. Any a de ladies a dem, dey jump in de circle an catch de spirit?

HUGH. Yer mean shake, an tremble? Yes, den dey just pass out, an dey lay dem on de ground?

ELSA. Yes.

HUGH. Yes, a lot, dey lie down on de ground an shake, an de others who didn't get it, was looking after dem, an talking ter dem, but it was a strange sound, I couldn't understand, and de drums.

ELSA. It was good den.

HUGH. I . . .

ELSA. You get a feeling?

HUGH. Yes, a tink so.

ELSA. Everybody does get it. An you eat manicu. Wit no salt.

HUGH. Yes. Why dey do' use salt?

ELSA. Salt fool we. So yer had a good time den?

HUGH. Yes, why dey kill de cock?

ELSA. Ter purify de grouwn, Mister Hugh, de blood is pure, and de cock have spirit ter release.

HUGH. Wit de blood?

ELSA. Yes, yer taste any?

HUGH. No.

ELSA. It do' tast a notting special just blood. An it do' waste, dey does cook it afterwards yer see an – How was me granmodder?

HUGH. She all right, I didn't know she was in it, wen we get dey everybody was making way for she an bowing an . . .

ELSA. Yes, she is a modder.

HUGH. Dey treat she like a queen.

ELSA. She's a queen, my father was a king, an my uncle was a duke all a we was royal family, it come from de old days de slaves had dey kings an queens an court meetings.

HUGH. I didn't know dat.

ELSA. Wen dey used ter hold court an dress up de plantation people used ter get frighten, an ban dem, an wen dey catch de spirit, dey used ter whip dem but den dey used ter meet in secret.

HUGH. Yes.

ELSA. You didn't know dat?

HUGH. No.

ELSA. Yes dey used ter do like de French and Portuguese an a tink de English, all a dem had king an queen, we had la reine and le roy too, yer see.

HUGH. Yes.

ELSA. Yer must go again wen de moon rise.

HUGH. Yes, an Marie say de only way dey could tell who was king an queen was wen dey find de crown in de bush, dey used to hide an wait an see who come fer it.

ELSA. Yes.

HUGH. Den dey used ter catch dem, she said anybody coulda be king, de people used ter choose him fer he fairness, he tolerance, he calmness, he advice . . .

ELSA. Yes, you could be a king if yer wanted ter, yer know Mister Hugh.

HUGH. Me nar? No way, no, no.

ELSA. Yer mustn't say dat, is up ter people ter choose yer, is not fer you ter say.

HUGH. No.

ELSA. No. Why you afraid?

HUGH. No, no, no, I do' know notting about dem tings dat is all.

ELSA. It en' have notting ter know, is what yer like.

HUGH. No, I is a town boy, I grow up in de city, I . . .

ELSA. Dat en' have notting ter do wit it.

HUGH. No, no, no.

ELSA. Is all right den.

HUGH. What happen if somebody say no?

ELSA. Nobody does say no.

HUGH. Not even . . . ?

ELSA. Dat is part of it.

HUGH. No, not me, I go watch on.

ELSA. Dat is all right, a tink a go make a co-coo ter night, a have de corn meal already yer want some green fig as well?

HUGH. Of course yer car' have co-coo witout green fig.

ELSA. Dat is true. Yer tink Miss Jean go want ter eat ternight?

HUGH. We could try she, what yer say?

ELSA. All right.

HUGH. Yer want me tell Marie anyting for yer?

ELSA. No, just tell she a all right an a hope she all right too.

HUGH. All right, a see yer later, a late already. (*He goes.*)


**Night**

*The telephone rings* – JEAN *enters, answers the phone.* ELSA *enters.*

JEAN. Hello. Oh what happenin'? Yes, yes, yer lucky ter catch me. Who? He in de bag, finish. (*She coughs.*) No, child, wen I finish wid he it go be caviar an cadillacs. (*She coughs.*) A come in wit style a go out wit style. (*She coughs.*) No, child, my hands full. All right, a go say you was with me all evening, but tell me where, where we was suppose ter be, oh dere, but I do' like dere. Yer car' tink a somewhere else? No is all right, no big ting, okay den, bye. (*She hangs up the phone.*)

ELSA. Evening Miss Jean.

JEAN. Hello, Elsa. Mister Hugh in as yet?

ELSA. No Miss Jean but he say he coming.

JEAN. Lord a starving girl. What yer have ter eat?

ELSA. A do some co-coo.

JEAN. Co-coo, oh yes, a remember dat.

ELSA. Yer want ter try some?

JEAN. No tanks, dat would kill me. If I eat one co-coo a would put on fifty pounds.

ELSA. A could do yer someting else.

JEAN. What I feel like is a nice chicken an chips.

ELSA. We en' have no chicken Miss Jean if yer had tell me . . .

JEAN. No child do' worry, I go get one. (*She picks up the phone, dials.*) Larry, yes, look do me a chicken and chips now, yes one, one, no, nobody en' move out, ten minutes, I tought you was a fast worker, all right. No you do' do it, get dat good looking half Chinese boy ter deliver de goods, yes a getting choosy in me old age, right. Tell him ter bring it by der pool. (*She puts the phone down.*) I going fer a quick dip, Elsa. (*She laughs.*)

ELSA. Yes, Miss Jean.

JEAN *goes*. HUGH *enters*.

HUGH. Evening Elsa.

ELSA. Evening Mister Hugh. Yer had a good day?

HUGH. Yes, Elsa . . . ?

ELSA. Yes, Mister Hugh.

HUGH. How you feel about working here?

ELSA. I do' feel notting Mister Hugh, I like it. Why yer ask, a do something wrong?

HUGH. No, no, no, notting like dat . . .

ELSA. Yer do' want me ter stay.

HUGH. No, no, do' tink dat. I glad yer come an everyting.

ELSA. It en' like work at all ter me.

HUGH. No, yer do' understand.

ELSA. I like it.

HUGH. I tink yer might have ter go home, fer a while.

ELSA. What a do wrong, tell me?

HUGH. Yer en' do notting wrong a tell yer, Marie say . . .

ELSA. Me granmodder say a must leave?

HUGH. Yes, yer have sickness in de family.

ELSA. Who, who sick, me granmodder sick?

HUGH. No, she all right, but yer modder not well and yer brothers and sister sick too, so dey car' look . . .

ELSA. What wrong wit dem?

HUGH. Nobody en' know, it just happen, a lot a coughing an weakness yer granmodder say.

ELSA. Well a better go.

HUGH. Yes, she didn't say how long for or anyting.

ELSA. I know.

HUGH. But a want yer ter know, an Marie agree wit me dat wen everybody get better, a want yer ter come back here.

ELSA. Yes, if me granmodder agree.

HUGH. Yes because I glad yer here an . . .

ELSA. A better go den, what bout de co-coo, yer want me serve it up first?

HUGH. No, I go do dat, a go drop yer ter de bus station.

ELSA. No Mister Hugh I go catch one down de road.

ELSA *goes.* HUGH *begins to serve food.* ELSA *retuns with a bag.*

ELSA. All right den Mister Hugh, I off now.

HUGH. Yes Elsa.

ELSA. Yer go tell Miss Jean.

HUGH. Yes an do' worry.

ELSA. No, all right den.

ELSA *goes.*

JEAN *enters wearing a bikini, with box of food. She coughs.*
*They both sit and eat.*

JEAN. Hi, what happenin' dere.

HUGH. Notting.

JEAN. Hmm, dis chicken taste good.

HUGH. Co-coo is good.

JEAN. Too good to eat.

HUGH. Yes.

JEAN. A like me chicken brown yer hear, an crusty, crusty an
brown, like me.

HUGH. You should try dis.

JEAN. A know what co-coo taste like. How de pipe lines going?

HUGH. All right, dey started laying terday, yer know dis is one
job I really feel good about. It wasn't just a straightforward
buying and selling ting.

JEAN. How yer mean?

HUGH. Well I never used ter tink a what happen, after we
deliver if de ting work or not, it was dere tough luck but dis
one different. I could see de whole process before me before it
even hit de people.

JEAN. Yes.

HUGH. I know, de water go up ter de sky an she go send it
down ter de mountains, de mountains go send it down, pass
de hills an through de rivers, ter de land an it go just stay

dere, so is up ter me ter do someting with it, we take on de job, we could waste it, spoil it, or just leave it, an dis is it, but people could benefit from it, Marie say dat . . .

JEAN. She still going bout wit yer?

HUGH. Yes. How yer cigarette ting going?

JEAN. It going all right, we have a few slight problems ter overcome. We en' sure how ter but . . .

HUGH. Yes? Like what?

JEAN. Oh. Some a de people say it making dem cough a lot, but dat is ter be expected, wit anyting new. We do' know if it just dem country people trying a ting on we, dey smart yer know, yer car' beat a country bookie fer smartness although dey look simple, dey quick, but I do' know what dey want. If dey want we ter give dem more, an dat go keep dem happy, I tell de American guy dat before he left, he say: You know your market. A tell him he dam right, dat's what he hired me for.

HUGH. Elsa had ter go home too.

JEAN. Why?

HUGH. Her people an dem sick, dey coughing.

JEAN. Right, yer see what a tell yer, everybody catching it now, yer know how Trinidadians follow fashion, one person do someting all a dem want ter do it. Anyhow, is you go suffer I car' cook no co-coo.

HUGH. Is all right, I just hope dey go be all right.

JEAN. Who?

HUGH. De people an dem.

JEAN. Dey go be all right, dem country people tough, all dat fresh air an good food, dey tough like leather, yer ever see dem walk up a hill, dey do it sideways.

HUGH. Yes.

JEAN. Dey hard, an dey does walk through all dat bush barefoot, is we who get soft, we used ter dis soft living everyting handy, if we spend some time in de bush, a bet yer we get like dem.

HUGH. Yes.

JEAN. Do' look so worried man, she go come back an cook up all yer nice food and yer miss she.

HUGH. Yes.

JEAN. Dat is all right, I like she too, so tell me nar yer keepin dis big secret.

HUGH. What secret?

JEAN. Yer birthday, what yer want fer yer birthday?

HUGH. I en' know, I en' . . . tinking bout . . .

JEAN. What about a power boat?

HUGH. Fer me? What I go do wit a power boat?

JEAN. A could afford it, yer know, if dat is what worrying yer. What bout a new stereo?

HUGH. De old one good.

JEAN. What bout one a dem new video recorder? Yer could record all yer favourite television programme, an show dem anytime yer like.

HUGH. I . . .

JEAN. All right, I go tink a someting, Lord, yer is a hard man ter please.

HUGH. What a might do is take a holiday.

JEAN. Where, Miami?

HUGH. No, a might go in de country fer a few days.

JEAN. Which country?

HUGH. Dis country.

JEAN. What dey have ter do up dere?

HUGH. A could just look around, an . . .

JEAN. At what, it en' have notting ter look at.

HUGH. Dey have a lot, de hills, trees, an lots a nice tings to take in.

JEAN. But yer car' swim or do notting.

HUGH. I could do odder tings.

JEAN. You an Marie?

HUGH. A might take she.

JEAN. Well if dat is what yer idea a having a holiday is fine. You might enjoy it, but you en' getting me climbing no hills yer hear, not me.

HUGH. Dat is all right.

   *A beat.*

JEAN. What about a new air conditioner?

HUGH. We have air conditioning.

JEAN. A new one –

HUGH. Jean I en' really interested in birthday yer know, or birthday party or birthday present.

JEAN. A wish yer would tell me what yer interested in, yer do' want ter party, yer do' want ter have a good time, all yer interested in is dis bush people, I en' know what happen ter yer, like yer going backwards all de time.

HUGH. I want ter know about dem people because dey have a lot ter teach we, about life, an we history, we life is based on how dey live how dey adapted ter life wen dey came here an after slavery.

JEAN. Hugh, I en' interested in dem tings, I know bout all a what dem people believe in Nanncy stories, superstition, an ignorance an . . . Souquiant sucking yer blood, an . . .

HUGH. But is what it's based on, dat matter.

JEAN. What it based on, eh?

HUGH. Survival, sanity. I do' know, I want ter fine out, dere's reasons ter know about.

JEAN. Yer en' go fine out a dam ting, an even wen yer fine out yer go still have ter come back an face de twentieth . . . Why yer do' ask me? I could tell yer.

HUGH. You. I went ter a Shango an if . . .

JEAN. You went ter Shango. Wen, wen? You never tell me. Before we married?

HUGH. No, de night a didn't a come home late.

JEAN. But yer didn't tell me – you went ter a Shango meeting, a big sensible, educated man like you. What happen ter you man? Yer went fer a joke, eh?

HUGH. No.

JEAN. No, a didn't tink so, I know a lot a guys does go up dere ter get dey kicks, watching dem girls shake, but you, not you, you realise who you is, you is a man of position in dis city, people respect you, if anybody had see you – you realise it reflect on me as well, dat my business depend on my good name as well, an if people even hear, oh shit man, I en' know what ter say, Hugh, de man I married went ter college, he went ter university, he got diplomas, he reads books, he like paintings, he tinks about tings, dat is de man I married, not a monkey man, yer know what, dat Elsa en' coming back here and as fer she granmodder . . .

HUGH. Marie.

JEAN. Whatever she name is, all dat foolishness bout food and she granmodder, it dead now yer hear, if yer want a cook I go get yer one if even I have ter get one from France I go get yer one, yer hear, is a good ting nobody en' see you or I woulda hear about it already, man you is really someting, if you want I could tie me head an catch spirit fer you, why yer do' ask me.

HUGH. Jean, I trying to tell you I make all de money —

JEAN. But you could make —

HUGH. More, listen ner.

JEAN. All right.

HUGH. A saying I make all de money in my life that I want ter make. An some a de ways I make it I en' too proud of. Dat might have someting ter do wit it. I do' know, but dat was de way I come an find it, I never stop ter tink bout de right an wrong way, a might of never make it dat way —

JEAN. But Hugh — we work hard for . . .

HUGH. A say listen.

JEAN. I know . . . all right.

HUGH. We have everyting we want, we have tings we en' even want, but we had ter have dem, why I do' know, I was lucky my family had some money, I en' know whey dey get it, or how dey get it, but dey was able ter give me a good education an, de rest was easy.

JEAN. You was so lucky, you know what my family had ter do ter give me a education, yer know what I had ter do, I went . . .

HUGH. What a trying ter say is what good it do me, Jean? I en' happy. I have tings I en' want, a big house wit rooms we never use, because everybody have ter have a big house, a swimming pool because everybody have one. Why? What fer? Who fer? Ter look big, feel big, I do' want dem tings, you take Elsa and she granmodder, dem people have so much, not in dey house, but inside dem.

JEAN. Hugh you car' be like dem, you know too much, you use to a different way a life, you car' change.

HUGH. Who say so?

JEAN. I say, I know dat, yer could admire dem, yer could try, but yer car' be one a dem.

HUGH. Dat en' true, dat en' true, dey life en' change.

JEAN. But yours . . .

HUGH. Why yer tink dey stay dat way? Dey stay dat way ter give us, people like me a chance ter see, ter see, how ter live, anodder way a living, I want ter live like dem, ter be like dem, simple, uncomplicated.

JEAN. So yer going ter live in de bush an tink dat go make yer one a dem?

HUGH. It en' where you live dat count, fer dose people.

JEAN. Hugh, what about us, our marriage? Everybody say how lucky we are, what a nice couple we make, people envy us, we have a successful life an marriage too, an you trying ter change dat fer what someting . . .

HUGH. Jean, what I talking bout en' go affect it go make it better.

JEAN. How, how, you want ter change tings? Fer I do' see how changing what we have go make it better, we already . . .

HUGH. I want to change what we do an what reasons we do it fer dat's what.

JEAN. You mean give up what we have, what we work for. Is dat what yer want? I do' know what yer want, ter tink dat old woman go adopt yer and give yer she grandaughter an everyting go be cosy, is dat what you want, ter give up everyting we have for dem bush people. I go tell you someting yer know, dem en' de only people who was poor an suffering. My people an dem was Portuguese but dey wasn't rich neither. Yer hear Perez an yer tink dey rich, but my father show me our family album an tell me how his granfadder come to dis island wit only a stitch on he back, yer hear, but dey en' lie down in de sun an drink rum, dey sell dis an buy dis an build up dey life. Yer know he was de first man ter bring a motor car on dis island eh, dey bring tings wit dem ter dis island too, culture, roads, an dey sweat an you want me ter give up what dey do fer some dream you have, everyting dey do, dey die fer.

HUGH. Jean . . .

JEAN. Yer want a virgin eh, well dat's normal, take she, but do' forget, fer everytime you horn me, I could do it twice, an a know how . . .

JEAN *leaves*.

HUGH. Jean . . .

**Morning**

HUGH, JEAN *having coffee. Long beats.*

HUGH. What kinda day yer have?

JEAN. Meetings – you?

HUGH. Meetings.

JEAN. What yer doing about dinner?

HUGH. I . . .

JEAN. Yer have ter eat, le' we have it together, I paying.

HUGH. I . . .

JEAN. What happen, yer fraid I eat yer? You choose.

HUGH. No, no, all right.

JEAN. Good den, a call yer.

HUGH. Yes.

   JEAN *leaves.*


**Later that night**

JEAN *enters.*

JEAN. I having a brandy.

   HUGH *follows.*

HUGH. I too.

   JEAN *pours.*

JEAN. Here, yer see dat wasn't too bad was it?

HUGH. No it was nice.

JEAN. Yer see, odder people know how ter cook too, yer might even get ter like French food.

HUGH. Yes, a lot a we cooking is based on de colonist meals, de French, Spanish, an even Portuguese.

JEAN. But is nice ter taste de original.

HUGH. Yes.

JEAN. Anyhow, wen Elsa come back yer go get all de good food yer want.

HUGH. Yes, a didn't see Marie terday.

JEAN. Why not?

HUGH. She didn't come.

JEAN. Well she must be take a day off, yer know . . .

HUGH. But she didn't send a message or anyting. A want ter clear some tings wit her.

JEAN. Yes, like what?

HUGH. De ministry want all de pipes we have. A do' know if ter keep any in reserve.

JEAN. Till de price go up?

HUGH. No, fer odder people, de nearest delivery date is six months, dey want dem now at de same price.

JEAN. So what is de problem?

HUGH. I en' know, but if I give dem all ter de Government an somebody else want some . . .

JEAN. Anybody else ask?

HUGH. No.

JEAN. So, dey go stay in de warehouse taking up space?

HUGH. Yes.

JEAN. An de rent?

HUGH. Yes.

JEAN. I en' see what you worrying bout, let dem have it, all a dem. Daddy always said dere's two kinda people in de world, dose who want to buy someting an dose who have someting ter sell, an whichever one yer is make sure yer get de best price. He . . .

ELSA *appears with a bag.*

ELSA. Evening Mister Hugh, evening Miss Jean.

JEAN. What you doing here child? I tought you'd be back in de village looking after yer people an dem.

ELSA. Dey do' need looking after no more Miss Jean, dey dead, all de sick dead.

HUGH. Oh my God.

ELSA. Dey was just coughing an coughing an wouldn't stop, we try everyting, all de people an dem help, it wouldn't stop dem, dey just dead.

JEAN. Oh my God.

HUGH. A sorry Elsa.

ELSA. Mister Hugh my granmodder say I must come back ter work.

HUGH. Yes.

ELSA. She say she want yer ter come up an see her.

HUGH. Yes.

ELSA. Ternight.

HUGH. Yes.

JEAN. Elsa why yer do' go an put yer tings away in your room.

ELSA. Yes Miss Jean. (*She goes.*)

HUGH. A going.

HUGH *throws up*.

A going. I have ter go, Jean, Marie wants me.

JEAN. Why? It's not true, it could be anyting, Hugh, it must be someting else, it must be someting dey eat or drink, dem country people does brew all kinda tings, dey do' know what it is just because it growing dey pick it an tink it good, dey too ignorant, look at Elsa, dey too ignorant . . . Hugh yer all right.

HUGH (*at the sink*). Yes, yes.

JEAN. Yes, you don't belive she do you? What she know? Dem country people, she is a little country girl, who . . .

HUGH. Jean, we know.

JEAN. She is a doctor, a specialist? We do' know she could be wrong, it could be anyting kill dem.

HUGH. Don't, Jean, you . . .

JEAN. Compensation dat's what dey want, dey make it up . . .

HUGH. You car' do dis, Jean, you car', I don't want ter see . . .

JEAN. Why yer believe she, dem people everyting dey say eh? What for ter get fool, ter let dem fool yer again.

HUGH. I have ter.

JEAN. Yer don't believe me, I'm yer wife. I need you here ter talk about dis.

HUGH. Jean.

JEAN. I know what yer tink. Yer tink it's my fault eh?

HUGH. No.

JEAN. We have ter kill dis lie, we have ter tell people it en' true.

HUGH. I car' do dat, Jean, we car'.

JEAN. Who say so? You want to see us in jail, everybody in jail, yer know how much people involved in dis. Yer know how much customs officers an Department a Health officers we bribe to get the cigarettes in? How high up we went?

HUGH. No Jean.

JEAN. What about dat guy in de Ministry, you give him de pipes, he have ter help, you could phone him, I could phone him, anybody, we could . . . I need you.

HUGH. I have ter go. (*He goes.*)

JEAN (*calls out*). I go do it yer go see, I go show you how it work, I go call everybody, every string I know, yer go see – I could do it . . .


**Morning**

JEAN *is going through the newspapers.* ELSA *enters.*

ELSA. Morning Miss Jean.

JEAN. Morning Elsa.

ELSA. Yer want anyting fer breakfast?

JEAN. No, just some coffee.

  ELSA *pours.*

ELSA. Yer know if Mister Hugh wants anyting?

JEAN. No Elsa.

ELSA. De papers say anyting bout de deaths, Miss Jean?

JEAN. No, Elsa, just some people died under mysterious circumstances.

ELSA. What dat mean Miss Jean?

JEAN. I do' know Elsa.

ELSA. Is de coughing what cause it, de cigarette smoke, Miss Jean.

JEAN. Elsa, a have ter go now, a have a lot a meetings terday.

ELSA. Yer want me do anyting fer yer tonight?

JEAN. No, Elsa.

ELSA. A could do you a nice piece a steak wit onions.

JEAN. No tanks, Elsa.

ELSA. Or anyting.

JEAN. No, tanks, child I go eat out.

ELSA. All right den.

> JEAN *leaves.* ELSA *clears the table, puts things in the sink, picks up the newspaper, reads.*
>
> HUGH *enters.*

HUGH. Goopoo moporuipin Eplsopa.

ELSA. Goopoomoporuipin Mipsteper Hupoo. My granmodder teach yer.

HUGH. Yes, she ask me ter stay fer de wake, last night.

ELSA. She didn't want me den? Yer keep watch?

HUGH. Yes.

ELSA. What yer see Mister Hugh?

HUGH. Notting, Elsa.

ELSA. What yer hear Mister Hugh?

HUGH. Notting Elsa, notting.

ELSA. I keep watch too.

HUGH. Elsa I didn't know de peole who dead was musicians.

ELSA. Yes all a dem was musicians. Yer hear dem?

HUGH. No, no.

ELSA. I keep watch too. Yer see how dey dead? Yes, I see how dey dead. Yer want me ter tell yer?

HUGH. No. I see, I see dem. When a get dere, dere was a procession going up de hills wit candles, a whole line a lights like a shining snake an Marie told me ter join she, an at de top a de hill everybody started singing and clapping den de drums started an we began calling out de names a all de people who died, an one by one de dead people started coming out a dey houses, a could see dem down de hill in de middle a de village an de blood, all a dem was covered in blood, dey eyes, dey nose, dey troat. I could see dem an de people ask dem ter play a tune, den a heard de music. First it was faint den it was up de hill ter de top, an we was dancing, dancing, ter music, an dey was smiling, den dey bow ter us, an before dey went in we ask dem: How can we help? What can we do? Dey said: Tell de story, tell de story. An went back in dere houses an we sat down till morning an kept watch.

ELSA. Yes. You keep watch . . .

HUGH. She do' want yer to come back, she say you must stay in town.

ELSA. Yes.

HUGH. She say de village need men.

ELSA. Yes.

HUGH. De village need music.

ELSA. Yes.

HUGH. She say yer must leave dis house.

ELSA. Yes, yer going back?

HUGH. Yes.

ELSA. Fer good?

HUGH. Yes, a going now.

ELSA. Yes Mister Hugh.

HUGH. Call me LeRoy. (*He goes.*)

## Night

JEAN *enters in a white dress, calls out.*

JEAN. Hugh, Hugh, Elsa. (*She switches on the radio.*)

RADIO. Such a massive reorganisation of the Ministry will not entail redundancies. The Minister stressed with the island's economy in such a strong position and expansion going ahead at such a rapid rate, it is necessary for his department . . .

*Slow fade on* JEAN *coughing blood.*